GOD ON THE GYMNASIUM FLOOR and Other Theatrical Adventures

WALTER KERR

Simon and Schuster   New York

Published by Simon and Schuster
Rockefeller Center, 630 Fifth Avenue
New York, New York 10020

First printing

SBN 671-21018-1
Library of Congress Catalog Card Number: 71-159133
Designed by Jack Jaget
Manufactured in the United States of America
Printed by Mahony & Roese
Bound by American Book–Stratford Press, Inc.

All articles in this book not otherwise credited first appeared in *The New York Times* and *The New York Times Magazine* and are reprinted here with their permission. Section 4 of "God on the Gymnasium Floor" first appeared, under that title, in *Theatre II, 1968–1969*, copyright © 1970 by The International Theatre Institute of the United States, Inc.; the introductory piece, "The Paradox," appeared in *Theatre III, 1969–1970*, copyright © 1971 by The International Theatre Institute of the United States, Inc. Section 2 of "Togetherness" was first published, under the title "Participatory Theatre," in *Harper's Magazine*, October 1969, and is reprinted here with its permission; "The Playwright as Existentialist" was originally published as a pamphlet entitled "Harold Pinter" in the Columbia Essays on Modern Writers series, copyright © 1967 by Columbia University Press, and is reprinted here with its permission. Section 6 of "Remembrance of Things Past" first appeared as "1919–1969: A Review of the Half Century of American Theater" and was included in *The Best Plays of 1968–1969*, edited by Otis L. Guernsey, copyright © 1969 by Dodd, Mead & Company, Inc. The article on Bert Lahr originally appeared in *Saturday Review*, November 1969, under the title "Close to the Dark Heart of Comedy," copyright © 1969 by Saturday Review, Inc.

*for Leo and Chuck
and Hugh*

Contents

# The Paradox

I DON'T KNOW which attitude staggers me more—today's almost total distrust of the theater, or today's almost total trust of the theater. Logically speaking—if we were logical creatures any longer—two such attitudes should cancel each other out. Instead, at the moment, they seem casually to coincide. There is the matter-of-fact requiem we daily intone: the theater is dead or as good as, it is a form worn weary beyond redemption. And there is the hard fact: in practice, and particularly in experimental practice, we behave as though the theater were the one form with the continuing power to save us all. The theater is empty of energy, and the theater has so much excess energy that it can be rushed to the rescue of every other part of our lives that is in danger of failing. Odd, very odd. And, in its oddness, a curious compliment.

I won't detain you long with an accounting of the "death" notice. We have all heard it all, very often. The theater *was* once a fine—if somewhat sluggish, primitive, and linear—medium for amusing, moving, or perhaps instructing a mob. When the mob had nowhere else to go, no other method of taking into itself the invisible impulses throbbing through the social air, the playhouse was a possible central meeting place, a sort of steam bath of the mind and heart. An innocent place, with its illusionistic tricks, its love of bombast, and its candy-butcher bustle in the aisles. It produced some genuine art, which we are happy to preserve on the library shelves, but mainly trash. The genuine art, however, was cast in a mold which is no longer ours.

It is not simply that film, say, has outpaced the clubfooted stage. The stage has been, can be, somewhat speeded up, enough perhaps to hold the attention of a television-trained, dial-dizzied child. Fundamentally, film—together with its various electronic brothers —has caught the new secret of working as our minds work, disjunctively, in overlaps, happy with collisions of fragmented simultaneity.

After Joyce, something happened to literature; what happened could be appropriated by film and by television and by music and even by the newly unstructured novel with its blown-feather-cage of words. And the stage could try, in a great multimedia heave, for the effect, could even produce something vaguely like it.

But the effort was patently laborious. With all strobe lights and soundtracks going, the stage was still a painfully slow, time-crippled giant. Imprisoned by its own continuity—we had to go to one place, take one seat in a playhouse, and *be* there until the course was gimpily run—the stage still had to make its way, not skipping, from A to B and down on through the hours, peopled by actors incapable of disintegrating and reassembling into something else on the spot.

The *conditions* of the theater were linear, verbal, hopelessly physical. They were conditions well suited to a neolithic society which brought the family for the day and took time out for lunch on the lawn, but not for a society in which perception had been McLuhanized. The stage was not quite as old as the wheel, but was like it. The wheel remained a valuable invention, but was only used now to get airplanes away from and back onto the ground. Art takes place in the air. The stage was no longer a medium for seeing as we see, feeling as we feel, thinking or nonthinking as we think or nonthink. It could not be *our* form, nor that of any increasingly sophisticated society we could foresee. And so it bored people. And so it was buried.

Buried in principle, if not yet entirely in fact. Mind, I don't say I believe all of this, that any of the conclusions we have drawn from actual change are irreversibly, necessarily so. But the evidence was more than theoretical. We had been losing playhouses all along, steadily, on the so-called road and at the professional New York center. We had been mounting fewer and fewer new plays each season. We had been having difficulty in interesting the young in the theater; the faces were fiftyish in the theater now and there was no one up in the balcony. The theoretical notion that the theater's peculiar energies were energies no longer suited to a radically transformed society was borne out, or paralleled, by an actual decline of interest. The theater had not been and was not to be a twentieth-century passion.

How astonishing it is, then, to discover that the very same heads that hold this position—twentieth-century heads, hooked into the circuit and responding reflexively—should regard the theater as its natural savior, outlet, regenerator, master matrix, and all-purpose adapter in almost every conceivable phase of twentieth-century life, particularly in those phases of life that seemed most in trouble, toppling into failure.

Was religion in trouble? Give religion to the theater and the theater would make it over. Was psychiatry not doing its job, failing to rid the harried of their hangups and giving them less freedom than it promised? Give therapy to the theater; the theater could relieve the bind much more readily. Was the science of politics collapsing in disgrace, breeding much more than disenchantment, breeding something close in spirit to anarchy? Give politics to the theater and politics would come away clean. Was there a credibility gap not only in politics, but in man's relationship with all media of information? Establish a Theater of Fact and get at the facts. Was the quality of life as a whole, the taste of existence, unsatisfactory? Blend life with theater—in happenings, on street corners, call the March on the Pentagon the "best play of the year," as one man did—and the quality of life would be improved, having become drama.

It has been our peculiar experience to see all things become drama, or try to become drama, or try to relocate or redynamize themselves in theater at the same moment in history we declared

the theater's energies to be spent. Theater, it would seem, has not
the power to save itself, but it does have the power to ransom the
world.

The suggestion that it can do what religion has failed to do goes
far beyond the simple, increasingly frequent use of sanctuaries as
stages. No theatergoer is surprised to find himself climbing the
stone steps of churches to see plays; he will have been to St.
Clement's, which is also the American Place Theater, too many
times, as he will have found Grotowski in an open chamber once
reserved for Methodists and Aeschylus' *The Persians* in one still
used daily by Episcopalians. Theater is not thought to be irrelevant
in these surroundings; in many cases it is thought to be rejuve-
nating.

Away from churches, the identification may be even stronger.
In the loft where The Open Theater works, a playgoer will be
handed a program in which it is explained that the actors are in
some sense priests, that the experience is in some sense a eucharist.
On Riverside Drive in New York City, at the Woodstock Center
for Religion and Worship, an ambitious new program is under
way devoted to the study of ritual "and particularly of the place
and future of ritual in the lives of millions of Americans groping
for a better understanding of themselves and their surroundings in
the midst of a technological-aesthetic revolution." Ritual, the
Woodstock brochure suggests, "is the expression in sight, sound,
rhythms, images, pulsations, spaces, and movement of what people
experience and believe." It is best approached these days, the
brochure continues, "by initiating a study of the comparative
relationship of the inner dynamics of the arts to the inner dynamics of ritual." If religion once gave rise to the arts, today the
arts—and the theater is in the forefront of this movement—may
help renew religion.

If psychoanalysis once seemed destined to take over many of the
functions of religion, today the stage stands prepared to take over
for psychoanalysis. Once again, practice is not confined to the
literal use of psychoanalytical techniques which have become
dramatic techniques, though this kind of direct therapy has in fact
found its way to the commercial stage, most notably in an improvised drama called *The Concept* which was performed—very

affectingly—by former drug addicts as a continuing process of rehabilitation.

The theater of "therapy" is with us everywhere, in the dithyrambic abandon of a suddenly topless bacchante inviting members of the audience (at *Dionysus in 69*) to shed inhibitions and join the players on stage, in the much more reserved and disciplined work of a Grotowski for whom "the performance represents a form of social psycho-therapy." Performance can lead, Grotowski says, "to a liberation from complexes in much the same way as psychoanalytical therapy," and his acting group is "concerned with the spectator who has genuine spiritual needs and who really wishes, through confrontation with the performance, to analyse himself." The actor who has worked well within the Grotowski method is told that, at last, "you will be pure, you will be purged, you will be without sin." And, by implication, something of this cleansing is passed on to the observer. "It is a kind of redemption," Grotowski explains, fusing in the theater functions that were formerly served by religion and psychoanalysis both.

Ernest Angel, writing in the bulletin of the Council of Psychoanalytical Therapists for January, 1969, points out that theatrical therapy is moving precisely parallel to certain advanced, and perhaps extravagant, techniques being used in analysis itself. Originally the Freudian concept of the analyst's approach to his patient was one of intimacy with detachment. Some experimentalists gradually altered the analyst's role to that of Participating Observer; here detachment was surrendered and the analyst began to do something with the patient (as actors now do with audiences), if only in game form. Other experimentalists pushed on, arriving at what was called a Corrective Emotional Experience. This took the form of an actual encounter, a release through the body, and led to the discussion of the possible benefits of sexual intercourse between analyst and patient. It would seem that Freud himself foresaw this line of development and referred to it, snappishly, as "the red light district of psychoanalysis."

Mr. Angel is just as snappish about what is happening in the theater. "Actors and spectators who fanatically strip in public are not really 'liberated,'" he says. "They merely betray their dire need for a more genuine therapy, fully clothed, on chair or couch." His objection to the new processes, both in analytical and theatrical therapy, is that "Transference is absorbed by intimacy, interpretation replaced by gratification, insight by insertion, catharsis by orgasm."

Be that as it may. Had the day been cooler, Mr. Angel might have wished to delete the phrase "insight by insertion"; it's a bit much, stylistically anyway. I do think, though, that some young philosopher, casting about for a theme for his doctoral dissertation, might well take a look at that "catharsis/orgasm" contrast. If we could satisfactorily distinguish one from the other, we might have learned something about both the theater *and* sex.

Whatever attitude one takes toward the exorcism of inhibitions on stage—whether one is put off as violently as Mr. Angel, or whether one wishes to burrow a while with Grotowski to see what psychic depths unshackled actors may disclose—the fact that the theater is now viewed as a replacement for, and perhaps an advance beyond, other forms of therapy is perfectly clear. One or another kind of salvation—it is not irrelevant that a free-form rock musical should be called *Salvation*—is envisioned as a natural gift of the stage.

Political theater is of course not new. Indeed, the principal obstacle to its reasserting itself at the moment is the clear memory we have of it from the Depression-ridden 1930s. We remember what it was like, that it was sometimes exciting in a melodramatically journalistic sort of way, that it left us, in the end, with no writers of note, no plays we continue to perform. We dimly sense that though our immediate concerns were served, art was not, and we suspect that direct political exhortation in the theater must, because of its journalistic nature, remain ephemerata, second cousin to the real thing.

The urge is with us again, though, and we are once more being told that it is impossible to make a theatrical statement that is not a political statement, *all* social acts being by nature political acts. If, therefore, the theatrical act is willy-nilly political, we had best examine it and our consciences to see what political thrust we *wish* any given performance to have. We must make public what may be hidden, speak out for fear of suggesting complicity by our silence. "It is no longer possible," Jean-Claude van Itallie wrote in *The New York Times* in 1967, "to 'simply write' or 'simply direct,' or 'simply act.' " These things do not exist as esthetic activities divorced from that other arena. "Any metaphor that an artist can construct for the theater which will cause public recognition of lost limbs of ourselves, lost dreams, parts of our own shattered, scattered, and shipwrecked bodies, minds and spirits, will be a political one." That the political nature of each metaphor must be made explicit is indicated by the increasing concern that The Open Theater, with which Mr. van Itallie is associated, shows for putting caption-style political tags to the rites it performs. In *Terminal*, images of death are not permitted to remain generic and all-embracing, but must narrow sharply, now and then, into explicit protest against the Vietnam War (even though the performers seem uncomfortable with this sudden reduction and are drawn immediately into awkward cliché where before they have been original and provocative). And, of course, we have *Viet Rock*s all about us, with a *MacBird!* or *The Cuban Thing* to go for a long run or a short betweentimes.

What interests me about this renewed effort to make the theater do political work is that it occurs at exactly the same time that we have despaired of making politics do political work. Political action proper has failed. Men marched on the Pentagon, but the war did not end; the Berrigan brothers went to jail, but the war did not end; Lyndon Johnson was toppled, but the war did not end; college students engaged in direct canvassing, but the war did not end. Today's world is filled with withdrawal symptoms—it is too easy to say from politics into pot, but certainly from politics into a polite dismissal of the machinery said to be at everyman's disposal. The political machinery we have, or are likely to get in our lifetimes, is antiquated, rigged, unresponsive. Forget it. But, but, but. . . . If the machinery leaves good men impotent, try the theater. The theater offers an activist a power he cannot exert elsewhere. Theater will do the job that political structures can no longer do. Does anyone dare to doubt it?

And so with Fact, the quicksilver quarry that eludes us in our daily newspapers and even in the depths of our libraries. No one has ever told us the truth about what Winston Churchill did or what Pope Pius XII did or what J. Robert Oppenheimer did. The truth is all classified, top secret, locked away in vaults which are not to be opened until twenty-five or one hundred years after all of us are dead. Can the theater, X-ray-eyed, read for us what we cannot read for ourselves? Yes, it can, possessed as it is—through the sheer pressing presence of actor and gesture—of the power to lift a hand and cry, "Let there be light!" That, at least, is the confidence.

And so with our lives, our everyday, role-playing, constricted, unsatisfying lives. By turning life into theater and theater into life, we can enrich the quality of what we are and what we do. Let chance encounters make the play, let the play be any act we really do perform, let us be conscious in back alleys and on boulevards that we are endlessly engaged in creating a drama of event, let us make theater of life rather than fiction in order to intensify—and become more aware of—life itself. I admit that I find this prescription a bit difficult to get hold of: I can conceive of the March on the Pentagon as admirable and even necessary, but I cannot quite see it in the Burns Mantle yearbook of best plays. I can sense what is sought, though.

And I see that it is sought in the theater—in the name of theater—even when it is out of the theater. More and more the theater is anywhere, everywhere, because we are asking it to enter, and to reanimate, more and more areas of our lives. We *do* feel "shattered, scattered, and shipwrecked." And we seem to know where the shore is.

I began by saying how strange it was that the theater should be granted such universal healing powers at a time when it can scarcely save itself. And there is a troublesome little kicker in the vast compliment. It is conceivable that, in the course of becoming everything else—religion, psychoanalysis, politics, fact, life experience—it never will save itself. It will simply disappear into all of the other things it is serving, may function as a catalyst in a dozen directions and vanish from sight as the new religion-form or new political-form or new life-form emerges. It may simply be used up in the transformation. No one speaks now of using theater for *theater*, no one is concerned that theater should have an identity of its own, and because this is so all of the other uses to which it is put should be scrutinized carefully, and even criticized mercilessly, to make certain that if theater is not being served at least *something* is. I want to know that the new adaptations *work* before I surrender the theater's last shred of independence or claim to a private character.

Nevertheless, I choose to take comfort from the compliment. I am pleased that theater should be thought so life-giving, no matter what it may be being asked to give life to. I am pleased that so many people in so many pursuits turn so instinctively to the theater when they are otherwise troubled, that they lean with such confidence on an old tool I love. I am glad that it is thought so *diverse,* that its energies are thought so adaptable, its face so flexible. I am glad that if it is in many cases a last resort, it is in so many cases a first. I like to see people trusting it, whether they be wise or foolish.

And I do notice that, in the proliferation of uses to which it is put, there is a physical proliferation of however underground a kind. We moan about losing playhouses. But if we are to count all the spaces in which plays are now performed—lofts, churches, garages, the lot—as playhouses, then the simple truth of the matter is that we have more theaters available to us today than we have ever had in the whole of American history. The theaters may be small, and they may be temporary; where a commercial house usually stands for sixty or seventy years, a church can become a church again tomorrow, a storefront a store. But the fact that they are there, right now, means that all of the promised uses we have been talking about are more than promises. They are at work and they are breeding.

No one should try to say yet what is to become of it all. To speak for myself, I am repelled by some of the current uses to which the theater's powers are put, puzzled by the contradictions in others, enormously interested in a few. That's probably par. But one thing exhilarates me: the theater is so little dead that everybody, absolutely everybody, is clinging to it for dear life.

PART ONE

PART ONE

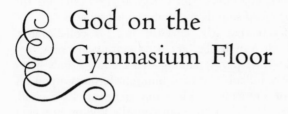

God on the Gymnasium Floor

I

IT HAD NEVER occurred to me that Cain would not know how to kill Abel.

I am now willing to suppose he would not have known, even if he'd slaughtered animals before. Men must have seemed to themselves radically different from animals then; and even if the connection had been made, how was one to be certain where the jugular was in a throat that spoke? Where would one begin to take the essential source of life out of a man? With the wrist, the power that held the bow and managed the plow? The back, with its strength to pull? The legs, carrying the whole man? Where do you strike?

I ask the questions, and suggest that for the moment I believe in them, because I have seen them worked out as harsh, straining, very tangible visual images on a stage, and they are—as physical presences—real. Strictly speaking, they were not on a stage. They were on an open floor in a loft on West 14th Street and they were mimed with spectators sitting crosslegged on the floor and cramped on benches all about. Joseph Chaikin's Open Theater is using the loft for its exercises, they are open to the public only

occasionally, there is no admission charge, and we are in that
undefined territory where playwright, director, actor, and audience interchange roles, abandon strictly logical texts, and go for
soul-broke with improvised sounds and unexplained silences.

Certain of the effects that Mr. Chaikin and his collaborator,
playwright Jean-Claude van Itallie, are now getting are most extraordinary, the Cain-Abel puzzle among them. Once Cain's heart
has become sufficiently inflamed to turn him murderously upon his
brother, the sense of desperate exploration is remarkably vivid.
Having begun his assault, Cain *must* complete the killing, however
that impossible objective is to be realized. His guilt, his intention, is
implicit in his having begun the act; there is no retreating, not in
the face of his own knowledge of what he has meant to do; *somehow* the mystery that is human life must be located in a uniformly
throbbing body and destroyed. Abel will not resist the attempt,
because, of course, he does not know what Cain is trying to do.

The Cain at The Open Theater first puts all of his sinew into the
profitless task of trying to break his brother by breaking off his
brother's hand from the arm. The picture is far more evocative,
even in some absurd sense mythic, than I'd ever have imagined.
Two spreadeagled figures, interlocked crazily at the wrist, seem
cave drawings, stick men in a struggle, rigid sources of embattled
energy that just might snap and fragment, even at the wrist, because they are so rigid. A fury of effort goes into the image; heat
flows from clenched fist to torso to face; if Abel does not splinter,
Cain will explode.

The investigation—the painful, necessary discovery of imposed
death—is pursued until at last, or near the last, Abel is little more
than a huddled bundle held high over Cain's head, perhaps to be
thrown at the spectators in a final spasm of frustration. We do not
exactly fear that the still-breathing body will actually be hurled at
us; neither do we fear that our belief will dissolve into cynicism, or
into laughter, now that we have come so close to the possible
boundaries of theater. We have by this time learned to trust the
imaginations of the people involved, and to trust the control they
are exercising over them. This is one gesture Cain might have
made, wishing to rid himself of his difficult task; we will wait until
he conceives another one, until he lowers his burden and looks for
its throat. We have lived through so many thousands of years of

violence, on and off the stage, that we are simply gratified to be put in touch with a sensed knowledge we'd forgotten: the news that it is in fact extremely difficult to kill a man. If you are going to do it yourself.

There are other provocative passages in the exercise, roughly rooted in Genesis, which is called *The Serpent* and which is, by design, unfinished, held in an improvisatory state. Tree and serpent are one, an undulating five-man Laocoön still in need of a victim. Adam and Eve discover one another with a wondering touch that is also an ignorant, hard, practical touch. And no matter what fingers the company is putting out, catching something or nothing in an ultimately closed fist, the work of reaching is itself disciplined, exact and exacting, made of firm lines. There is nothing of the sloppiness here that disfigures Tom O'Horgan's work and that will apparently dog to the death The Living Theater (Mr. Chaikin comes, at some remove now, from The Living Theater and may yet be the man to give certain of its original impulses an orderly form). Nor does the evening try to subsist on the merely coarse enthusiasm Richard Schechner in his *Dionysus in 69* and his *Makbeth* has brought to so much of the business of letting go. Of all the work now being done in this vein, The Open Theater's seems to me plainly the best and for quite plain reasons. I'll jot down three of them quickly.

1. It has humor. Over and over again it smiles at itself, smiles at its sorrow, smiles at its involvement in a universe that does not yield logical answers. When, in this instance, it softly concludes its intense engagement with Adam, Eve, the serpent, and Cain with an extremely friendly chorus of "We were sailing along, on moonlight bay," you smile with the realization that you've smiled before during the evening, it's really been all of an emotional piece. Humor is rare in such experiments, and I think it is a guarantee of seriousness. It is the humorless companies that quickly become ridiculous.

2. It rests solidly upon the word. It claims not to. Though Mr. van Itallie is himself a writer, a word man, he insists in his program notes that words are not to be regarded as "dominant" in the experience. Fortunately, they are so—in the sense that they are there, they are well put together, and they serve as a base for the visual and physical opening out. For instance, a chanted but

entirely intelligible litany introduces us to the Cain-Abel motif with the thought that "it occurred to Cain to kill his brother, but it did not occur to Cain that killing his brother would cause his brother's death." (Think about that for a second. No, never mind. You will think about it if you hear it in the theater, which means that word and thought are controlling what you see.)

This is followed by the more explicit statement, apparently taken from Louis Ginzberg's *Legends of the Jews*, that "Cain did not know how to kill Abel." With these somewhat startling suggestions ricocheting about inside our skulls, we now attend to movement, to pattern, to iconographic representation. True, the visual flowering takes up more time than the words did. But the words have dictated and they continue to dominate. They are our one true clue to the gesture that is forming, the grunt or the groan that is beginning to be heard.

3. The words, like the gestures, are respected by the performers. They are not trampled on or turned into useless sound. There are, still, rather too many self-hypnotizing silences for my own taste; I don't care to wait too long while performers make private arrangements with themselves. But when the action becomes public, it is honestly public—spoken and mimed for the benefit of others who are present. No one is catatonic yet, and many are accomplished.

In fact, although The Open Theater's more recent work, *Terminal,* has to do with the dead and the dying (as we sit in the theater we are in the process of dying; below the theater building itself lie bones long buried), its paradoxical effect is to intensify our awareness of the body as body—alive, dimensional, vulnerable, and certainly doomed, but pliant and firmly fleshed, rhythmically moving.

There is no need to reach out and touch the actors, or any need on their part to invade the bleachers where we are; their physical presences somehow reflect *our* physical presences and we become immensely conscious of our common hands and skins and shoulders and capacities for bumping one another. It is curious, but there is a greater degree of *interchangeability* between performer and viewer here than in any other experiment I have seen, though the borderline between playing space and watching space is never once transgressed.

The fusion is intuitive, a matter of being forced to breathe in and out together, a result of attending to the swaying forms before us under sometimes hypnotically blinking lights so that we are mesmerized as we might be by a magician making pendulum sweeps with a glinting watch. This is literally the case at least once in the evening: a girl who has gripped a rectangular flat so that she seems impaled on it rocks slowly right and left behind the near-prostrate form of an executed man who realizes that he has been perfectly willing to be rid of himself.

Now the effect of common tangibility, of inhabiting similar structures that can both breathe and cease breathing, is everything in *Terminal*. Working hard to make a schematic statement, an intellectualized proposition, out of the occasion is useless (and when *Terminal* does come near doing so, it is at its least effective). The two-way current is evident from the outset—"we come among the dying to call upon the dead" is the chorus' first announcement—and by simply attending to the double motion, death going one way and resurrection coming another, we can catch all the clarity we need.

We are shocked into realizing how close we are—how close we always are—to the edge of things. "This is your last chance to use your eyes," a young man in white is told as his nameless nemesis stands ready with eye patches that are, in an instant, going to seal away sight forever. One patch goes into place. The man's last searching, anxious but not panicky, glimpse of what is left of the world comes through a single, rolling, uncertain eye. At the final moment, the one eye does not know what it is most important to look *at*. Given one chance to use his voice before ultimate silence descends, what does the same human being do? He hesitates a long time, then does not use a word. He arrives, however he does it, at a sound that might be taken for a noon factory whistle, something shrill and deep and central and conclusive.

We are made aware, simply sensually aware, of the preparations we make daily for dying without acknowledging to ourselves what we are doing. The imagery here is cosmetic. Rather than wait for the embalmer (though we do several times see an embalmer at work), we—through our representatives—line up to be made to look better. The eyes are touched up in anticipation of death, the cheeks turned healthier, the lips firmer; we know how we wish to look to others when we are no longer ourselves and we make ready. ("The lines of a lifetime may be erased in less than an hour.") Sitting in the theater you stop to wonder which of the things you did today were cosmetic—anticipatory efforts to conceal the truth—in exactly the same sense. You are not badgered into doing this; you are provoked by overtones into reflecting on it for yourself.

When Joseph Chaikin's Open Theater succeeds, which is much of the time, it succeeds by this sort of radiation. Sounds are heard on stage—fourteen voices clacking nonsense syllables in counterpoint until the cumulative clamor is, incredibly, the terrible thrust of church bells—and the sounds are permitted to suggest whatever they do suggest to *you*. When the incantation of the living has, in *Terminal*, at last succeeded in summoning up some of the dead, the phrases of the dead do not announce meanings or tell stories. Rather, a dead figure, now blindly, impulsively animated, repeats not only his lurches through a limited and binding space, but his words as well. The repeated words: "Pa, why don't you do something?" "Oh, but I do, I go from the bedroom to the kitchen." We do not get beyond simple variations on these two lines. But a life—a dead life, if you like—is heard as on a record. The needle is stuck but our knowledge is complete.

It is only, I think, when the collaborators who have conjured up the evening together—directors Chaikin and Roberta Sklar, writer Susan Yankowitz—feel some need to politicize the content at hand that *Terminal* falls into cliché. "I saw a child choking on air, what did I do? I saw a man on fire, what did I do?" becomes the chant of one of the ritualistically exhumed. Precisely because it is so close to the slogans of the moment, this sort of interpolation seems less than what we have been hearing and feeling. Scale drops away, as indeed does mystery, and we feel that a moralist has been lurking among us all the time, waiting to rap our knuckles or take up a collection. Even so, the moment is somewhat redeemed by the enforced candor, the prose music of the same guilt-ridden figure's reiterated "I saw, I can't say I didn't, I saw, I can't say I didn't." Here the phrasing seems personal, that of a conscience, and we feel we have moved away from the placard.

"The judgment of your life is your life," and Gabriel's thought, spoken through a trumpet that is actually a bullhorn, that whatever you wanted most in life will become your eternity, are similarly both familiar oversimplifications, more pontifical than evocative. One other criticism. When speech *is* to be used—and there are, for instance, interviews conducted with the soon-to-be-dead—it should be thoroughly professional, projected speech; although the members of The Open Theater can score nonverbal sound and chant litanies with remarkable force, they tend to mumble a bit when written *scenes* are offered them.

Terminal is a matter of contact. While you are there, I think you will find yourself immersed in it, teased by it and rested by it at the same time. I do not find that I remember it to the same degree that I remember *The Serpent*, however. Its aftereffect washes away quickly; I confess I have had to go to my notes to jog my memory about some of the gestures I liked best during the actual experience. The best sequences of *The Serpent* do not vanish so quickly. Months after seeing it, I find myself continually reverting to its bold ambiguities, particularly to its notion that Cain did really wish to kill Abel, all right, but that he only wished to kill him, he didn't wish him dead. He expected him to be around next morning, to talk to, perhaps to kill again. *The Serpent* starts the mind off on tangents that keep extending themselves; *Terminal* seems to turn in on itself and conclude where it began, in bleak silence and a blank stare.

If you are at all interested in the theater's latest attempt to remake itself, this is the company to watch.

2

WITH The Living Theater, you were never lonely.

You could be quiet for very long periods of time, if you cared for quiet. Each of the three productions I saw at the Yale University Theater during the group's last visit to this country opened in prolonged silence. The *Antigone* began with members of the company, in twos and threes, appearing against the naked backstage wall to hesitate, stare at the audience, shield their eyes, move again ever so slightly, hesitate again. The staring continued for ten minutes. Four members of the company then dropped to their knees, scratched at the floor, and uttered low moans. The moans continued for fifteen minutes, after which the first word of the play was spoken.

The *Frankenstein*, a company improvisation rather than an adaptation of Mrs. Shelley's novel, had already found its silence before we'd entered the theater. The company was seated—had been seated for how long?—crosslegged on the stage, staring at us once more. It was meditating and we were told, briefly, that the purpose of the meditation was to enforce the levitation of a girl, long blond hair bathing her expectant body, at stage center. If the girl levitated, the event would have been consummated and nothing further need have been done; we would presumably have got up and gone home. After fifteen minutes of wordless concentration, the meditation gave way to three minutes of yoga exercises; we were assured, in a sentence, that following these three minutes the girl would levitate. On the evening I attended she did not levitate, which meant that the play had to go on, as indeed it did for some hours afterward. (I was forced to leave at eleven; the third act had not yet begun.)

The opening of *Paradise Now*, an improvisation meant to take the theater into the streets whenever the police are willing, opened less quietly, though at a whisper. Members of the company rustled through the auditorium, leaning solicitously over those in aisle seats, murmuring, "I'm not allowed to travel without a passport," "I don't know how to stop the war," "You can't live if you don't have the money," "I'm not allowed to smoke marijuana," "I'm not allowed to take my clothes off." Each of these statements was developed separately, in ascending repetition, ending at last in a roar; each roar subsided suddenly, however, to a new whisper, so that hush tended to predominate over clamor. The practice continued for one hour after the announced curtain time, at which point the members of the company took off their clothes.

You were, at certain moments, interested. You were not interested in the players stripped to G-strings, for their bodies were in the main ugly, the males scrawny, the girls underdeveloped. (An exception had to be made for Rufus Collins, whose physique would have pleased a sculptor; he also possessed the company's only distinguished speaking voice, which he was likely to destroy if he continued to scream as required.) You were interested, at least during the *Frankenstein,* in gimmickry. Once the eighteen-minute silence was over, murders erupted everywhere on a three-story jungle-gym: a man swung into space by the neck, others were garrotted, gassed, guillotined; a girl was hurled alive into a coffin and carried through the house. You probably hadn't heard a girl screaming inside a coffin before. There was a slight prickle to it.

Tubes were now attached, tangled as on a telephone switchboard, to a male corpse in an effort to restore destroyed Man to life. While a blinding, spinning, pure white light rattled at our eyeballs, the corpse turned green, red, green, red, with a lantern representing the human heart flickering and fading as hope soared, faded. The corpse was given a foot, a brain; a red eye was placed in its navel. The tubing began to pulse, pale yellow, then to run a new course away from the experiment, climbing the high scaffolding until it led us to eight or nine silhouetted bodies, suspended in midair, forming the outlines of a moving man. The massive image was unexpected. There were visual busynesses to attend to.

But, quiet or mildly bemused, you were not lonely. The players were always with you. They were in the aisles with their feet arched high, ready to kick you in the face. They were behind you, massaging your head. They were beside you, having crawled to the center of the row of seats, to touch you—touch your hair, touch your cheek, touch whatever happened to be in your pockets as they explored them. "Holy pencil," they said as they found your pencil, "holy glasses" as they found your bifocals. When the words happened to call for sibilants, it was sometimes necessary to wipe the players' spittle from your face. In this theater, this "free" theater, we were all one. There were no actors, no spectators, no critics—thanks be to God, no critics—only "human beings." Human beings being together.

It was right here that lightmindedness vanished and, if you were a human being with human sympathies, your heart began to break. For there was no togetherness, no secret sharing, no impulsive return of the performer's intimate gesture, no yes. Though you were not alone, these players were. It is true that a few students at Yale, seated on the stage to begin with, did partially strip and join hands with the company to go into the streets on the opening night of *Paradise Now;* one or two were arrested along with directors Judith Malina and Julian Beck. But these were *efforts* at joining, attempts at participation to see what participation might be like. I doubt very much that any of them returned to Europe with the Becks when their American journey was done, transformed, absorbed, committed to the cult. I doubt that the experience *was*.

Plainly it was not for the hundreds of spectators who sat patient, tolerant, willing, detached on three nights. The audience was calmly, responsibly, even respectfully neutral. It did not laugh openly very often. It did not shout out many ripostes. It did not become irritated; those who slipped away generally did so unobtrusively. If there was no hostility in the house, there was no commitment either, no fusion with the event. But it was not the spectators who were isolated. They had each other. They exchanged glances with one another, little jokes with one another, friendly reassurances with one another. They knew who they were; *they* constituted a body. It was the Becks and their companions on the stage who were isolated—alien, earnest, believing, begging, trying, trying, trying so hard, sharing with one another something they could not project beyond themselves, hopeful, self-hypnotized, phantoms on an empty playground.

The almost unbearable truth was that life and the theater had passed The Living Theater by. Their group gropings, hands sliding over loinclothed bodies piled high as a funeral pyre or clutching at their genitals in masturbatory dance, no longer seemed adventurous; they seemed a mild, if not senile, form of O'Horganism. Who would arrest these vacant-eyed children? Their gimmickry, even when it still caught the eye, was ancient, incredibly innocent, camp: the business of arranging seven bodies to look like one, or of putting curled and twisted bodies together so as to spell out the word "anarchy," was Aquacade stuff, Busby Berkeley come late; it is done better every Saturday afternoon on football fields.

The application of this technique to regular dramatic passages, as in the *Antigone*, was achingly literal: to show that Creon was trampling on men, Creon walked on the back of a man; to show that Creon was catered to by sycophants, five or six performers crawled on their knees after him, licking his thighs and rubbing their heads against his stomach.

It is small wonder that Creon (Mr. Beck) could not speak well in the circumstances or that Sophocles' play was reduced to kindergarten level, but speech was no better when the principals were freed of their barnacles. The mystique had swallowed speech, made it cheap; the confrontation between Mr. Beck's insanely grinning Creon and Miss Malina's petulant and bewildered Antigone seemed, in the reading, a confrontation between a Halloween pumpkin and Poor Pitiful Pearl. Nor was the sacrifice of speech compensated for by acrobatic skill. A girl spinning off a revolving line of bodies came away clumsily; a flutter of fingers seemed almost arthritic; a man solemnly stepping backward should not really have stepped on the hair of the nearest kneeling girl, not if he had been rehearsed.

At one time, before The Living Theater lost its quarters here and was exiled to Europe, Miss Malina, as a director, had often been able to impose a clear discipline on a production. Whether one cared for the materials being produced or not, a firm, skilled, passionate hand could be felt at work: *The Brig* had been a drill, expertly organized. Now, in the new freedom, all disciplines had gone soft. In her infrequent appearances on stage, Miss Malina herself seemed lost, somehow hurt. Mr. Beck continued to seem pontifical—and untalented. The majority of the performers did not seem to be actors at all. They were converts, only converts.

The intellectual life of the group had been reduced to this: On the second night at Yale, there were some two hundred students who had not been able to buy tickets; the house was sold out and more—perhaps a hundred and fifty additional spectators had been permitted to sit on the stage. A chant went up outside: "The theater belongs to the people!" (Were there no people inside, filling every inch of available space?) The Living Theater performers became very agitated about the exclusion of those others who wanted admission. They proposed, heatedly, that the doors be thrown open to all who wished to enter. (The aisles, bear in mind, were already filled with members of the company.) Word came back that the theater was overcrowded and that the Fire Department would admit no more. Fury now raged from the stage. How could the theater be *free*, how could the country be *free*, so long as there were Fire Departments?

This theater of freedom meant to be a theater of joy. It was more nearly a matter for tears.

3

THE FIRST production of Jerzy Grotowski's Polish Laboratory Theatre that we were given an opportunity to see in this country was a ritualized reduction of a seventeenth-century Spanish play, Calderon's *The Constant Prince*, partly as adapted by Polish playwright Julius Sowacki, partly as compressed into a hydraulic-valve hiss by Grotowski. It was in Polish. It was not only a constant series of physical tremors, a near-naked rib cage fluttering like an immature animal in panic, it was also a foaming overflow of words, words spat out at Speed Speech. (If there is Speed Read, why not Speed Speak?) Because no adequate translations were available to cue us into the Spanish or Polish originals, because the adaptation was so free that it would not have mattered if there had been, because the whole verbal content was cried at us with such garrulous and pained force that we were inclined to say "What's the matter?" rather than "What's the meaning?", there was no way of accounting for the occasion totally or intimately. It was only possible, at first exposure, to watch, wait, describe.

What *can* be described? An exposure to the body that is almost fusion with the body. A prince is being tormented on an open rack—in reality a highly varnished platform reflecting the glare of two crossed spotlights—by the ordinary people of this world, the ordinary people including such kings as may rule it.

The prince is stripped to a loincloth, crucifixion style, flogged with his own greatcloak, jabbed at with an umbrella point, lifted, dropped, danced circles about, reviled and caressed. Ribs are counted with prying fingers, nostrils examined.

The prince, sputtering his anguish though not resisting his tormentors, speaks with his lips pressed directly against the floor. The effect of contact, though it is only a contact with wood, is immediately visceral. (We seem to remember what it is like from having done it as children.) The prince rises, lifts one heel to throw his angular body out of balance, wrenches himself sideways as though he could continue to stand broken-legged, scourges himself, groans like a pierced bull, topples, salivates, quivers, slips without warning into a *pietà* relationship with a seated woman, expires.

The performer who is undergoing all of this, Ryszard Cieslak, seems to have the shoulders of Frankenstein's monster, the ascetic elongated torso of a John the Baptist, the head of Prometheus; his veins, under stress, are as defined and simple as those of Michelangelo's David; we are aware that we have been invited to look at the human body as sculpture unstylized, unabstracted, as a thing that is both modeled and breathing. Usually sculpture diminishes the body by being so much more than the body is. Usually the body, when exposed, diminishes the body by being only the poor thing it is. Here nothing is diminished, not the body, not sculpture either; the two meet as exchangeable partners, the relationship is discovered to be true.

The surrounding figures make less point, discover less. Swathed in black, heads sometimes covered with cloth, chanting insults that still have religious vibrations clinging to them, leaping spastically from corner to corner of the arena and then lunging at one another as well as at their victim, they are bleak, noncommittal, automated zeros, authoritative nobodies. They *look* as though they understood their own out-of-kilter postures, their feet are securely grounded no matter what attitude they have now lurched into, they command the space they land on; but, without language, they do not say much about themselves.

And so we watch, our eyes wandering now and then but always coming back, our ears caught mainly by the incredibly sustained rhythmic groaning of the prince (can the voice be made to do this without destroying itself, we wonder). We watch from behind high partitions (so high that we are meant to have the feeling of peeping over them, staring downward into a kind of bear pit) or lean forward on still higher crossbars that keep us from tumbling outward and over into the spare, sterile scene of operations below. We are unfamiliarly passive, detached, remotely committed. We are not hypnotized. We are halted.

Here we have come to the theater, here is some sort of theater going on without us though in our unacknowledged presence, here is that theater disappearing from view after an hour and a half (or less) as swiftly and silently as an unlooked-for short circuit, here are we rising and shuffling off our platforms quietly, without discomfort, not amused by the experience but amused by our common aloneness once the event has abandoned us, moving off down the street again without agitation or regret.

The Washington Square air is peaceful as we go. We do not really wonder whether we have been provoked or rewarded; we feel that we have come as to a necessary appointment and that we would honor the appointment again.

As of course we did. And now I have been searching back through my notes and my random memories of the three performances The Polish Laboratory Theater offered us to see if I could say whether any one moment was more representative for me of the company's special qualities than all the others I'd been exposed to. I think I have found one. It occurred during *Acropolis*, the piece in which Jewish and Greek legend run together like a blood puddle at Auschwitz.

The center of the stage, a construction of gas pipes, bathtubs, and wheelbarrows gone rusty, was for the moment emptied of actors. We, sitting directly on the stage, were closer to the core of things than the performers were. We were aware of one another and in occupation. The performers were all behind us, scattered in the unidentified dark, making rushed whispering sounds that felt as though the walls of a room were hurrying to meet at a corner.

A sudden sibilant raked my ear; the speaker was near my shoulder; I didn't turn to see who it might be. A body was thrust violently past and above me, to land with a thud in the wheelbarrow an inch from my head. I didn't shy, or think I was going to be struck. I looked at the audience faces opposite, and to the left. Almost all were open-mouthed as the actors emerged into light again, wooden soles stomping, eyes heavy-lidded and vacant white, shoulders thrust forward to jab at other bodies in erratic rhythm; otherwise, the audience faces were entirely composed.

That is to say, Mr. Grotowski has altogether succeeded in achieving at least three of his promised effects:

He has put the audience and the actors together in an extraordinarily close relationship without insisting upon that false intimacy, that overbearing directness of contact, that marks and mars the work, say, of The Living Theater. The actors are next to you. But they never invade, or so much as threaten to invade, your public privacy. You are you, they are they; our functions are distinct even if our bodies should touch. We tumble together, so many checkers in a glass, without dissolving into one another and ending up mud. Atoms interplay, but retain their stability.

He has arrived at a discipline in performing that breeds confidence in the performers and in the occasion. Though all protective forms have apparently broken down and we are absolutely exposed to the violence of performers manhandling properties where we sit, we are not fearful that performer or prop is going to lurch out of control and do us damage. To play our parts we need only be still; the action will wash over us but leave us intact. In honoring his own skill, the actor honors us. We trust him.

He has created composure, rest, openness, ease in his audience. This is established, a bit mysteriously, even before the performance begins. The auditorium doors are kept locked until a few minutes before performance time. The audience gathers on the steps, standing, seated, smoking, chatting—and waits. By all the laws of logic, this should be irritating. Instead, the mood becomes unusually sociable. I wouldn't be surprised if people who haven't spoken in years speak while waiting for Grotowski. Why? I'm not certain. It is conceivable that those who have cared enough to come (or tried desperately to get in, the seating being so limited) have come precisely because they are open, or wish to be open, or wish to *seem* to be open, to a radical rethinking of what theater might be. The willingness makes them homogeneous. It makes them docile, patient, bemused, friendly.

Once inside, the interior quiet continues. One may be seated on stage in a very sharp white light without being made to feel self-conscious. Woolgathering during the performance, one may catch another pair of eyes across the way woolgathering in just the same way. There is no guilt in this, nor is there sly connivance. Both pairs of eyes are apt to redirect themselves to the action, as if by common consent and with the tacit acknowledgment that they'll be woolgathering again a little later.

Cruelty or suffering within the action does not agitate anyone looking on; the cruelty, the suffering, is studied, passively, reflectively, without engagement. The audience remains throughout the performance in repose, and afterward leaves with a psyche as unruffled as the actors' faces. The effect is that of time out from living. Apprehension has been outlawed for an hour or so. If this is a theater of "trance" for the actors, to use one of Grotowski's phrases, it is nearly that for the spectators too.

Control in the performing, trust in the watching, detachment in the close relationship, finally a kind of peace for both actor and spectator (for the actor because he has completed his act, for the spectator because he has let himself be calm and undemanding)— these are good things to have, in and for themselves. It should be stressed that, in Grotowski's theater, they exist in and for themselves. They are not meant to lead us on toward any other value, to play servant to any other thing. They are the end of it, except for whatever indirect private therapy can be read into the qualities themselves. The experience is a closed one.

The actor's function, for instance, has been entirely altered. He has ceased being an instrument and has become an object. Normally the actor is thought of as an interpreter of what someone else has prepared; he is an instrument of the playwright, a servant of the public, a tool used by a director in bringing playwright and public together. Here he is forbidden to "play to" the public or show them the least concern. In Grotowski's "poor theater" everything that might interfere with the actor's concentration upon himself is pared away: costume that might make him pretend to be another person, lighting that might shelter him in atmosphere, a text that might demand he serve another man's psychology. He is his own man now, alone. He is alone with his own body, his own capacity for making sounds, his own personal stripped-down truth.

For Grotowski only the act of the actor dare be regarded as "theater." Brushing everything else aside, the actor trains himself to be responsive to whatever impulses stir at the "innermost core" of his being, taking care that his reflexes work so quickly that "thought has no time to intervene." The face, normally expressive of thought, becomes a mask. Words, which "are always pretexts," are to be subordinated to preliterary sound. And, since the actor must forge his "score" out of his own body and nothing else, the text written by another (the play proper in our usual understanding) either vanishes altogether or is treated as a malleable plaything with no authority of its own.

Work "without a text," Grotowski asks? And answers: "Yes; the history of the theater confirms this. In the evolution of the theatrical art the text was one of the last elements to be added. If we place some people on a stage with a scenario they themselves have put together and let them improvise their parts as in the Commedia dell' Arte, the performance will be equally good even if the words are not articulated but simply muttered." Grotowski's special bogey is literature. "Faced with literature," he says, "we can take up one of two positions: either, we can illustrate the text through the interpretation of the actors. . . . In that case, the result is not theater, and the only living element in such a performance is the literature. Or, we can virtually ignore the text . . . reducing it to nothing."

Here we come upon a problem, a serious one. In closing off the performed act as he does, closing it off particularly to the intrusion of the dramatist, Grotowski forces us into the paradox that what is good for theater is bad for drama, or that what we have always called drama (the verbal structuring of the act by a writer) is bad for theater. The two are not bedmates but mortal enemies, unrelated, mutually corrupting. With his either-or fiat Grotowski declares theater to be—always and in all ways—a simple thing, not a complex one, much as Elizabeth Hardwicke does to opposite effect when she declares that drama is first and last literature and nothing else.

Is the interplay between drama and theater which we have come to call casually by either name actually capable of being reduced to this simplicity? At this late date in time I rather doubt it, since the evolutionary process *has* been at work. Mr. Grotowski, perhaps a shade disingenuously, claims that theatrical history proves his point because in the evolutionary process words came last. Does that mean that they don't belong? Or could it mean that they are an organic extension of the original impulse arriving through increased complexity at a new richness? The evolutionary movement is always toward complexity. In most cases the new complexity achieves a higher order of existence, of perception and the capacity for action.

It is impossible to prove now what the Commedia dell' Arte, with its improvised performances, was or was not for the simple reason that no one wrote it down. Such descriptive fragments as survive do not suggest that it was superior, *as theater*, to Molière, who did write it down. Molière worked on a Commedia base; the time and intelligence he spent writing it down most probably constituted an improvement. I do not really suppose that the first playwright, or any playwright thereafter, marched in upon the actors and took over, stealing the form they had developed. I think the actors asked for his help, begging him to come in because they didn't know what to say or didn't feel they were saying it all or saying it well enough.

This process, subliminally and ironically, is already repeating itself in the Grotowski laboratory. The third of the pieces shown here, *Apocalypsis Cum Figuris*, was improvised, subverbally and then verbally, by the players. When the entire "score" was worked out in terms of movement and sound, Mr. Grotowski turned aside to the library and, helping himself to substantial passages from Dostoevski, T. S. Eliot, Job, and St. John, substituted "literary" materials for what the actors had been saying on impulse. Why, if not to increase the profundity and the power of the sounds coming from the actors?

It isn't possible for someone who does not understand Polish to say exactly how these insertions affect the experience. And they are in any case used impressionistically, not for narrative purposes. Nevertheless, and quite plainly, in this particular case it is the director who is taking on the task of the writer, as in the cases of Shakespeare and Molière it was the actor who did; he is here *selecting* what is to be said, consciously structuring it if not actually inventing the words. I suspect that this is how the complex organism of the "play," theater and drama simultaneously, came into being in the first place and how it is likely to continue coming into being so long as the evolutionary impulse continues to press us forward.

I found myself content with all three performances of the company, content to be there, content to experience this much, content to go away contented after the hour or so of playing time. I did, however, find myself less interested in the third than in the first. I did not become bored. I simply found myself thinking my own thoughts oftener. The closed experience is a real experience (as it always has been with a clown or a serious mime), but it is not, by definition, an expanding one. It is capable of infinite variation but not much advancement.

I wondered, as I sat on a bench with my back to a radiator

watching a black-clad Simpleton carry an apostle in flaring white robes about the open floor on his twisted shoulders, whether my attentiveness might not be diminishing simply because it was being given nothing more complex to feed on. The human mind, whether on its way to the moon or to the Washington Square Methodist Church, says more, more. That's the way of it.

4

THE TERRIBLE struggle of the theater to give birth to itself all over again can be seen on a dozen fronts today. The fronts tend to be floors, the floors of garages, lofts, and school gymnasiums, and the floors, in the process, come to resemble snake pits as much as anything. Sweaty bodies rise and fall, murmurs and moans ebb and flow in incantatory rhythms if not the rhythms of parturition, a tangle of bodies seems to become a single heaving body straining to rid itself of the fetus it hopes it contains.

Be literal about it. The theater, believing itself to be dead in all of its older manifestations, has plunged or is trying to plunge into its own womb, seeking out a fresh identity, looking for a third coming. It remembers, plainly, that in its first two comings it came out of a religious or ceremonial impulse, out of mythic rite and sometimes out of god-induced ecstasy. To find itself again, to find a new way of being itself, it must go back to its sources, beyond Euripides as much as Albee, beyond form and even coherence into the dim intuited gropings by means of which flesh became spirit and spirit flesh.

That current experimentation means in some sense to be religious is inescapable. Richard Schechner, defending the dithyrambic frenzy of his *Dionysus in 69*, reminds us that Jerzy Grotowski "speaks of his theater in religious terms, of 'novitiates' and 'disciples.' " Jean-Claude van Itallie, introducing us to his mime-drama *The Serpent*, insists on restoring the theater's "original religious function of bringing people together in a community ceremony where the actors are in some sense priests or celebrants, and the audience is drawn to participate with the actors in a kind of eucharist."

As I sat, not long ago, in a college gymnasium watching yet another group of performers approach each other in sackcloth to make silent gesture or utter single syllables divorced from linear content, I understood—or thought I understood—that the patient, attentive response of the students around me was as much religious as anything else. It was not theatrical or esthetic in any overt or definable way: no laughter, no tears, no leaning forward, no turning away in contempt because of the lack of these things. The student spectators were of course merely curious in part. They will always opt for the new whether it rewards them—yet—or not. But there was a willingness to be silent, to be respectful, to be worshipful of an effort at least, that existed above and beyond these things. They wished, I think truly wished, to be incorporated in a ceremony, to be embraced by myth if any such thing could be arranged, to be opened to what they were later quickly willing to call spiritual possibility.

I know because I asked them later. The performers on this occasion had not really been good, had not arrived at anything persuasive on the floor. They were amateurs and it was necessary to indulge them. But they *had* been indulged and when I suggested to the assembled group that they had been indulged out of a religious rather than an esthetic wish, the students instantly agreed. They were more than willing to enter into a religious experience simultaneously with a dramatic one, or prior to a dramatic one if it had to be that way. Why not have all experiences at once? Why not submit to a state of mind that might, perhaps, one day produce drama? If it did, well and good; the patient submission would have been worth it. If not, well and good again. *No* state of mind, least of all the one called religious, ought to be neglected by anyone interested in making contact with what is. I did not really need Andrew M. Greeley to tell me, a month or so later in *The New York Times* magazine, that "there's a new-time religion on campus," that, no matter how bizarre or occult current preoccupations might seem to be, "the return to the sacred" was real.

The "return to the sacred" can exist independently of drama, of course, or of the effort to make drama. But it has helped to give drama's own new effort houseroom, it has created a tentative audience for it, it has nudged open a psychic door at the very time drama wanted to go through it. And, superficially at least, drama theorists can make a good case for the desire to go through.

It's true that drama did twice get itself born of religious ritual. So far as we can tell about the Greeks, a band of worshipers began by singing and dancing in honor of a god—Dionysus or some other—and ended up by impersonating him. Mime leapt from liturgy. Certainly this is what happened in medieval times, long after drama had been lost and needed a whole new matrix. Several minor portions of the mass were elaborated to allow for a responsive exchange of dialogue lines and from dialogue mimetic performance sprang up.

Logical, then, that we should wish it to happen a third time. Perhaps there is no other way to *get* drama, no alternate source. And so we drum ourselves into the incantatory, attempt to dance ourselves into the ecstatic, reduce dialogue once again to ritual repetitions, mime our ways toward the mythic. We speak urgently, and in some groups exclusively, of priest or celebrant, of ceremony or rite rooted in myth, of eucharist.

There is one bothersome catch. The two earlier religions that gave birth to drama believed in themselves. Whatever the Greeks may have privately thought about their gods, they believed sufficiently in a force named Dionysus to personify him graphically and then to stand in awe of what had been personified. Dionysus had, for this audience, a concrete, tactile presence. (It is still powerfully sensed in *The Bacchae*, written at a time of relative skepticism.) For medieval Christians the eucharist was truly the body and blood of Christ, which they ate and drank. These were functioning religions, consensus religions, most literally "deposits of faith." Being alive in this way in the minds of worshipers, they possessed procreative power. They could generate expressions of themselves (dithyrambic structures, hymns, masses) and expressions rushing beyond themselves (plays, dances, paintings) of authentic style, feeling, animation. The authenticity—and the heart to *do*—came from the religious guarantee.

Drama at the present time has no such functioning consensus available to it, no new mainspring charged with the specific religious energy to set the whole vast procreative process in motion. We are trying for a third drama though we do not live in the time

of a third religion. We haven't a new impulse to guarantee the
birth of a new mode. This is immediately obvious when one
glances at the materials being worked over by those now in the
vanguard. *Dionysus in 69* is, of course, a reworking of Euripides'
The Bacchae. Vanguard? Mr. Schechner has gone all the way
back—as far as our literary history permits—in his search for a
religious impulse capable of breeding a fresh form of drama. He
really does wish us to act on the impulse he has attempted to
borrow: to get up from our places on the floor and to enter, to
feel, the interior Dionysiac pressure toward abandon that the
Greeks felt and that exists as a record in Euripides' play. We do
not in fact feel this specific religious impulse today, however; we
do not bring it into the theater with us as deposit or guarantee.
The specific religious impulse is dead. It has been dead for a very
long time. Because it is dead, the gesture dependent upon it must,
for the most part, be empty, effortful, artificial. We can try to let
ourselves go, but there is nothing genuine pushing us.

The Serpent is more fortunate though no more '69, ceremonially
speaking, than *Dionysus. The Serpent* depends almost wholly upon
Genesis for its inspiration—Adam and Eve, Cain and Abel, man
begetting—and in so doing draws upon two religious traditions
that are ancient rather than new: the Jewish and the Christian.
Ancient as these two are, they both continue to possess procreative
power of a kind. Audiences may have long since dropped literal
belief in the stories being told, but they have not lost imaginative
rapport with them. The Genesis narratives remain familiar, they
have belonged to us personally from childhood on, they are shared.
Because they do constitute a common heritage they can, when
they are well used on a stage floor, unite an audience, consciously
or subconsciously. The religious substructure of *The Serpent* is a
substructure we have not lost touch with.

Bear in mind, though, that it is not a '69 substructure, not a
hitherto untapped source of energy. Attractive as it may be, it has
its roots in something old. Which means, to me, that we cannot be
at all certain of getting something new out of it. We might. Then
again, we might simply arrive at the medieval morality play all
over again. Indeed, the "play" I saw performed by another group
in a gym turned out to be exactly like Yeats without words.

Society at the present time does not offer the stage the *original*

religious grounding it is looking for in order to create a wholly
original drama. The situation is not comparable to that in which
the Greeks or medieval Christians found themselves. Rather, the
stage is confronted with the kind of audience I sat with in that
school gym one Saturday afternoon. I have said that the students
were willing to describe the occasion as some kind of religious
search. But it would not have been possible to assign to the assembled audience a religious character of any definable kind. There
were probably believers in the group, though of various persua-
sions. There were undoubtedly unbelievers, in goodly numbers.
Religiously speaking, the group was amorphous, diffused, structurally incoherent. No formal name could possibly have been put
to it, no credo devised capable of gaining its uniform assent. All
audiences are like that today. How, then, do you create a ceremony to represent it that is not in itself amorphous, diffuse, and
structurally incoherent? How do you create a *ceremony* at all? A
ceremony describes and articulates a belief. Here there is so much
indeterminateness that it would not even be possible to construct a
ceremony of unbelief.

The stage goes on trying, as perhaps it must. The people who do
the work, of course, know all about the fragmented nature of the
audience, the absence of consensus, the hollowness of the merely
adopted myth. They embrace nonstructure willingly, accept in-
explicitness as inevitable. What they really hope to do is uncover
whatever residual binding belief may be found to exist in the
group subconscious, to tap through their exercises a kind of
dramatic/religious common denominator, to excavate the two
kingdoms at once and possibly as the same thing.

That is to say, they have reversed the old process, the only
process we have thus far known. Drama once grew out of religion.
We are trying to grow religion out of drama. We are trying to
grow religion out of drama so that we can grow drama out of the
religion once we have got it.

Backward, back-breaking, self-consuming. Not enough for
drama to have to reinvent itself through religion. It must reinvent
the religion too. Drama is being asked to derive itself from an
experience it must first create.

Is this possible? To be honest, I doubt it. History doesn't suggest
that things are likely to happen so. We can endlessly debate the

priority of the chicken or the egg, but no one has ever seen them come to birth at the same moment, out of sheer will power. Am I out to discourage the effort then? No, not that, either, as I discovered talking to a student audience that day. I couldn't see the profit in the process, yet I didn't want to try to curb it, not yet, not too soon. History is no absolute. If it offers us few surprises, we may yet surprise it; we may have to, in various areas. And theoretical processes that do prove to be impossible when tried very often throw off valuable by-products in the trying.

What I would like to do is underscore the extraordinary difficulty of the task being attempted. It is very easy to toss about words like "myth," and "ritual," "ceremony" and "eucharist." Untalented woolgatherers can do it. It is made even easier by the fact that these very words have so little real content for us at the present time, carry such little weight in our actual lives. It is their weightlessness that makes them so manipulable.

But the thing being attempted is so far from easy, so far from being a matter of picking up handy coins and tossing them casually onto the floor, that if we are to avoid frustration and fury and premature failure we'd best recognize the effort as the unprecedented, the entirely radical, the utterly fundamental gamble it is. As my ten-year-old, a budding scientist, tells me, the first step toward solving a problem is to state the problem.

Togetherness

I

Now that I have my lower lip, my two legs, and my right arm back in working order, I may be able to set down a few reflections on the most ambitious and amply endowed product of the Megan Terry–Tom O'Horgan–Cafe La Mama combine to date. The project was called *Massachusetts Trust;* it was improvisationally arrived at during six weeks of experiment at Brandeis University (with the staging done *first* and the text thereafter), and it opened as the *pièce de résistance*, to considerable resistance, at a Brandeis summer festival. After seeing it, it did take a while to get back in writing trim.

You must understand that there had been no violence involved. All of the evening's violence—or "Vi-lence," as it was generally pronounced by Mr. O'Horgan's actors—took place on the stage. There, actors were seized, turned upside down, and had their heads inserted into other actors' crotches while loyally continuing their unavoidably garbled speeches, actors who may have been representing men of the Mafia were shot down in cold ketchup, and what seemed thousands of supernumeraries raced hotly up the aisles to assault a possible political candidate in a free-for-all that was really quite convincing. Where a melee is wanted, O'Horgan is your man.

The evening was roughly political, generally unintelligible, devoutly gymnastic. But it must be said that whenever the assorted acrobats left the stage to join those of us who were being responsibly attentive in the auditorium—this happened approximately every one and one-half minutes by my watch—they behaved with admirable discretion. They looked closely into our faces, demonstrating eyeball-to-eyeball contact, they crawled down the aisles clutching at us only occasionally, they offered us cookies—but they did nothing to account for my own eventually paralyzed condition.

The problems I continued to have with lips, legs, and formerly stout right arm were all problems of response. Obviously we'd been meant to respond in some way to the visual, aural, and physical inundation, to the fact that we were totally surrounded by blaring microphones, booming drums, performers dangling directly over our heads from swinging cranes, feet, feet, feet forever. (All performers went barefooted and were rarely upright, which meant that dirty soles became our most familiar companion.)

Response, however, was not meant to be uniform. Text and staging were carefully uncohesive, rigorously fragmented, so that nothing—neither political comment nor abstract visual image—could come into the kind of focus that might have bound an audience together. Massed eyes and ears in the auditorium were denied the definition that would have made them see and hear the same things, with the result that each onlooker responded as *he* responded, and hang the fellow on the other side of the house. It was every nervous system for itself.

This was undoubtedly the intention of the creative spirits behind the enterprise. Engagement ought to be *personal*. For me, it became very personal. For instance, as a person, I am fond of hearing what is being said. This is mere habit, I know, and somewhat outmoded; but *I* leap for joy whenever a string of words escapes the cacophony in the general form of a sentence or a thought. And I did leap when, the cross-sound having subsided for a moment, an actor was to be heard discussing how he'd been stretched out with a girl, happily sucking on her lower lip while she sucked on his upper lip. Ah, I thought with relief, something tangible, something to cling to as a memory when next all hell broke loose. Because all hell promptly broke loose again, I had time to cherish this one little remnant of straightforward speech, of remembered life, and to think about it. That was my downfall. You *can't* chew on a girl's lower lip while she is nibbling on your upper. It's not possible. I began trying to imagine it in the theater and for days thereafter found myself unable to pass a mirror without rehearsing it, with the result that one of my lips—it was becoming harder to tell them apart—soon looked as though it had barely survived the ministrations of a particularly unfeeling dentist. I report this simply because it may make Miss Terry and Mr. O'Horgan happy. They did engage me.

My legs had become engaged because I am accustomed to crossing them in the aisle. The principal advantage of being a reviewer with aisle seats has never been the proclaimed one of having easy, immediate access to the nearest exit; reviewers are people who sit *through* shows, and, after all, if you are firmly determined to get out of a theater you can get out no matter where you're sitting. The principal advantage is that you can lop one knee over the other and let a leg dangle in the lovely aisle.

Unfortunately, if the aisle is going to be occupied by racing, gyrating, tumbling bodies, you are going to have to get that one foot out of there in a hurry or run the risk of maiming an actor, which no decent man would wish to do.

Now it would have been perfectly all right at *Massachusetts Trust* if the actors had *stayed* in the aisles. You'd have adjusted very quickly to the new state of affairs, tucked your knobby knees back where other people put them (pressed against the seat just ahead), and rested content. But Mr. O'Horgan's gymnasts were inconsistent in this respect, never making up their minds where they most wanted to be, and it was *up* onto the stage, *down* into the aisles, up, down, up, down, the whole night through. And, since leg-crossing is by this time a reflex with me, I was thoughtlessly lopping and then frantically retracting until the nice lady sitting next to me began to look at me most peculiarly. I had not been doing my set-ups conscientiously that summer and I may possibly have come out of the theater in better trim, though with a twitch. Whatever the upshot, I did have muscles that *remembered* where they'd been that night. They knew they'd been involved.

As for the matter of my right arm, the trouble came about this way. I'd been paying close attention to the stage, hoping to discover why one of the political parties involved was searching so assiduously for a "tiny-titted" candidate, when a performer who was crawling stealthily down the aisle reached out and put a hand on my arm, whether for solidarity or support I cannot say. He held it there quite a long time, so I assumed that this was yet another example of the contact so many theatricalists are groping for these days.

Well, I didn't mind. He wasn't brutal or anything. Just one thing happened. I became terribly, terribly conscious of my right arm. I couldn't think of anything else. I couldn't think about the actor or what he might be doing in relation to the play. I couldn't think about the play. I just thought about this thing that was *mine*, buzzing there all by itself, imprisoned, detached, improbable. Even now I still look at it nights, when I'm alone. You see, it had somehow left me, divorced itself from what was once an unthinking, unselfconscious unit. My arm had been isolated, and I waited a long time for it to relax and go back about its business.

I am sure that if I'd told Mr. O'Horgan about this, he'd have said fine—if the evening had made me conscious, really conscious, of *anything*, even my arm, it would have accomplished its purpose. The current avant-garde has a standard reply to everything that may be said about it, whether hostile or friendly. Raise an objection and that was the objection you were expected to make, supposed to make; the event brought you alive so that you could make it. This is rather a bottomless well and it led to an incident at intermission time on the steps of the handsome circular building that houses Brandeis' three theaters. One theatergoer was proclaiming his dislike of Megan Terry's random text, which was politically a great deal less trenchant than, say, *Of Thee I Sing*, and of the planned unintelligibility in the staging which kept him from being able to say just *what* he disliked about it. A gentleman connected with the production overheard him and immediately snapped, "Well, are you going to boo at the end?" The first man, trained to politeness in the auditorium, said no, he thought not.

"Well, you should!" snapped his interrogator. "You're sitting here all evening, and you should do *something!*"

There is a certain logic to this; and, in fact, there was a good bit of booing, mixed with fairish applause, at final curtain. The difficulty with this bottomless-well position, the assertion that any response is the right response, is that it turns booing into victory, makes good and bad drama, good and bad performing, good and bad reaction, indistinguishable.

Pass that. The most curious sensation I had, listening to the split responses and paying some attention to my own constant distraction, was this: the more public the experimental theater tries to be, the more private it becomes.

2

I AM TOLD that when Joseph Heller's *We Bombed in New Haven* was running on Broadway, Jason Robards had one rather unsettling evening. Mr. Robards was playing an air force captain whose duty it was to send pilots to their probable deaths, but he was doing so in a play that insisted upon two actor-audience intimacies now much in vogue. One intimacy had to do with the fact that an actor is not just an actor or a character, but a *person.* ("I'm Ron Leibman" said Ron Leibman, stepping out of rank and out of role, just as in *Dionysus in 69* downtown the supporting players continually reminded the actor playing Dionysus that he was not Dionysus but a student at NYU.) Mr. Heller's point, in the play, was that whereas actors and characters always wind up safe in their dressing rooms, *persons* can be killed. He wanted us to remember that in actual warfare there are no actors, only people.

The second intimacy had to do with acknowledging the fact that we, as an audience, were present at the play and could, if we wished, take a hand in it. There came a time in the evening when Mr. Robards understood that all of the fictitious killing was quite real. Appalled, he tried to put a stop to it. He was informed by his immediate superior, however, that orders could not be questioned, that the bloodshed must go on. Mr. Robards, thoroughly angered, retorted that it would not go on because—turning to those of us seated out front—*we* wouldn't let it go on. We would halt the vicious cycle, now that we knew.

Mr. Heller was, of course, here using the actor-audience relationship for the purposes of irony. He assumed that we would certainly not intervene on Mr. Robards' side, that we would continue to sit there as we always do sit there, allowing war to go on as we always do allow war to go on. Our silence was to indict us, our refusal to act in the theater was to become our refusal to act in life.

Except that on this particular evening Mr. Robards is said to have finished the scene with his usual bitter discouragement, starting toward the portals to execute his orders and make way for the next sequence, when he was suddenly summoned back to the footlights. A little knot of audience members had got up from their seats, come down the aisle, and were now standing grouped at the edge of the stage. He had been quite right, these unexpected activists told him, and they were *not* going to permit the fighting to continue.

Apparently Mr. Robards, who at least wanted the play to continue, tried gentle persuasion, urging the interlopers to return to their seats quietly. They wouldn't. They'd been invited to protest and they were protesting. If the way to stop war was to stop this play, they would do it. That's what the play had been asking them to do all along, wasn't it? On they went, refusing to heed Mr. Robards' plea that there were other scenes to be played, until, out of his element and at last out of patience, Mr. Robards exploded. "What do you want *me* to do?" he cried, "I'm only an actor!"

I am also told that the author of the play was present that night and was overheard reflecting, on the sidewalk afterward, "Maybe I ought to write something for Jason to extemporize."

Two crises, two contradictions. The actor proclaims himself more than an actor only to take refuge in his limitations as an actor. The author urges a response to his play that his play is not prepared to contain.

Now these are rather light instances, more amusing than theory-shattering. But they do reflect in miniature a curious double effect that seems to haunt almost all of our current attempts to experiment with a participating audience and a spontaneously creating acting company. Experiment of this kind is by now fairly well developed, albeit with differing emphases from group to group.

As Richard Schechner, director of The Performance Group, has pointed out, methods are eclectic, the ultimate ends not sharply focused just now. He writes: "We have not yet answered the questions—when during a performance should the audience move; when should it stay still; when should it talk to the performers; when should it remain quiet; when should everyone see what is going on; when should only some people or no one see?" The answers Mr. Schechner eventually gives will no doubt part company with some of those Mr. O'Horgan or Mr. Beck or Mr. Chaikin give. It is too soon to be certain; and it would be unfair to imagine all companies as one company moving in one direction.

But it is probably fair to say that at least two propositions are common to, and fundamental for, all of the organizations now working at what has been called "participatory theater." One is that a higher degree of intimacy, of union or communion, than now exists between actor and audience is sought. The other is that in the process of seeking, and to help the process along, the audience must become more active than it has been in the past.

Simple enough propositions, and rather readily accepted in theory. The puzzling thing is that, in practice, each tends to produce its opposite. The effort at fusion tends to fragment the audience. The demand that the audience become more active tends to make it more passive.

Consider. An actor fixes his eye upon me, comes up the aisle to speak to me or touch me, all in the interests of a new kind of embrace. He wishes to destroy my aloofness, my detachment, my aloneness. But, to speak for myself, the one moment in the world when I feel most alone, most isolated, most conscious of myself as an individual, is the moment when an actor in an aisle starts directly toward *me*. Suddenly I am cut off from the group, even from the person I came with. I am exposed in space, I am no longer audience and I am certainly not actor. I am only I, unrelated, singled out, limited, confined, achingly conspicuous. I do not leap forward into that embrace; I retreat into a shell deeper than my customary shell.

Naturally I at first attribute this reaction to my own inhibitions;

here is the very hangup from which this kind of theater is attempting to free me. I quickly notice, however, that my reaction is by no means special. From the apprehensive shifting of bodies, the studious looking away, the transparent sheepishness of expression which afflict the next person—and the next and the next—singled out for a performer's personal attention it is clear that virtually all who are approached are upon the instant uncomfortable. Some have become uncomfortable enough under pressure to swat the actors away with their folded programs; most endure, try to grin, and pray for release.

More important than my own response or any subjective response I may wish to attribute to others, however, is what may be observed objectively about the audience as a group. It ceases to be a group and becomes an uncohesive assembly of individuals. During the performances of The Living Theater at Yale, for instance, the audience did not, as a unit, respond to the invitation to mount the stage or to disrobe. During *Paradise Now* a few students straggled to the stage to join the throng of students who had been there from the outset because there was nowhere else to seat them. I saw one young man begin to unbutton his shirt; he stopped at the navel, unimpelled to go further. I understand there have been occasional responses more robust than this (Richard Schechner is known to have stripped at the Brooklyn Academy of Music). But responses seem to come, when they come at all, *singly* (Mr. Schechner was of course predisposed). I have heard of no spectacular group fusions with an acting company. At Yale the audience was inclined to remain on its traditional side of the house, where it was entirely tolerant and composed.

It was also entirely decomposed—as an audience. People *did* talk to one another, freely, openly, from seat to seat and row to row. ("Listen, George, what time tomorrow are you going to—?") They addressed one another by name and when they struck up bemused conversations with strangers sitting near them they sometimes introduced themselves. They smoked, apparently without thinking about it; and when efforts were made to get them to stop smoking because of fire regulations, they put out their cigarettes only to light up again, reflexively, shortly after. There was no uninterrupted focus upon the activities on stage, no welding or blending, no fusing into a unified body in the auditorium. Everyone remained himself, as he had been on the street before coming in, an individual with an isolated identity. Behavior was social, but social in the cocktail-party sense, a society of loners meeting and exchanging pleasantries behind the customary smokescreen of cigarettes.

Ironically and unpredictably, an event intended to encourage the maximum engagement had produced the maximum detachment —the greatest I have ever seen in a playhouse. An event aimed at fusion and communion had finally arrived at something like the perfect alienation Bertolt Brecht had struggled for so long. Over and over again Brecht wrote of the audience he would have liked to create: an audience so uninvolved with matters on stage that it would sit back and smoke, reflecting upon what was happening but not participating in it emotionally. Here it was.

Instead of a thousand people becoming one, one among themselves and then one with the players, a thousand people had been returned to their thousand separate selves. Was this atomization of the audience the result of newness, inexperience, inhibition—a first stage to be overcome? Is it perhaps necessary to destroy the audience as a unit in order to pave the way for individual conversion? Or is there something in the nature of the attempted form that inevitably produces isolation instead of fusion? If I suspect that this last is the case it is because I detect a tendency toward privacy, aloofness, singleness and separation in the very structuring of the form itself.

At *Dionysus in 69,* for instance, spectators were admitted one by one, not two by two. Tom O'Horgan, working elsewhere, has finally arrived at a production to which only one spectator is admitted per performance. The play is done for him alone. Acting companies are in some important cases apt to ignore audiences altogether. Even The Open Theater does not care very much whether spectators come. *The Serpent* is performed for the public rarely, though it was two years in preparation; when it is performed for the public, no public announcement is made. Though this is the play and performance intended as a "eucharist," the eucharist is not offered very often or very urgently.

In this The Open Theater merely reflects what Peter Brook considers a characteristic of Jerzy Grotowski's Polish Laboratory Theatre. Our very first exposure to the company came in the form

of a necessarily unsatisfactory television appearance. But in introducing that appearance, Mr. Brook—who has himself staged improvisatory plays in London—spoke warmly of the company's
utter indifference to audiences. The company is not eager for
public performance. In public performance it does not address
itself to spectators. It is, rather, content to make its statement and
let that statement stand whether anyone overhears it or not,
whether anyone responds to it or not. Spectators are admitted
simply as "witnesses" to the statement, to the self-contained act.
They may look on—in Mr. Brook's image—in much the same way
that apartment dwellers have sometimes looked out their windows
on murders without engaging themselves even to the limited
degree of telephoning for the police. The actors make their action.
The onlookers observe. They then part, having acknowledged
each other not at all.

The two impulses—toward announced engagement and toward
actual disengagement—are in some sense the same impulse, almost
as though current had been sent along a wire only to rebound
instantly with shocking force, or as though a man had walked into
a mirror and bumped into himself coming back. The first impulse
seems to produce the second, perversely.

But there *are* times when actual engagement takes place, when
one or another spectator is willing to do what he has been asked to
do, when one or another acting company does mean, however
briefly, to make room for intruders from the auditorium. What of
these?

In the instances I have been able to observe, our interior contradiction immediately crops up in another way. We hail the participating spectator as someone who has ceased being a passive
creature sitting listlessly on a bench and become active. Yet the
first thing such a spectator notices about himself as he invades the
production is that he is more passive than he was; in fact, his
passivity increases in direct proportion to his "activity."

Let us say that he has, in Joseph Papp's free rearrangement of
Hamlet, been sought out by an actor, lured from his seat, placed at
center stage, handed a revolver, and invited to shoot Claudius.
Clearly he is now in a position to affect the action on stage, to alter
the very course of the play, to exert a new kind of power over

performance. He is free to make a decision, to pull or not to pull a trigger, to dispose of the king on Hamlet's behalf—or for any wild reason of his own—or to let the king live. For this high suspenseful moment he is in charge.

He is nothing of the sort. As he soon realizes, he doesn't even know whether the revolver is loaded, whether or not it will fire a blank if he does pull the trigger. Supposing he pulls it and the gun fires, he doesn't know what Claudius will do—drop, or grin smugly and remain standing. He doesn't know what the next move in the pattern is meant to be, how the company around him is going to treat his participation, how quickly he is going to be hustled back to his seat.

He is a blind pawn, entirely under the management of the directors, players, and property men who have arranged an overall schedule without consulting him, without letting him into the creative secret. When he finally retires from a situation in which he did not know how to behave because he could not know the rehearsed master plan, he most likely feels a put-upon fool. He should feel a fool, for he has been lured into a pseudocreativity that has been essentially a fraud. You will notice that in Mr. Schechner's remarks, quoted earlier, there is a recurring "we": *we*, the producers, have not yet decided when the audience should move, when it should speak, when it should be quiet. Everything is decided at the top, by the management, as indeed it must be if the evening is to progress or acquire shape or mean anything. The management would be—and I understand on occasion has been— seriously embarrassed by any participation that could not be quickly controlled, just as Mr. Robards was embarrassed by the acceptance of an invitation that was never sincerely meant.

All that is being offered is a limited *illusion* of participating— and this in a theater formally dedicated to the destruction of illusion. The Living Theater has become notorious for its treatment of creative upstarts in the audience: whenever one or another audience member rises to voice disagreement with something said from the stage, a roar erupts from the actors that rides roughshod over the dissident, drowning him out altogether, though he has in fact been invited to express himself, to dissent. So much for participation that goes against the grain of the preset

schema. "The 'trip' for the audience must be as carefully structured as any ancient mystery or initiation," Mr. van Itallie has
written. That, I think, is the fact of the matter.

But this is not participation, it is paternalism—and the audience
knows it. I have seen and heard audiences respond variously to
invitations that it regarded as less than genuine. I have heard an
audience, at *Tom Paine*, angrily order the players to "stop all this
damned nonsense" of chatting directly with the customers and
"get back to the play." Or I have watched members of the audience submit to coaxing and allow themselves to be drawn into the
arena, whether to level a gun at Claudius in *Hamlet* or to engage in
a group grope at *Dionysus in 69*. One male member of the
audience who did surrender to three or four girls of the *Dionysus*
company and let himself be stroked by all of them at length may
be as representative of the "active" spectator as any joiner I have
seen. He went along with the game. He looked embarrassed but he
was halfway willing. During four or five minutes he made no
effort to escape the groping. *But he did not grope back.* Has anyone, ever? If he did, what finally happened to him? If he did not,
can he be called active?

Even the most ardent enthusiasts—letters inform me that there
are some—must eventually be got in hand, put back into their
private playpens. All, the willing and the unwilling, the interested
and the embarrassed, are at the mercy of the company, Keepers of
the Score. They are not only passive before the planners, they are
more passive than they formerly were. Formerly, as observing but
not participating spectators, they acted as judges, deciding for
themselves what they thought of the performance, granting or
withholding applause, sitting as gallery gods in a position of power.
Now they have either rejected an invitation, in which case they
are apt to feel guilty or inadequate, or they have exuberantly
accepted one and been absorbed into the event, in which case they
can scarcely applaud the event (themselves) with any justice or
objectivity. The traditional power of the audience has been dissipated without being replaced by any real power inside the event.
One active role has been surrendered to a passive role.

Why? Why should each of these experiences—at *We Bombed
in New Haven* or *Paradise Now* or *Dionysus in 69* or *Hamlet* or
whatever—contain a built-in rebound? I suspect because all human

participation short of murder or sex is arrived at not on a one-to-one basis, by means of direct confrontation, but through the presence of a third thing, an artificially arranged, mutually agreed upon, virtually invisible catalyst. Murder is a direct blow, sex a direct penetration. They are absolutes; something comes to an end in them. But participating in a baseball game is not a direct, spontaneous, improvisational meeting between team and team, between pitcher and batter. Between the teams, and between pitcher and batter, stands an invisible but understood third entity, the rules of the game, the pattern of play. On a basketball floor violations of the unseen pattern are instantly penalized by a referee. Even a conversation between friends, intimate as intimate can be, is not a one-to-one event. It is impossible to walk directly into another's mind. Participation is made possible by the presence, once again, of an immaterial though fiercely present third factor, the subject of the conversation, the thing that is being talked about. One participates in a friend indirectly through the matter being discussed.

Much of the work being done in the name of participatory theater labors mightily to eliminate this third thing, which in the case of the theater is of course the (invisible) play. It is the play that has been regarded as the barrier to communication, to communion, to oneness. When the actors stopped playing *Tom Paine* to converse out-of-frame with the audience, the play was being broken, deliberately. When a spectator was asked to take aim at Claudius, *Hamlet* was being broken, as Euripides' *The Bacchae* was being broken whenever, at *Dionysus in 69*, Dionysus was identified as an actor by name. A hole is punched through the invisible mesh of the play so that actors and spectators can crawl through it toward each other, meeting head on. When the participatory staging of *Massachusetts Trust* is done first, and the text later to suit, the very concept "play" has been broken in advance. Confrontation is the essence of the experience; any third thing can only appear as subordinated fragments, shards kicked about beneath the actors' feet. The play has ceased to exist in the way that the unseen pattern of a ballgame exists.

I have been stressing the invisibility of a play, even of the most traditional sort of play, because we are inclined to forget how intangible, if present, a play is. We speak of "going to see a play,"

but when we get to the theater we do not see the play. We see the
actors. The actors are performing the play but they are not the
play. The play is an elusive movement in midair between us, something like a Fourth of July sparkler twirled about to make a
pattern that never comes to rest and can never be seen whole at
one time. We watch an actor make a line in space and try to
imagine the play he is trying to describe. The actor speaks a line he
cannot see and hears it hit the audience and make a bump. The two
parties—actors and audience—are totally and immediately exposed to one another, separated only by a gesture that is hypo-
thetically taking shape between them. They are very close, but
their closeness comes of being fastened together by intense focus
on the third thing, a transparency called a play, that hovers between them. Indeed, they build this third thing together by mutual
consent and mutual challenge, testing its truth each step of the
way.

The film critic André Bazin makes much of this peculiar relationship. He points out that film is the medium with which an
audience actually identifies. Because the actors aren't there, which
means that nothing can be done to or with them, the film audience
is left with no option but to attach itself imaginatively to the
images on the screen and go where they go, do what they do. In
the theater, however (and here he is quoting a fellow theorist
named Rosenkrantz), everything is reversed. The actors become
"objects of mental opposition." They do so because "their real
presence gives them an objective reality and to transpose them into
beings in an imaginary world the will of the spectator has to intervene actively." A spectator must engage *himself* in the activity of
turning Jason Robards into an air force captain or an NYU student
into Dionysus; it is not all that easy. It is a contention, really. We
challenge the actor to make us believe him, he challenges us to dare
not to believe, we fight it out, building ever so imperceptibly a
structure out of the struggle. It is a precarious business, one that
can crack open at any moment (then we will laugh or hoot or
become bored and go away), both sides are on a tightrope from
which either can fall. The tightrope, again, is the play, the hidden
line, the vanishing point, upon which we can meet. Make any
image you like of it. Audience and actors are matchsticks, pointed

at each other, touching. The heat of the unseen play makes them flare—and in the flaring fuses them.

I think the presence of this third thing may be an indispensable requirement for a true meeting of actor and spectator. So far from being a barrier, the play may serve as an invisible conductor for both parties. And this may be especially true at a time when we are trying for that most difficult of all unions, the joining of the audience's subconscious with that of the actors. "Don't lose any thought in wondering what connects the scenes or what logic applies from one scene to the other," Joseph Chaikin has counseled audiences of *The Serpent.* "There is no logical progress," he says. "The connections are in our head."

Our head? Is there such a thing as a group head? Can one man's subconscious know another man's subconscious directly? Can I even know my own wife's subconscious (we will not speak of knowing the children's) without introducing that third factor, a subject to be discussed, which will, by contrasting our separate responses to it, drag to the surface subconscious roots that can be compared? I can know love without words, and perhaps death without words. Can I know anything else of life without the intervention of a touchstone?

My own best guess is that the double effect we have been talking about, the sudden reversal or contradiction that presents us with the opposite of what we have sought, occurs always at the moment when the play is being broken. It occurs automatically when no play is present, when only actors and audience are present, unescorted, unserved.

And I am inclined to think that The Open Theater is the most effective of the groups now working in the general vein precisely because it means to sustain a structure, some kind of structure, throughout the experience. Mr. van Itallie would like to dismiss the conventional word "play." Instead of "writing a play" he would prefer to "construct a ceremony." He is somewhat suspicious of words, though he is himself a gifted writer of words. He is willing to use them, but would like to subordinate them to a ritual arrived at by director, actors, and writer in rehearsal.

Allow him his ceremony and his looked-for eucharist. The fact remains that the ceremony is very carefully built; it stems from and heavily depends upon the use of introductory words (the remarkable "death of Abel" passage in *The Serpent* would be nowhere near as effective if we had not been given the objective, Third Thing statement at the beginning that "Cain did not know how to kill Abel"); it employs throughout a familiar and fusing mythology (much of Genesis). The fact that director Chaikin's images are superimposed upon one another in a "non-logical" way, as he says they are, does not matter; audience and actors are together focused on a vision between them that can be shared, that serves as a root connective: a vision of Eve, of mankind begetting, of Cain killing. The fact that this vision is intangible, a web spun somewhere between us that is not a material web, does not matter either. That has always been the case.

The new experiments tumbling about us mean to alter many things: our posture in the theater, our sense of what a stage is, our understanding of what it means for actors to be present when we are. Something of use will surely come of them. Perhaps no more than five or ten minutes of *Dionysus in 69* were persuasive in this regard—the five or ten minutes in which whispers rose around the room until they had drowned the man trying to dominate the room—but that is a little something. Much more of *The Serpent* is persuasive, perhaps an hour and five minutes of it, perhaps all of it except, significantly, those passages in which the actors do finally move among the audience, staring directly into the spectators' eyes. Something quite arresting becomes silly on the spot.

As we experiment, and on the evidence thus far offered, we'd best avoid the broken play, the broken ceremony, the broken mystery. A sustained mystery held aloft in the middle distance may, however mysteriously, envelop us. A broken play tends to kick.

3

I COME reluctantly to the conclusion that there is a great deal of naïveté in some of our most advanced theatrical attitudes.

At the moment I'm thinking of one in particular: the attitude we take toward illusion on the stage. We're against it. We distrust it. We fear it. From Brecht onward, at least, we have held that sustained illusion—continuing and unbroken belief in the images moving before us—is a trick and a trap and a sop. It means to lull the audience into something like total gullibility. Slowly surrendering its wits, the audience permits itself to be wrapped, cocoonlike, in an artifice it accepts as reality. Its critical faculties are dulled; its awareness of the world outside—or even of the real world back-stage—is put to sleep; Barbara Bel Geddes is not Barbara Bel Geddes but truly that girl making pretty conversation on the telephone, as George C. Scott is truly that scoundrel corrupting everyone in sight. The action of the plot sucks us into it, the setting persuades us that we are where we aren't; at eleven o'clock we must make a fearful effort to return to our senses again.

And because this sort of illusion is so self-contained it is irrelevant: irrelevant to the politics we must live by before seven-thirty and after ten, irrelevant to not-so-dreamlike problems we must solve if we are to survive, irrelevant to anything that could remotely be called fact. It cheats us into temporary satisfaction. When the opiate wears off and we return to fact, we are worse off for our unthinking, palliative, merely distracting time of self-indulgence. We have lately become terrified of illusion because it entices us to share a sham.

And so we have become preoccupied with the business of shattering illusion, breaking down the scenery so that it can be seen as shabby canvas, intercepting the narrative with placards or projections announcing that it is no more than a contrived narrative, forcing the actor out of "character" so that he shall be known by his right name. In *Dionysus in 69*, as we've seen, the actor appearing as the Greek god Dionysus frequently interrupted himself to explain that he was really, or also, William Finley, who grew up not far from the garage in which he was performing and went to the movies regularly, where he saw Laurel and Hardy cartoons. (Did he really, by the way, see Laurel and Hardy cartoons at the movies, or are these more recent figments of the television imagination? When we are going after fact, we should see to it that it is fact, I think.) Later, reproclaiming himself Dionysus, he was stopped by a fellow-performer's challenge, "Dionysus? Bullshit. You're Bill Finley." A third dimension has been added, presumably, to our experience of the play. Has it?

I don't think so. I have several questions about all of this. I have noticed, to begin with, that it is thin. That is to say, we do not really get two identities in place of one. I still do not know who William Finley is, or what he thought of the movies he went to, if he went to them. Although he has been identified by name eight or ten times in the course of the evening, I still have no full-bodied sense of him as he is outside the theater; I have, in the end, learned little more about him than his name and I could have got that from the program. I haven't added a new man. I have merely halved the one I was looking at. Dionysus has had time and substance taken away from him, and this has diminished the space he occupies in my eye. But I have not been offered a compensating personality of any richness, scale, or detail; I have barely shaken hands in the shuffle. Even so. It may be more important to us just now to clear our heads of the old mesmerizing patterns, to throw off the drug, to be utterly honest with ourselves about the nature of the picture in front of us than to waste time worrying about weight losses suffered in passing.

But here comes the key question. What, in fact, is being challenged? *Has* the audience ever subscribed wholly to the pretense set before it? Has it ever been confused, for a single moment, about the true identity of the actor so cunningly disguising himself up on stage? Is the audience ever absorbed into the illusionistic action to the point where it forgets that it is an illusion? I suggest that it is not, has not been, and never means to be.

Take an example from a most illusionistic, stubbornly realistic play, recently revived. George C. Scott played an abominable scoundrel in Lillian Hellman's *The Little Foxes* and played it with all of the leers, sneers, and ruthlessly arched eyebrows that were necessary to persuade us of his unmitigated wickedness. He cheated the poor, cheated the rich, cheated his relatives, and kept a sharp eye out for anyone he'd missed. As Ben Hubbard he was morally horrifying. Following the line of the plot, we were honor bound to detest him. Until, after getting off a particularly nasty speech, he made an exit. On the instant the audience broke into enthusiastic applause. It was not applauding Ben Hubbard. Heaven forbid. It was applauding George C. Scott—virtually by name. Somehow or other those entranced people out front had managed to keep stored in their heads the information that Mr. Scott was an actor and not Ben Hubbard, and that no matter how one felt about Ben Hubbard one could feel quite differently about Mr. Scott. The circuit was double the whole time. Nor did the interruption to salute Mr. Scott cancel out, or destroy, the so-called illusion of the story still to be followed. Having signaled enthusiasm for Mr. Scott, divorced from Ben Hubbard, the audience promptly turned back to the other Hubbards who were being so viciously out-witted by Ben and continued worrying about them. Off, on. No problem. Multiple vision is easy to come by.

There is of course nothing unusual about the instance. It happens nightly in the theater, is the commonest commonplace of all our theatergoing experience. It must seem unusual only to those who imagine, out of their own feverish fears, that the audience is incapable of this sort of simultaneous translation and is actually conned into behaving more or less as that sadly deceived spectator in *Showboat* was. If you remember *Showboat*, one of the Mississippi spectators attending a performance on the *Cotton Blossom* apparently had never seen a show before. Watching the villain manhandle the extremely attractive and extremely vulnerable in-génue, he mistook play-acting for fact, rose in the balcony with his nobility all a-tremble, whipped out his six-shooter, and began giving the villain what for. *He* believed in illusion. But that is a joke, a preposterous extravagance. Even for *Showboat* it was always a bit broad.

We may have laughed at that fellow but we have never really believed in him because nothing similar has *ever* happened to us. From the time that we were first dragged to the theater in the company of maiden aunts—perhaps to be chained to the theater forever and to be forever grateful to the aunts—we have always understood exactly who the players were and what they were up to. They were play-acting in exactly the sense that we had always play-acted, in basements or backyards; how were we to be fooled by something we'd been so deeply engaged in from the dawn of consciousness? The least sophisticated member of the audience comes fully equipped to handle the situation. He is aware of the sustained event as fiction without ever having surrendered fact.

The notion that the playgoer is a potential patsy who may re-quire frequent dislocating to remind him that there is a truer world behind the scenes simply isn't so and—much to my surprise,

I'd quite forgotten—isn't new. It's in *A Midsummer Night's Dream*. I was startled, being so forgetful, during a recent performance to hear Bottom and all his play-acting friends worrying about the very same problem. One of Bottom's company is going to play a lion and he is going to roar most fiercely. It suddenly occurs to the assembled weavers and tinkers that the roar may be much too fierce, that it may in fact frighten the spectators out of their illusion-enchanted wits. There is a hasty, troubled discussion. Snout thinks there had better be a prologue (a Brechtian placard?) to say that in the coming scene the lion is not a lion. Bottom has a better suggestion:

> Nay, you must name his name, and half his face must be seen through the lion's neck; and he himself must speak through, saying thus, or to the same defect, "Ladies," or, "Fair ladies," "I would wish you," or, "I would request you," or, "I would entreat you," not to fear, not to tremble: my life for yours. If you think I come hither as a lion, it were pity of my life: no, I am no such thing. I am a man as other men are"; and there indeed let him name his name, and tell them plainly he is Snug the joiner.

Same fear, same solution. But Shakespeare assigns both the fear and the solution to amateurs.

It is possible that we may discover things we are not looking for as we continue our post-Brecht, double-Pirandellian, Bottom the Weaverish investigations of the two-faced psyche. Who can ever say what experimentation may or may not stumble upon? But when we are theorizing about our experimentation, providing it with excuses and justifications and rational underpinnings, we had best not lie to ourselves. As we work out remedies for situations we say we don't like, we'd best doublecheck to make certain the situations actually exist—and are not, in themselves, mere illusions.

4

I AM eternally filled with admiration for the extraordinary sensitivity of the most ordinary audience, for the quickness, the delicacy, the curious subtlety with which it responds to what is happening on stage, and I hope that some of our newer experiments with audience response aren't going to corrupt the sensibility that is actually there.

I was fascinated one evening, for instance, to listen to an audience *not* listening when something more important was at stake. During an off-Broadway play in which a highly nervous, indeed almost completely unstrung, character was to be seen lighting cigarette after abandoned cigarette, one match missed the ashtray to which it had been consigned and nestled instead in a box of Kleenex.

Slowly the Kleenex took fire. The fire was never of blaze proportions, but its steady black curl with wisps of menacing orange flutter seemed not about to subside and remained threateningly unpredictable. The actor playing the part, engrossed in a long passionate speech and now standing away from the table, didn't notice.

The audience was first quietly tolerant, composed, experienced enough to suppose that the limited conflagration would burn itself out. It didn't. The audience then, without undue anxiety and even with a trace of amusement, tried to signal the actor visually, raising fingers and pointing to the table—but never speaking aloud. It held its peace, refrained from actually interrupting the actor's train of thought, hoping that a mere gesture would send him casually back to the table—skipping no dialogue beat—to take care of matters. That is to say, it was enormously cooperative, not wishing to embarrass the actor or wantonly destroy the performance rhythm.

It could no longer listen wholly to what the man was saying, of course; his passion was provoking little dramatic response. Two minds began to function out front: one that recognized a reality that seriously needed dealing with, one that wished to sustain an artifice that actor and audience had come together to create. The audience was able to sit still and wait, holding things in suspension, until one or the other should come to its natural termination, whatever that might be.

As it happened, the actor never did see any of the signals offered him and the wait was a longish one. He may ultimately have noticed, as actors subconsciously do, that the words he was speaking were not quite taking root in the auditorium, were skimming without landing. Whatever turned him toward the table, he did in due time discover the event he was competing with and, of course, damped the blaze out without dropping his intensely assumed role. Immediately, almost with the click of a recorder turning on, the audience began listening again.

I'm not talking about the audience's bravery, or anything like that. Given the physical materials on stage—no soft gauzes nearby, no hanging scenery—it was unlikely that anyone was going to be in any danger, though, of course, you never can tell. What impressed me was the courtesy, the continuing participation of the audience in a stylized relationship the actor had struggled so hard to build, the niceness of the distinctions that audience was making. It was balancing in its head a half dozen or more things: an actor's pride, memories of theatrical disasters begun as casually, the cadence of performance, the importance of the audience's own role in a theatrical event, statistical information on the probability of things getting worse, dangers of panic, possible methods of communication, the probable necessity of the actor's returning to the table soon, the internal logic of the play proper. It arrived at a very nice balance.

The audience is also extremely sensitive to formal lapses in the art of playmaking itself, whether it could explain its sensitivities or no. On several occasions I've noticed a most peculiar thing. An audience immediately detaches itself from the proceedings, if the proceedings are meant to be serious, whenever a character in a play begins to talk about the making of plays.

I'll have to give you an example. In Joseph A. Walker's *The Harangues*, done by the Negro Ensemble Company, a devious, pretty devilish, plot was afoot. A young black was about to marry into a white family with the private intention of killing off his fiancée's father. In order to work out the deception properly, he drew into his confidence a black friend. The friend was at first reluctant to go along with the proposed, perfectly cold-blooded murder. But he was persuaded. He was persuaded, in part, because he was an unproduced playwright and, as soon as the rich white father-in-law had been done in, there would be cash enough to back one of his plays.

It just wouldn't take, not as serious motivation. The audience had been paying macabre attention to the plot as a whole, fascinated by its relative intricacy and some very smooth playing; but the moment producing a play was given as a *reason* for committing murder, the house giggled, inside if not aloud. From fairly intense melodrama the whole thing dropped, on the instant, to absurdist comedy. The audience had been perfectly able to take murder— that unlikely event—seriously. It announced, in its abrupt psychological withdrawal, that it was not prepared to take producing a play seriously. Not in the same context.

The play, you see, had turned in on itself, committed a kind of incest, exposed itself as artifice by reminding us too openly that plays are only things that cost money to get on. It took the play and performers a considerable time to win the wary back, now. The audience had made a swift, silent, formal judgment on what constituted the world of onstage as against the world of backstage and it insisted that its nuanced distinctions be respected. A game is a game, and goes by rules.

The audience can, however, be enticed, or pushed, into behaving falsely, self-consciously, synthetically. This is, as we know all too well by now, a time in the theater when those of us who sit out front are being urged to participate more and more actively in what is going on onstage. This is also a time when we are encouraged *not* to distinguish theater from life, but to see the two as one and the same thing (thus happenings, thus planned dramatic events acted out among unprepared people on the streets).

Whatever we may or may not learn from the exploration of these attitudes and/or possibilities, they are in some instances capable of unsettling an audience's usually fine sense of proportion altogether. During the first production of Le Roi Jones's *Slaveship*, I was seated behind a girl of perhaps eighteen or nineteen, white, inconspicuously dressed. Mr. Jones's pageant made use of a great deal of physical brutality. Slaves were knocked down, dropped through a trapdoor, kicked. The stage was surrounded by several

low bars, separating us scarcely at all from the violence done regularly to the blacks during the performance.

At one point a black lad—let's say he was fifteen or sixteen—was
hurled savagely across stage so that he spun headlong into the
surrounding bars. He crumpled over these, head bowed, hands
hanging limp, for the remainder of the sequence.

Within a minute or two the girl seated in front of me had fished
a handkerchief out of her purse and was softly and soothingly—
and I would say condescendingly—wiping the perspiration from
the actor's brow and hands. There was pity in the gesture, sorrow
in it, kindness in it.

Fake, fake, fake. The actor wasn't hurt; he was dramatizing a
hurt, but he was himself hale and hearty. He wasn't perspiring
because he'd been maltreated on a plantation in the sun; he was
perspiring because he was performing on a stage and it's hot under
stage lights. Furthermore, his precise role in the play at that point
was to illustrate white inhumanity to blacks; he didn't want an
overly solicitous white girl mucking up the image. In fact, he
probably didn't want any girl, white or black, pawing at him while
he was trying to keep his mind on his performance.

As for the girl, whom we shall call well-intentioned, she wasn't
doing anything for a put-upon black, except perhaps make him
feel a bit of a fool. (I am glad to say he didn't hit her, but I had
forgiveness ready in my heart in case he did.) Doing things—and
doing things means arriving at justice rather than pity— is for the
streets and everywhere else. Else. In the theater the girl's gesture
was false through and through: useless, inappropriate, unproduc-
tive, presumptive, ostentatious, sentimental. It was humanly artificial as opposed to being esthetically artificial. And it *was* opposed
to it, hurting what might have been horrifying if she'd kept her
theatrical wits about her and just let the image stand.

An audience's theatrical wits are quite wonderful tools, rich in
intelligence when they are behaving normally, responding adroitly
out of sure instinct and long experience. We must be careful not
to addle them. Whatever new things we may demand of audiences
—and some of our requests for a reawakening are legitimate
enough—we don't want the customers rushing towels to bloodied
actors. It's going to ruin their makeups.

5

THE MOST moving theatrical experience in New York in 1968 was *The Concept*, an off-Broadway experiment that achieved exactly what most serious drama is forever trying to achieve: deep involvement without cheap rigging, ultimate tears without any sort of sentimentality. It did so in a way that might well have been thought impossible.

The word "theatrical" must be stressed because at first blush it seems the wrong word. None of the actors in the three companies which rotated weekly was a professional. All were former drug addicts, now members of a rehabilitation project known as Daytop. We knew before we met any of them that the three groups had spent a combined total of one hundred seventy-six years on heroin and forty-one years in jail. Their average age was twenty-five.

As they began to act out fears and angers that had led them to look at themselves by looking candidly at others, we were entirely aware of their amateur status. Speech was casual, unprojected, overlapping. Gestures were not trained for effect. The text had gradually been improvised and we could hear it still groping, slips of the tongue and all. If we found ourselves moved in these circumstances, weren't we being moved by the fact that we were in the physical presence of people who had suffered most savagely and then behaved heroically, by a literal actuality that had almost nothing to do with art?

In part we were. We were held through the opening loosenesses, the occasional but quite obvious stylistic gaucheries, by a kind of voyeuristic curiosity and by a natural, extratheatrical, sympathy. While a couple of foolish braggarts (one boasted of having a house in Westchester that required fifty-three servants) were getting drunk at a bar, while a passionate jailee was failing to persuade his weary wife that he was ready for another try at coming home, while an obtuse and apoplectic father was screaming at a judge that it was *he* who was suffering most over the misdemeanors of a son, we did spend time speculating. What could this performer's case history possibly have been? Were there telltale signs to look for? We were conscious of persons, and of an immediate purpose to the demon-ridding reenactment. We were meant to be.

Then a curious shift in the quality of belief took place. As the residents of Daytop finished showering and dressing in rhythm to come together for an encounter (a group session in which the participants fiercely and deliberately attack one another not for their failings, but for their lies about their failings), we began to forget—we had to remind ourselves forcibly—that they were themselves former victims. They did not so much become actors playing roles as clear, naked intelligences, sources of light. So long as the group was concentrating its fire on just one member, yanking out secrets, swiftly mocking any attempt at evasion, drowning dishonesty in a roar of calculated obscenities, we could perhaps feel that the target of the current attack was or had been sick—not sick in the way described, but somehow sick. But it was not really possible to remember that those doing the mauling were, or ever had been. They became, for us, the norm: highly skilled, extraordinarily perceptive, infinitely loving symbols of health. They were wisdom incarnate, trustworthy surgeons, ruthless and *right*.

Thus it was dramatically shocking each time the focus changed. Suddenly the girl or boy whose protective layer of pride had been knifed away was dropped, let free, abandoned to recuperative reflection. Without warning, mathematically, the pack whipped off after another fox. The very fellow who had so intensely, so rationally, so successfully led the last charge was instantly cornered, hilariously humiliated for having been embarrassed about wetting the bed one night, ravaged for having felt so guilty about leaving a burning cigarette in a linen closet that he hadn't been able to bring himself to confess the careless act. Our heads snapped back. They can't be turning on *him*, we said to ourselves; he's the "doctor," he is sanity. The sensation occurred again and again. We had ourselves become so involved in the therapy that we successively accepted each practitioner as our teacher; in time it became unthinkable that such a "teacher" might not know himself.

Toward the end of the evening I think we worked as hard as the encounterers did to try to persuade a pretty, secretive, shyly affected girl that she might conceivably have deserved any love offered to her. The girl did not really suppose no one could love her; she supposed that if anyone loved her it would be a misdirected, stupid, mistaken love; she knew herself inherently unlovable, her distaste was for *herself*.

The prodding began, became quiet and dry and relentless. The girl's eyes flew upward in fake exasperation, her tongue ran over her lip as though to wash away the spurious sweetness of hope. She fought, fought hard, to keep her hated image of herself intact, fought to keep her own unhappiness alive. The others, including ourselves, fought back until, out of stammers and twistings and broken protests and tightly gripped disbelief, the girl was forced to face affection because there was no space around her in which it did not exist. Trapped by it, she could not move unless she was willing to walk into an embrace.

The concentration of the sequence was so absolute, the pressure inward so great, that its successful release released suppressed emotion in the audience as well—to a point I have never before or after experienced in a theater. The actors, having expelled the self-images that no doubt helped them to become drug addicts in the first place and having acknowledged themselves as possessing value, walked into the audience to test that value. As they did, members of the audience, here and there, rose to greet them, voluntarily. "Do you love me?" the actors asked, directly. The members of the audience who had risen embraced the actors. They had been brought to this pitch, beyond pity. I would not have thought, if I had been told of this ultimate gesture earlier, that it could be anything but synthetic. Instead, it was serious, and simple.

And how was any of this theater, or anything like art? The fact of the matter is that whatever was literal or actual or a record of continuing life had already been formalized—and not once but twice. It had first been formalized in the performers' own therapy; the people on stage had long since taken themselves out of themselves for a good look, held themselves up like art objects to be examined dispassionately. They had recognized themselves by taking one giant wrenching step backward from their earlier adopted skins, from their postures, their rationalizations, their habits, their self-portraits. A bold degree of detachment had come into being while they were curing themselves; it was the principal thing that had cured them.

And they had now put their knowledge through a second transformation by distilling it for representative exposure on the stage, selecting it, joining it, moving it another degree away so that it could be seen—seen deeply—by other eyes. If there was still a personal factor present that is not usually there when an actor assumes a role, it was not quite as dislocating as one had imagined in advance. Good playwrights, after all, invariably feed something of their own flesh, under whatever disguises, into the constructs they build. If one thought of these young men and women not as actors, but as playwrights, still growing their own play, one came closer to the secret of the evening's theatrical authority: we were being given two levels of formality with the breathing source still inside them.

It rather reminded us how often, in the merely fashionable products of the contemporary theater, we miss the sense of breath. When we say of a play that it is tired or stale or old-fashioned or empty, we probably mean only the last word: empty. That is to say, it is merely a formalization; quickness is no longer in it. Life was once there and it is gone, leaving only a patterned gesture behind it. Life was all too obviously still there in *The Concept*. There was no need to overinflate the work and call it mature or sophisticated or even professional as drama. But I think it was necessary to recognize that we had been affected by something controlled, and that the residue of actuality that lingered in the play's raw reach after conscious shape did confront us, there and then, with a most unfamiliar power.

# Trouble in Wonderland

I

EVERY age of the world is "the modern world" to the men who live in it, and we know that. Even so, it's a bit of a shock to leaf through Hegel, who died in 1831, and come upon the sentence: "Vexation is the sentiment of the modern world." How did he know us so well?

Hegel was speaking directly of drama when he wrote the line, and he was trying to explain an exasperation in the body politic, and in the contemporary psyche itself, that tended to keep playwrights from producing work as great as the Greeks, say, had done. The Greeks had known all about doom and had had intimations of early death (even Achilles' horse wept in advance over what was to happen to his master, foreknowledge and foreboding were so omnipresent); they knew that the universe did not play fair and that men played most foul. But they handled these certainties in a certain way. They took them more or less for granted, sighed a little, nerved themselves to necessity, and then lunged forward to accomplish everything in the way of private or public improvement possible before the roof caved in. By resigning themselves—to some degree—to the fact that the world was the world

and woe was a part of it, they freed themselves for immediate
action, for practical work. They didn't immobilize themselves by
sitting down and moaning over the hopeless nastiness of it all.
They could be "sad, but only momentarily." They could not be
"vexed or annoyed."

No doubt Hegel is romanticizing the Greeks somewhat in supposing that they were *never* exasperated, *never* driven to the mood
in which they'd just as soon have knocked down all the temples
and defaced all the symbols of hope in order to get the jump on
what was coming anyway. All men have surely known the mood
at one time or another. I once watched a woman leap in fury at a
garden she'd very carefully planted and tended months before and
rip from the ground every shred of remaining vegetation. The
children, who were small, had been idly pulling up the flowers one
at a time. Better to wipe out the intention and the hope entirely, in
one wild swoop, than to watch it vanish inch by inch, daily, before
still yearning eyes. The urge is familiar.

Still, there's a difference between an impulse of the moment and
a sustained, determined commitment to the principle that all plant-
ing is useless, all ordered activity absurd. One makes for a brief
fine flurry, the other for impotence at the heart.

Modern man, Hegel goes on to say (so long ago), decides that if
he cannot have his immediate end, an absolute perfection here and
now, he will have *no* end, seek *no* perfection. Never mind perfection. He will not even seek improvement, for, having been cheated
out of his instant satisfaction, he comes to regard improvement as
sheer illusion. Instead, he sits and spits.

"Thus the modern man easily gets into the mood in which he
loses heart with regard to everything else," Hegel continues, "and
does not even seek to reach other things he might quite well have
made his aim. . . . All else that belongs to his nature and destiny
he abandons, and in order to revenge himself destroys his own
courage, his power of action, all those ends of destiny to which he
might otherwise have quite well attained. This is vexation. . . ."

Recognize it? The theater's been shot through and through with
it in recent years—the sound of spite has been a familiar hiss on
our stages, the counsel of helpless surrender its ready companion—
and the theater has housed it because it exists outside the theater,
which means it must be taken in. The stage is not to be blamed for

inventing vituperation that has no object except to display spleen
(vexation cannot have another object because it holds all objec-
tives futile), nor can its dramatists be faulted for reporting the
precise sound of the whirlwind. Indeed, the stage can be praised
for being honest about the weather beyond its doors, for being
responsive to a streak in man that every once in a while gets the
better of man.

The streak, the screech, the urge to splatter in all directions
because the promise of shape itself is a fraud, exists now. I was
much struck by a good bit of the mail that came in after my
review of Barbara Garson's *MacBird!*, particularly the mail that
took me sharply to task for suggesting that, however out of control some of our emotions may actually be at the moment, the
organization of those emotions into a "play" ought itself to be
controlled. It may be advisable, even necessary, to state on the
stage that an undisciplined state of mind truly rages through seg-
ments of our society; the statement, however, by its very nature
involves a discipline, *is* a discipline. "But you don't understand,
Mr. Kerr," one reader wrote at fever pitch, "We are in despair!"

I believe that. *MacBird!* had, unmistakably, been a work of
despair. It wasn't really an attack on specific political abuses or on
particular political personalities. It was an attack on politics as
such, on the possible art of governing. As Peter Brook said at the
time, the author was talking "about the mechanism of power,
about this and nothing else." It was "the entire structure of ruling
she wished to hold up to the light."

By scattering her fire unselectively across the landscape, leaving
no motive or course of action or personal characteristic unassailed,
the author wiped the slate clean (or muddied it irremediably).
Political processes engage all men in compromise. Compromise is
filthy. Ergo, the process itself is filthy, structured government a
moral impossibility. There is nothing on which to build. Vexed,
cheated of our hope, we can only blow off, shrilly, wantonly, at
random.

Mr. Brook, in his comments on the play, went on to praise the
blowoff as productive. "The fact that the material is flimsy, the
idiom pulp, the expectation of literary immortality nil, is a source
of strength," he concluded. In Hegel's view of things, it would be
nothing of the sort. It is a sign of impotence and a carrier of

impotence. When we refuse to believe that any good can come of our eternally dirty arrangements, when we permit ourselves to become frustrated beyond endurance by our certainty that perfection is nowhere in sight, we can do nothing but wash our hands of the whole mess, make our plays messier for spite, submit to a vision of universal human incompetence, and subside. Samuel Beckett has already made graphic for us the perfect stasis our despairing streak must drive us to: we sit on the sand or in locked chairs, urinating, immobile.

The mood, as Hegel says, is essentially one of revenge. This is how we will treat a universe that has treated us so shabbily. And what it leads to is the destruction of the "power of action." We will match the indecency of the universe with our own immobility, like a child refusing to eat its dinner and going, in deeply satisfying self-pity, straight to bed.

This is not, of course, the whole story of the contemporary stage or of our contemporary lives. It is one impulse among a dozen impulses, interlocked and thrashing for mastery. Vexation as a response to the forbidding complexities of our days is also related to, and sometimes entangled with, a stronger, more vigorous, more direct kind of response—the kind that bluntly calls a spade a spade in hopes of getting some work done with the spade. Some voices speak to be heard, others simply to make noise of their annoyance.

As we listen, it is worth while trying to distinguish, I think, between the play that successfully forms itself into a fist and the play that merely pushes its open hand into our faces—mugs us, as it were. Random outrage doesn't really mean to cope with matters; neither does a whine. If we can gently separate what is merely a mean streak from the many urgent sounds that bombard us, putting it to one side as no more than an excess of the tongue or a confession of lost courage, we may be able to attend all the more carefully to the genuinely productive boldness, the undespairing and disciplined candor, that is sometimes at hand and always badly needed. One clue to genuine energy, as opposed to wantonly distributed exasperation, lies in the shaping of a play. The act of forming anything well is already an act of courage and an assertion of hope. Despair, by contrast, is invariably on the sloppy side. What else should it be?

Meantime, it's some small comfort to think that the man who

described one of our moods so perfectly was born in the eighteenth century. That's two hundred years ago and we're still here. And still complaining, of course.

2

I KEPT wanting to avoid reviewing the Theater of the Ridiculous on the grounds that it was ridiculous, but clearly that wouldn't work. Experimental groups that insist upon mindlessness as the essence of each gesture performed and each necessarily unintelligible word spoken are indeed always one up on anyone who wishes to make comment on them. Since all norms have been abandoned or carefully inverted, comment is irrelevant. One either joins the irrationality, in which case coherent reviewing becomes impossible, or one attempts to treat the irrational rationally, in which case one is plainly a damned fool.

I speak, then, as a plain damned fool when I suggest that, if one listened closely enough to the intentional nonsense being shouted and mimed on weekends at the Gotham Art Theater high up on West 43rd St., one might have picked up a few clues toward measuring the quality of the work if one could have measured the quality of the work.

Listening closely wasn't easy, partly because all lines and lyrics were screeched at the top of everyone's lungs at the same pitch and rate all night long, partly because the stage was inundated with garish visual distraction meant to split possible attention in any case. Girls with green faces gone spastic shook the oak leaves in their hair while revolving the red dust in their navels. Siamese triplets clawed first at their own crotches and then at each others' while their dirty brassieres gradually became undone. A girl in a blue robe trimmed with ratty white fur sat on a toilet chewing at her blue-stockinged toe, abandoning the toilet only when an urgent man wished to put his head in it. A chap in bloody shorts who might or might not have been castrated eventually acquired a pair of papier-mâché breasts, a fellow in a frock coat sported an enormous and apparently overused phallus, a gypsy in drag battered the heads of her/his fellow performers with a tambourine while mouths and elbows and ankles and hips twitched all about

her/him and about a thalidomide baby with leather-jacketed half
arms. If the shrill and flailing anger of the ruthlessly splattered
evening seemed directed at anything other than mind, it seemed
directed at a world in which sex and thalidomide babies are possible. But that is a conclusion of the witness and must be stricken
from the record.

I did, however, in the process of listening more carefully than
was probably wanted, come across a few lines which may suggest
what the quality of the enterprise might have been if it had permitted itself to be an enterprise open to judgment. One sassy
dialogue exchange:

"You know, you look like Myrna Loy."
"Nobody ever told me that before."
"Hold on to it, boy. I have a feeling no one ever will again."
Hilarious innuendo, begun with a haughty sniff:
"A girl of your bearing!"
"What bearing?"
"Ball bearing."
Sly pun:
"You are unique."
"You mean a eunuch?"

Hearing these things, and knowing what would happen to them
if they were exposed in open court rather than drowned in a
dervish busyness, I had a feeling that the piece (called *Heaven
Grand in Amber Orbit*) had been very, very wise to adopt its
policy of total unaccountability in which all standards are automatically retired. When there is no evident trace of wit or talent at
hand, the posture of witlessness is a life saver.

And because I'd missed an earlier camp epic by Ronald Tavel
called *Gorilla Queen* (I am fond of put-ons and put-downs when
they really work), I made a special trip to the Judson Poets'
Theater, which is situated in a choir loft that shakes whenever the
actors do, to see a romantic tragedy called *Arenas of Lutetia*. I
have the press agent's word for it that it was a romantic tragedy.

I admire that press agent. I really do. He had composed, in his
advance blurb for the play, one of the most imaginative, most
genuinely creative pieces of writing of our time. "The story is
simple," he began, achieving quite a high level of invention right
there. "Twin brothers, St. Sebastian and the hunter Actaeon, are

abducted by a blundering bird of fate and brought to a fabulous
empire ruled by an Aphrodite called Lutetia. Rivals in love, as well
as odessy [*sic*], the brothers unravel their dualism and confused
identities though, predictably, they fail to equal the undying
transcendental value embodied in Lutetia's symbolic figure of
Woman."

Now, to have got all that, and to have got it so limpidly, so
evocatively, so *confidently* (and with only one misspelling) out of
what was actually going on at the Judson was a literary triumph of
some magnitude. Only a terribly insightful man could have dis-
cerned so much. How, for instance, did he know those two
brothers were St. Sebastian and Actaeon, or even that they were
brothers, especially since they both first appeared in crash helmets
futilely trying to silence a peculiarly shapeless dance of protest
performed by peculiarly shapeless women? They could have been
Mayor Daley and Norman Mailer for all of me, and you're lucky
you don't have to rely on *my* interpretation of these events for
any sort of guidance.

True, if you stuck it out until the second act (as a rather pretty
little thing sitting near me did not, but she probably hadn't seen
the press release), you'd have realized that one of them—the one
now dressed like Spartacus in bloomers—was St. Sebastian right
enough. By this time he was hanging broken-wristed from a cross
and people were shooting arrows at him. We hadn't taken all those
art appreciation courses for nothing.

But Actaeon, first act or second, was another matter. His only
distinguishing mark for quite a long time—until he was finally
wrapped in a piece of mangy hide left over from a D. W. Griffith
film about man's genesis—was that he was plainly wearing lipstick,
and quite a lot of it. Now I have just looked up Actaeon in the
Oxford Companion to Classical Literature and there's nothing
about lipstick. If anything, Actaeon got himself into trouble on
other counts: surprising girls at their bathing, being a better hunts-
man than the nearest woman, that sort of thing. At the Judson,
however, he was a pretty backward type, keeping his distance
from the "Medea-madonna" of the title until she finally nailed him
and dribbled either blood or pink water all over him, and we
needed interpretative help to get hold of him.

Probably the only place we didn't need it was in the matter of the transcendental Woman, whom we would surely have recognized even if we hadn't had a press agent holding our hands. Transcendental Women are always very leggy, which this one was (though she seemed to have fur-bearing knees; at least Sebastian, who kept nibbling at her knees the night I was there, also seemed to keep spitting out fur, which surprised me but nevertheless occupied him). She also had breasts. Not for long, but she had them. When someone, who had been paying attention, remarked, "You are pretty well appointed," she snapped back, "And you are pretty well disappointed," removing her breasts as she spoke. (Breasts have to put up with an awful lot these days.)

I see that we have now touched on the language of the play, which I'd hoped to avoid. The language was either pop art ("pop art is flop art" one of the more intransigent chorus girls kept saying), or insufficiently imitated Joyce, or one hundred per cent pure minstrel show—you could take your pick.

"I hope you're ratisfied," one actor said to another, and though all of the acting was very, very bad, I don't think the line was fluffed, I think it had been written that way. "If I may denture to be so told . . ." another began. "I take reception to that!" a third concluded. (That is pure minstrel show and was last delivered in 1904 by a gentleman named Mr. Bones.) Otherwise there were references to Sidney Queenstreet and jokes (I *believe* they were jokes, though remember, this was a romantic tragedy) like, "I believe we've kept the status quo," "Or the status low."

The attitude, whether it was pop or put-on or in-between poetic, was presumably smart. Nothing inside it was smart or even remotely professional. It is high time that a supercilious tone of voice was ruled out as a substitute for wit, or wisdom, or competence.

3

EITHER the people who were performing *Alice in Wonderland* knew what they were doing, in which case they were not doing it well, or they didn't know what they were doing, in which case they oughtn't to have been so long about it.

The amateur acrobats who first drew us down a rabbit hole (a door we had to duck through) at the Extension Theater (really an unused room in a church) on Park Avenue South were, to get the best over with, rather well trained. Under the direction of Andre Gregory, and with enough assistance from the Rockefeller Foundation to enable them to spend two years at it, they had learned how to fall softly, to tumble tables quietly, to curve themselves into croquet balls and go rolling through arched-spine wickets.

Let me list at once four effects that came off. A chap in coveralls that seemed to have been made of bed ticking pronounced himself the Dirigible Prince, was immediately punctured, and then skittered to the floor like a deflating balloon, twisting every which way as the busy air took its leave of him. Four sturdy performers bent over, backsides touching, to form a comfortable mushroom upon which a Caterpillar could sit; the Caterpillar, wanting another draw on his hookah, simply reached down to unsnake the limp arm of one of his doubled-up supporters. Humpty Dumpty, actually perched upon a tower of interlocked chairs, was supposed to be held in place by invisible wires straining from the taut arms of four temporary stagehands; eventually the unseen wires gave and the tower toppled over. The Dormouse, wishing to speak, had his mouth promptly stuffed with bread in vaudeville style; Larry Pine, who played him and had also played the Caterpillar, managed to make the process of becoming breadlogged seem funny.

What was done was done with at least reasonable agility, though the speech was always inferior (sometimes intolerably so, as in the case of a morose and ultimately unintelligible White Knight) to the knocking about. But what was being done? Lewis Carroll's fantasy was, first of all, being "confronted" in the modern manner, which is to say that the text was taken simply as a point of departure, to be chopped up absurdly, to be challenged. In the present instance, however, this was no more than a parasitical activity; if it hadn't been for our clear memories of the two Carroll books, not an image on stage would have conveyed anything to us, comic or cruel or whatever.

And to attempt a reduction of Carroll to the absurd was surely a work of supererogation. To do it, the members of the Manhattan Project had to assume that when Carroll wrote nonsense, when he trained little girls to see the universe as preposterous, he hadn't *really* known what he was doing. They were going to tell him.

They did it with a snigger. They chalked upon a blackboard
LEWIS LIKES LITTLE GIRLS. As if this weren't clear enough, when
Alice was offered the cake that reads EAT ME, the phrase was given
current and most explicit visual illustration. In general, an Alice
who adopted the ample smile of an idiot (or a nymphet, as she
growled a lusty "Come on!") was tossed, fondled, mauled, and
Manhattan-handled in such a way as to suggest that a certain
bachelor mathematician had had something quite shocking in mind
when he had gone boating with his underage Victorian friends.

Well, well, now. We do keep hearing this sort of thing these
days: Freud discovered no actual forms of neurosis but simply
projected his own neuroses onto his patients—that sort of thing.
And, in fact, any such rearview-mirror gazing is likely to have
some degree of truth in it. Some degree. Lewis Carroll, like James
M. Barrie, is almost too easy a target for the clayfoot crowd (I
hope to God they'll leave *Peter Pan* alone because *Peter Pan*
already is its own farthest extension, its own most complete
revelation).

But men perceptive enough, sensitive enough, aware enough,
and talented enough to write masterpieces generally have some
notion of what they themselves are about, what dark sides—if
any—bother their dreams, what quirks of makeup account for the
quiddities they are. The very first thing they do is incorporate
these burrs of self-knowledge into their work, exorcising them if
you will, making use of them most certainly and making use of
them—if dark they be—*as darkness*. Do you think there is nothing
dark in *Alice in Wonderland?* The man made mock of every
virtue of his mind. That is why adults have always been able to
read the book.

In order to go him one better, to see him more clearly than he
likely saw himself, one would have to be more imaginative than he,
more generously endowed and even more generous in spirit. One
would have to dig a well, not piddle in the surface mud. That the
people at hand were not quite so endowed was indicated by the
indulgences they permitted themselves when they had run out of
Carrollisms to borrow or smirk at. Now they suggested that the
Caterpillar with his hookah was really on a "trip," now they
slugged the phrase "No chance" as every tired nighttime comic has
done, now they began a speech "May I make one thing perfectly

clear" in Nixon's voice. In the process of skinning Carroll they were willing to skin any old cat that came to hand. It made children of them, and I rather thought they needed a man to tell them stories.

Lewis Carroll once wrote:

> Let me take this opportunity of answering a question that has often been asked me, how to pronounce "slithy toves." The "i" in "slithy" is long, as in "writhe"; and "toves" is pronounced so as to rime with "groves." Again, the first "o" in "borogoves" is pronounced like the "o" in "borrow." I have heard people try to give it the sound of the "o" in "worry." Such is Human Perversity.

Amen.

4

I WAS GLAD to learn from Joseph Papp's program notes for *Mod Donna* at the Public Theater that the musical was *not* to be construed as a profeminist entertainment. I was glad, because if it had been a feminist entertainment anything I might have had to say against it would have been taken as male-oriented, biased, vengeful, near-sighted, thick-headed, and disloyal to that half of the population which has been making so much noise lately and to which I have for so long been so intensely devoted. I was off the hook. Right?

I was also grateful for Mr. Papp's program notes because, having directed the play, he seemed to understand it. Pointing out that the author, Myrna Lamb, was an activist in the Women's Liberation movement (she simply hadn't bothered to write about it, if I understand the situation), Mr. Papp told us that she had nevertheless dug "into the very core of the matter." I continue to quote:

> The heart of *Mod Donna* is the heart of the male-female relationship in our society: the use of sex as the ultimate weapon, the final solution in the bedroom and on the launching pad. Sex and murder are partners in crime. Whores and Wars are heads

and tails of the same coin. Orgasm is substituted for fulfillment and Penis Power corrupts both men and women, turning them both into objects. Having more options, the man finds alternatives outside the boudoir, while the wife, who has been turned into a witch, wields the knife of castration.

Well, wow, I thought to myself as I got out my Pep-o-Mints and settled back for the revelation, wait'll I get home and tell them what I saw tonight! (My wife had not accompanied me, having decided to stay home on the launching pad.) And as things started off, I was quickly able to identify that castrating witch. She and her husband came riding into view on little coffee-table-type seats, scooting a bit jerkily across the pretend-marble floor inlaid with tracks and interrupted only by cool gray pillars. He was smoking a cigar. So, by the way, was she, which led me into wondering what all his extra options were. Anyway, good looking as she was (Sharon Laughlin was cool enough to have been carved from cold cream, with faint wisps of hair brushing her ivory cheeks in the best Charles Dana Gibson manner), it was clear that her doe eyes were killers, her smile a crusher, her composure a limpid insult.

At first meeting this wife didn't seem at all injured that her husband was currently playing about, if that isn't too modest a phrase in this age of total candor, with a misleadingly virginal little thing named Donna, a girl who couldn't say no to any man provided he asked her politely. The husband, however, *was* upset that his wife had recently invaded his office, "where he lived," to take up with (oh, these circumlocutions!) his business manager. His business manager was married to Donna, probably to keep costs down.

The wife had a suggestion. Why shouldn't Donna come and live with them? Three in a bed would be nice indeed: it might help the wife toward orgasm, it might even increase the husband's potency. (I should add that between these conversations a chorus of girls— is it all right to call them girls anymore?—came leaping onto the floor, clad in trousers and belts and brass-studded jackets, to announce in acrid song that they were earthworms and were sick of it. Virtually all of the music in this musical was provided by these unrompered rompers; the principals sang very rarely, very wisely.)

The notion struck the husband as quite jolly, it struck Donna as even jollier, and it didn't seem to bother Donna's husband much until later on (he turned out to have an unreasonable streak).

So they copulated as one (it was all very ladylike, you could have taken the children if you'd really had it in for them). For a time it was pretty dandy, and then it degenerated into the same sort of standard quarreling we all have at home:

HUSBAND: Come to bed with me.
WIFE: Will we have ecstasy?
HUSBAND: Something like it.
DONNA: Oh, go to bed and get it over with!

You could see that Donna was getting just a bit miffed by the whole layout (*Note to Editor:* That is not a surreptitious naughty pun; there is just no word in the English language that doesn't start talking dirty the minute you try describing these plays), but she nevertheless consented to the castrating wife's decision that they must all three have a baby. (Donna was going to get stuck *having* the baby; the wife was just going to cooperate in its conception.)

These developments tended to enrage the chorus girls, causing one of them, one with a lot of frizzy red hair, to leap onto a platform wearing a spiked crown resembling the Statue of Liberty's and calling out that the others had to help her to "get Creon." (This was either a reference to *Antigone*, in which Creon gives an early feminist as good as he gets, or Mr. Papp had omitted something from his program notes. I find the latter unthinkable.)

Donna became pregnant (April Shawhan was a lovely thing to look at in her pink silk and pink breasts, but she did an increasing amount of snarling as the play dug deeper into its core), Donna got ditched (the wife decided that she and her husband would now go off on a second honeymoon together, *alone*), and Donna's husband began taking pretty firm rhetorical stances. "Now hear this!" he said, "You've got to be alive and breathing to make the motherhood scene, and you're not going to make it!" This, by the way, was a song cue.

After the song, in which the girls flattened their hands backwards at the wrists in imitation of Theda Bara imitating Cleopatra and in which the husband flipped a girl about while keeping a lighted cigar firmly clenched between his teeth (that girl was going to get burned if the play ran any length of time, and I didn't want to be there), Donna's husband did return to prove that he had meant what he said. He killed Donna with a blunt instrument (not the text).

The last thing I remember was the chorus madly running through the auditorium injuring no one but throwing their flowered hats into the central ring. I did not understand the significance of this particular gesture.

I suppose it's half true what they've always said, that women hate women. It certainly looked like it in this particular instance, what with Susan Hulsman Bingham's nagging, grainy, broken foxtrot score and Miss Lamb's insistence that the world is ruled by two kinds of women, bitch goddesses and idiot bedfellows. The men, who were both patsies, came off a little better simply because they didn't *start* anything; they simply went along for the ride, as more or less cooperative victims. Indeed, if any one plaint loomed larger than another during the evening, it was the chorus' wail, "All right, what is it about men? They want to be dominated by women."

So much for Penis Power.

5

For real cruelty, you've got to have heart.

Let's indulge ourselves in a paradox, briefly. Our minds are much on the Theater of Cruelty these days, and with the visit of Yugoslavia's Atelje 212 to the Lincoln Center Forum we were at last given an opportunity to see the grandfather of all plays belonging to the Theater of Cruelty, the Theater of the Absurd, or the Theater of Whatever Self-torment One Happens to Prefer.

Alfred Jarry's *King Ubu*, first produced in 1896, is perfectly heartless and comfortably obscene. It couldn't care less that a king is killed, an abandoned queen is left to die, a loyal friend betrayed, sons lost to the four winds, all usurpers condemned to fouling themselves in the pits they crawl into at night. Insanity is the accepted norm of the human condition, success and failure are equally detestable if not in fact interchangeable, feeling is a joke and so is any action that might spring from it.

Life is literally anarchic, and *everything* should hurt. The lively Yugoslav players did not mince manners in letting us know the plight we are all in. Got up as tatterdemalion clowns, with curled painted mustaches on the men and cat's whiskers on the women, they investigated with a cool indifference the inner workings of ambition, fear, love, luck, the whole beastly lot. It was all child's play, with excrement. King Ubu used a chamber pot for his crown, and his crown for a chamber pot. The youngest son of the man Ubu had murdered, an heir to the throne with whom we might ordinarily sympathize, was a peak-capped horror, a little princeling made of ice. He watched his brothers go to their doom with simple childish excitement and he comforted his mother with a detachment Machiavelli could not have managed. The great white bear with alligator's jaws that threatened to dine on the ousted Ubu, with his wife as dessert, was a very modest creature who daintily drew his skirts about him as he clung to a ladder, waiting for supper. Not even terror could be taken seriously when all emotions were transparent frauds. What a man might do, think, or feel was meaningless, merely a turn in the exacerbating circus through which he perforce had to romp, willy-nilly, under the whip. The lash struck everywhere, denied everything.

And how did we respond to this image of ourselves and our self-deceiving dreams? Giddily part of the time, indifferently the rest. We tittered, we giggled, and then we just looked. But—and this is the point I'm coming to—we did not feel any pain. Somehow or other a totally cruel image, one from which every trace of sentiment has been rigorously removed, has no power to disturb us. We may even give assent, in an abstracted way, and say yes, this is more or less what it all comes to. But we do not shudder and certainly we do not weep. The cold, cold surface and the terrible single-mindedness have anesthetized us. The most we can do with an uninterruptedly savage view of things is find it, now and again, mildly amusing. Perhaps that is why the gifted players anticipated us and presented themselves as clowns.

Shakespeare's *Henry IV, Part Two* was being performed in Central Park the very same week, and *Henry IV, Part Two* is quite a different kind of play. It has not precisely heard of hopelessness as a way of life, it believes that Doll is truly fond of her Falstaff and Hal truly fond of his father, it is skeptical of power and yet not so skeptical that it would sniff at the crown; it permits emotion. And it is much the crueler of the two.

I suggest it is the crueler because it permits affection, because it proposes that justice and rectitude and honor are also—and most terribly—a part of the scene before us.

It does have cruelty on its mind. The evening opens with the needless, meaningless ravaging of a man. Henry Percy is anxiously awaiting news of his rebel son's fortunes in battle. News comes. The son has been victorious and is safe; he has killed his enemy, Prince Hal. The father is elated. But the news is false. At the peak of his elation and his gratitude more accurate news thrusts its way forward. The son is dead, the battle lost, Hal secure. The blow would have been bad enough in any case; it is gratuitously intolerable now, made so by nothing more than idle rumor. (Rumor is a character in Shakespeare's play, and for this production director Gerald Freedman placed him, in a clown's cap and streamers, high above the scene, crooking a leg casually and grinning maliciously as he surveyed the wanton damage.)

There is cruelty coming for Falstaff and he senses it; that may be why the fat old man brings such a tart tongue and impatient eye to the fools about him, half wishing to wound first. We know that the chimes of midnight are catching up with this aging sport (when a dog barked in the park on the night I saw the play, it did truly seem to be nipping at Falstaff's heels).

There is cruelty in the crown. When Prince Hal has innocently tried the crown on, only to be caught out by his dying father, the King's savage physical assault on the boy, catching him with a clout while he is suppliant on his knees, is genuinely shocking. A man's last breath can be greedy. And there is, of course, the all too familiar final cruelty of the play: Hal's wintry rejection of the Falstaff he has loved, in public, before the very people to whom Falstaff has boasted of their friendship. Humiliation could not have been more scathingly arranged.

But hold a minute. How effective, how cutting, would this last scene be if it were not for the scene just before it? In the scene just before it Prince Hal, now ready to be crowned king, meets the Lord Chief Justice who has been the scourge of his wild youth. The Chief Justice fully expects that Hal will take his revenge; having come to power, he will even the score for all those old whippings. And Hal, imperious, still resentful, is angrily tempted to do so. The elderly justice makes a speech in which he points out that he was simply doing his duty, that Hal fully deserved the earlier treatment he got. And Hal listens. Hal is intelligent. Hal is fair. When the speech is done, he gives the Justice justice. He commends him for his strictness and increases his honors. There is integrity in the world too.

It is the integrity that kills Falstaff and makes all of us ache. For, having seen justice done once and been very much moved by it, we now realize that we are seeing it done twice: Falstaff deserves disgrace as surely as the justice deserves praise. That is what is so terrible about it, so intolerable. We can raise no protests, offer no sympathy, work out no rationalizations. Virtue itself is cruel, rectitude is cruel, justice is crueler than injustice because there is no possible escape from it. If Hal were being merely capricious or callous, we should not take it so hard; we should simply dismiss him as an ingrate, as demonstrably inhuman, and keep up our old love affair with Falstaff. As things stand, we must accept the verdict. And that hurts, really hurts.

Cruelty here becomes a condition of the world when the world is going right. Isn't that a harsher piece of information than any contained in Jarry, or in any other demonstration of the world gone wholly wrong? We can't titter now; we've done well and are still smarting for it. We've permitted ourselves to feel for the Lord Justice and to see goodness in Hal. Now we're really trapped. There is no way to heal the scar. It is when we open our hearts that we are finally, and necessarily, horrified.

6

It DOES strike me that one whole strand of the current experimental theater may be superfluous because it is straining terribly hard to get us where we already are.

It is trying to give us the sense that we are *there*—there where the action is, there at the precise moment the happening happens, there where immersion in the immediate is total, there under bombardment, there on the spot, there before thought has had a chance to tidy things up.

We are at the center of the melee, with impromptu voices calling over our shoulders to "Tell it like it is, man," caught between
forces that have not yet become coherent, subject to violation by
soundtrack and players, part of the script before the script has
been written, participants in an action that no one has quite
planned.

Advocates of this kind of theater are in passionate earnest, and
they have a premise. The theater we have known bores us because
it displays a dead life, life cut and trimmed and dumped on the
meat counter where it has already gathered flies. The only alterna-
tive is to enter a live life, before the callous and merely money-
minded butchers have got at it. Catch life before anyone else has
caught it and codified it, killed it, for you.

Working from the premise, one such advocate has, as we've
reported, announced that the 1967 March on the Pentagon was
1967's only genuine play. Those who marched had met and
mingled with drama instead of observing, distantly and indifferently, its interment on a stage. Those who were unable, or who
failed, to march on the Pentagon may be able to take up the slack
by marching, or being marched upon, in auditorium or garage.
The important thing is that, wherever you are, it's *now*.

But the one wrestler's grip that life has already got on us, the
one awareness no modern man is without, is the grip of the now,
the actual and unyielding pressure of the instantly present. I'm not
going to recatalogue McLuhanisms for you here, or talk about
telestar making a global village of us all, sharing the anger of
Prague before Prague can quite clear its head of bewilderment.
One needed only to flick a television set on—and off—during the
Democratic National Convention of 1968 to deal with nowness
directly.

Flicking it off said as much about the living instant as flicking it
on. Here was a speech in progress, not a film. An empty speech, a
speech making its way through ritual, unfelt motions. (The living
now can be as mummified in its immediacy as the dead *then*.) It
was going to go on for a while, stretch into a new, not yet
counted, nowness. Snap it off, for now. I have a *now* of my own: I
can speak to someone, write a check, write a letter, while waiting
for nowness in Chicago to catch up with mine here. Half the time
I am ahead of it, so fast does my world go.

When I snap it on again, I am there—as those old record albums used to say—while helmeted police maul ministers and hurl them into waiting wagons. No blood is dry yet, no scalps stitched. The shocked faces of bystanders are my shock, coinciding in time. They have not reflected, I have not reflected, we are joined, locked in simultaneity. Someone in my house went to the bathroom and missed seeing Dan Rather knocked down. No, not seeing. *Being* at the knocking down. The dizzy totality spins on, and we are breathless from it. Multiply it by a ringing telephone—another *now* message—and we scarcely know which way to turn. Chances are the caller will say, "Are you looking at what's happening *now?*"

More than the television image is blurred in the frantic swing of the camera to catch what has never been rehearsed, what cannot be predicted. The eyes blur, comprehension blurs, the antennae of the senses blur (what is that sound? a gavel at the convention or some-one banging on the front door?). In time—and this is very much what some theatrical experimentalists are after—the distinction between the rehearsed and the unrehearsed blurs. You may have read, in *The New Yorker*, a neck-snapping account of a motion-picture actor, an actor who had appeared in *The Dirty Dozen* and similar films, getting out of his car on the highway, smilingly approaching the driver behind who'd lightly touched his bumper, and clouting the driver full in the face, drawing his fingernails across the man's eyes for good measure. Sincere experimentalists would have to approve the actor and the action. He was not con-fined to dead film, the film was *now.*

We are all of us in it all of the time and a sniper may tag us on the Long Island Railroad. In our homes, in our cars, on trains and on the telephone, we are centers of a thousand trajectories, hostile, friendly, demanding, beneficent, irrational, logical, random. We have been pushed up forward, and that is where we try to cope. We speed-read the signals, and have no time to look back. We no longer have to look at our watches. We are everywhere the second hand is, when it is.

That is already our experience. The attempt to reproduce it in the theater—to reproduce it as it is, man—exposes the theater to three swift self-denials. The attempt, quite literally, to make the theater indistinguishable from life, as in calling the March on the

Pentagon a play, deprives the theater of an identity of its own. Life goes on, the theater does not.

To the degree that such theater succeeds in duplicating the precise conditions of our lives, it also becomes superfluous. Why go to the theater when we are already there?

And, lastly, it becomes synthetic. The process, trying hard not to be a manufacture but a continuation of fact, remains a manufacture: the sounds are manufactured, the sights are manufactured, the performers are only performers, feeble alongside the sniper, the cop, the shocked bystander, the real bore. We have duplicated what did not need duplicating, and in general duplicated it lamely.

This is not an argument for evasion of the real. It is an argument for understanding of the real. Obviously the moment of least comprehension is the moment of greatest inundation. Even as we watch bodies being clubbed on television, even as we are caught up—our heads swimming—in the violent, unfocused, swerving, jarring immediacy of it all, we want to stand back. Stand back just a little, just for a moment. We want to *see* what we are seeing, see it in its wholeness, its shape, its meaning. We want to know what orders were given, where and by whom. We want to know, at the very least, which victims may have deserved a tenth of what they are getting, which have deserved nothing at all. We want to relate the action *now* to the actions that preceded it, and we want to grasp its implications for action that will follow tomorrow. We want the event to take form, and only distancing will do that for us.

Form, through distancing, is of course what the theater has always been about. It has never denied *now;* it has simply put it in the intelligible perspective of *and then*. It may have sometimes, it may have very often, falsified the *and then;* but even when it was clumsily falsifying it was not losing sight of its function. If we are rebelling in the theater now, it may be a good idea to ask what we are rebelling against: the act of distancing itself, or a merely outmoded method of distancing, one we have come to see through and one which may very well be replaced by a better.

The issue seems to me critical just now. It may be that this is the very time when we most need the theater on its own terms. The more we are plunged into nowness in our lives, the farther we are pushed toward an unfamiliar and even incomprehensible frontier, the more we are desperately engaged with unexpected blows struck by an invisible hand at an unpredictable hour, the more desperately do we need a space in which we *may* stand back, or even sit down. Standing there, or sitting there, we need accept no lies about shape. But unless we have a reflective, judging, distancing place in which shaping may be attempted, or even experienced, we won't be able to tell a lie from a truth.

The Theater
of Fact

I DO NOT KNOW that I had ever before felt exactly the strain, the unreleased and in a way doubled tension, that I felt whenever Conor Cruise O'Brien's *Murderous Angels* touched one of its bitter, relentless turning points. Mr. O'Brien's rhetorical play, which has been seen in Los Angeles and Dublin but not yet in New York, is a parliamentarian's exercise, an exhaustive brief worked out to say that Dag Hammarskjöld, playing God on earth because he had been given God's job to do, permitted the murder of Patrice Lumumba in order to keep the Congo from turning into a nuclear Sarajevo. Hammarskjöld's own death in a plane, Mr. O'Brien intimates at the sharp top of his lungs, came about as a direct result of his virtuous, cold connivance.

The evening, then, is a case made—and, as such, not a mere trotting out of fact, but in part a work of the imagination. The imagination is used, however, in a very special way. It does not try to know Hammarskjöld as a person or present him as one. We first see him dropped down—almost literally dropped down; he seems to have been deposited like baggage on an airstrip platform, half buckling at the knees—in Katanga, where he has gone to meet the secessionist Tshombe before paying a diplomatic visit to the man he should have recognized first, Lumumba. Tshombe is all too plainly the puppet of white copper interests; Lumumba is the true saint and cement of the Congolese people. An irretrievable error has been made.

Thereafter Hammarskjöld appears whenever his formal, symbolic chess-maneuver presence is required: to say that because Lumumba, in retaliation, has sought help from the Russians, Lumumba must go; to say that decisions made are not subject to humane discussion; to say that sometimes Abraham is required to put his great sword to Isaac, without intervention from an angel; to say that he himself cannot afford human emotion because he has been made trustee for the species, not for individuals.

And so the play proposes to deal not with individuals but with the long, naked, dry outline of Things Done. We look at positions and justifications, waverings and absolute commitments, as though these things could walk (certainly Mr. O'Brien makes them talk). An industrialist aristocrat who has said "I am power" ultimately preens himself on his success in saving Katanga for white money by marching solemnly along a red carpet (Agamemnon's, no doubt) calling attention to the medals and the braid that almost conceal his nonexistent heart. Lackeys lapse into choral yes-ings, actual filmclips of Congolese events in 1960–61 are flashed onto a six-panel screen overhead.

The play's language is explicit, formed in long rolling periods, candid in a way that vulnerable human speech is never candid. "The time is coming when men will die for what you think and for what I feel about what you think," a minor functionary remarks. "As in the opening of games, it is for white to move," announces a two-man team, white chess knight held by one, black by the other. We are not pretending to speech but attending to the illustration of an argument.

This argument, in essence a remarkably coherent position paper dealing with almost unmanageable complexities, is always clear, always interesting. It does, before it is through, build in the playhouse a sense of controlled, helpless anger. But the anger, the increasing tension, has two targets, shuttles back and forth in two directions. It is directed at the sorry sequence of events. And it is also directed at the ignorance we are finally left in, the fact that we still cannot *know*, for all our attentiveness, whether what we are hearing is true or not.

The evening straddles the two kinds of truth that are possible, plunging into neither of them. There is the truth of fact, of strict historical accounting; but Mr. O'Brien isn't after that, he knows he can't for certain read Hammarskjöld's—or anyone else's—mind. There is also ordinary imaginative truth, the truth that gains at least temporary assent because the people on stage come to exist as intelligible objects in their own right, men and women who smell when they don't bathe and who miss nuances when they're hungry—quirky, idiosyncratic, half the time unknowing and all the time temperamentally unreliable creatures. But Mr. O'Brien has at the same time waived this way of being true in favor of detached and impersonal statement.

Waived and not waived it. He knows he has a play to write, audiences to hold, some tricky private motivations to account for. Whereupon he lets slip into the action, though it tends to contradict the abstractness of line he has set for himself, bits and pieces of "people" behavior. He is most successful at this with Lumumba, a cynical, proud, careless, honest, passionate man in shirtsleeves and bowtie with his feet on the table when the Russian ambassador calls. In other places the incidental humanizing comes up false. When, for instance, Lumumba's white mistress, half out of her head since the death of her lover, manages to make her battered way into Hammarskjöld's U.N. office to challenge his God-playing directly, the clash between the impersonal political brief and the savageries of private passion turn the moment into straight ten-twent'-thirt'. The confrontation is neither believable nor wanted; it is garish and off-key, a reminder that this sort of emotion has been ruled out for tonight and that it is interrupting a spare intellectual exercise gratuitously.

The author runs into other theatrical difficulties. A great deal depends upon the fact that, at the outset, Mr. Hammarskjöld simply shares a platform with Tshombe. Death on the double is going to come of it. But the visual image itself—several men standing about while drums beat in the background and a routine speech of welcome is piped into a microphone—is not suggestive enough, not sufficiently self-explanatory, not *dramatic* enough to account for its aftereffects. Hundreds of words are going to be needed thereafter to say how crucial this moment was; looking at it, we see nothing crucial at all. Hearing and seeing have been separated; they don't reinforce each other. On a stage that is an unfortunate weakness.

On the whole, however, we understand that we are focused on thoughts rather than acted events, and that the thoughts are all really in Mr. O'Brien's head. The thoughts themselves are tantalizing, we hang on to discover the precise nature of the moral crisis the author has envisioned for his heroic antihero, we do enjoy the syntax and the deliberate verbal thunder. Then, with each thunderclap, we arrive at our double desperation. We are appalled by the events as they are arranged for us. And we are disturbed and frustrated by the knowledge that they *are* arranged—not factually, not imaginatively in the sense that a new dimension has been created, but argumentatively. We have been shaken up by a good debater without a chance to ask questions. Which means that in a piece about a man who played God, Mr. O'Brien has played God-plus.

Perhaps there is no way of resolving the emotional ambiguities stirred up by this kind of playmaking, this use of the stage. But the ambiguities are there and it is altogether possible, at any given moment, that they are worse than that, that they are injustices. There is an ugly moment, for instance, when we see an actual newsclip, high overhead, of Adlai Stevenson at the U.N. being interrupted by a violent outburst among the blacks in his audience. The real Stevenson is transparently upset and as he calls for order he says that the demonstration has obviously been rigged for political purposes. Because of the hypothetical "inside track" that we have been following, courtesy of Mr. O'Brien's personal interpretation of his materials, Stevenson seems, in the fleeting instant, both dishonest and a fool.

But it is Mr. O'Brien's preparation, his imagined sequence of events, that makes him so. Actually, Stevenson's role in the events of the play has never been examined at all, indeed not so much as mentioned. And Mr. O'Brien doesn't bother to say whether or not the demonstration *was* rigged. It may well have been; his simple silence suggests that it was not. Thus an actual man in an actual filmed situation is in effect calumnied by context. When slivers of fact are dropped into extensively developed hypotheses, the hypotheses tend to *use* the fragmented facts without having to make a responsible accounting for them. Hypothesis here dominates fact; it may as easily distort it. Watching the sequence, one wonders uneasily how much of the rest of the evening—how much of Hammarskjöld, how much of Lumumba, how much of many people who once existed and now serve as an author's pawns—has been created for us by the same swift sleight-of-hand.

I came away unsettled in what I think is the wrong sense.

This contest between fact and imagination, in which both lose, persists in all current stage documentaries with which I am familiar. Most playwrights beg the question before they have quite begun the play, as Rolf Hochhuth did a few years ago in publishing his historical footnotes to *The Deputy* simultaneously with the acting text. "As a stage play the work requires no commentary," he announced in his opening paragraph. The ensuing sixty-five page commentary, then, was presumably required by the work's existence as scholarship.

But we were immediately embroiled in a contradiction: "What is offered here is not scholarly work and is not meant to be. But since neither the Vatican nor the Kremlin as yet permit free access to their archives, historians will have to wait before they can present a comprehensive account of these events. To intuitively combine the already available facts into a truthful whole becomes the noble and rarely realized function of art."

The play, then, was to be composed partly of fact that could be documented, partly of "truth" arrived at intuitively. But these two "truths" belong to entirely different intellectual orders which cannot be interchanged without mutual damage. Used in the same context, one subverts the other. The introduction of imagination corrupts the purity of the factual base; the insistence upon factuality impedes imagination. This mutual subversion can, in certain circumstances, arrive at the wildest of inversions, creating effects quite contrary to those intended.

Mr. Hochhuth fell victim to just this turnabout in *Soldiers*, the play in which he assigned to a man he himself regards as great, Winston Churchill, the moral responsibility for the fire-bombing of Dresden and the death by remote control of the Polish general Sikorski.

His evocation of the personality of Churchill was to a degree genuinely dramatic; personal color was added to it in the fine performance given by John Colicos. We became intimate with this baby of a bulldog. Mr. Colicos' rolling lip dipped and surged like a vessel at sea as he chomped out his insistence that civilians be burned to death; his driving tilt forward as he lurched out of bed or bore down on Sikorski made him seem a toppling weight crushing the hesitant consciences of the world; the wit and the nerviness and the cold pain in his restless eyes told us that the man felt, all right, but kept his feelings tightly held between his teeth. The two "crimes" that occupied this man—cremating whole cities and ridding himself of a man who was a political embarrassment—were in fact thematically unrelated. They had to take turns being dramatized. But Mr. Colicos at least made them the moral crises of one person.

Nevertheless, the closer Mr. Hochhuth came to drama—to an imaginative identification with a man—the more hopelessly did he compromise his point. The last third of the evening was mainly taken up with a debate over fire bombing between the Bishop of Chichester and the stubbornly ruthless Prime Minister. Rhetoric flew fast and thick: "I kill because there is no help for it!", "Kill the enemy but not his family!", and so on, slogan for slogan.

Because Churchill was *not* going to be dissuaded from his policy of fighting the war on the enemy's terms, the Bishop, for all that he was plainly virtuous, inevitably became a repetitive bore: he could only return and return to his theme, profitlessly, reiterating arguments that were going to be dismissed rather than met.

But that was not the worst thing that happened to him. Churchill was the dramatic figure, the complex one. He was the man we knew best. Knowing a man is next to liking him, being interested in a man's personal complexity becomes very nearly the same thing as siding with him. Theatrically—even if only theatrically—we are always rooting for the richest image.

And so, on the production's opening night in New York, there was applause for a spat-out line just once. It came at the point of Churchill's total exasperation with the Bishop, his refusal to listen any longer. Mr. Colicos filled with a rage his stocky form could not now contain, he turned on his badgering opponent with a glare that announced he would happily burn *him*, he abandoned any pretense at rational argument and, virtually strangling on the words, barked at his secretary, "Helen—a car for the Bishop—at once!" Hoary as the line was, bull-headed as the hero was, the audience clapped its approval. And Mr. Hochhuth had written the play in support of the Bishop's cause.

Heinar Kipphardt's *In the Matter of J. Robert Oppenheimer*, also a documentary careful to call itself not quite a documentary, had a strong odor of anesthetic about it—not in the sense that it was apt to be overpowering, but in the sense that it was determined to be clean. No cheap rhetoric, no false moves that would cause it to turn turtle. The performing—both in Los Angeles, where it was first presented in this country, and in New York—was spare, dry, controlled, quietly intelligent. The lines, whether invented or from the transcript of Oppenheimer's security-clearance proceedings in 1954, seemed to have been tucked into place with a scalpel. Spectators tended to listen with a kind of concentrated detachment, alert, careful to preserve an appropriate hush, aware that they were invited eavesdroppers who had best respect the delicacy of the occasion. There was a sense in the air that the situation was iffish, that the outcome of surgery might in the end be ambiguous.

Gordon Davidson had directed for as much ambiguity, and just as much subtlety, as the text would allow. Joseph Wiseman, as Oppenheimer, sat lofty and prim as an articulated mechanical man in an industrial exhibit, feet held close together, head cocked as though listening for sounds from the stratosphere. His tone was High Mandarin, his pipe was handled not nervously but ritualistically, his candor was calculated ("I can't understand why," remarked a hostile counsel of one of his indiscretions; "Neither can I," snapped back the man in the spotlight), his arrogance and his humor seemed to hold hands in the dock. We were inclined to honor his outbursts; they came from such infinite reserve.

The text was not uncommitted. Whenever an unfriendly witness appeared, he was likely to be a bit of a boor or a bit of a boob. Witnesses friendly to Oppenheimer were a great deal more likeable and a great deal more persuasive. But the acting on both sides was kept in very low key, insisting that bias of any kind be allowed to slip in only through the back door, suppressing sentiment and pointing no more than a sly finger at scoundrels. There were no poor performances and the evening was interesting from gathering to dismissal.

It was interesting, that is to say, until we had been dismissed.

Then the sensation of not really having been fed was sharply felt. We had not actually been given undiluted facts. The evening had opened with a disclaimer. A voice in the dark, between newsreel shots of bomb tests and twelve flick-on panels ready to remind us visually of the year of Hiroshima, told us that this was not to be "a documentary sandwich," that certain of the scientists and counselors who were to appear on the stage had not actually appeared at the hearings.

At eleven o'clock we had no way of knowing what had been reported and what had been arranged. At the same time, we had been denied an imaginative dramatization: speech had been cropped too close to fact for that sort of freedom. We were not truly certain what we had seen, how responsible or how manipulated the ending had been, how representative the residue might be taken to be. A chalked blackboard introduced one passage as FROM THE PROCEEDINGS. It introduced another with the announcement that THE PROCEEDINGS ENTER A DECISIVE STAGE. Was the first actual transcript, the second a dramatist's attempt to form fact into "play"?

The upshot was ambiguous in a final sense; not only did we wonder what the characters had done, we were also forced to wonder what the author had done. We had been held, often fascinated, in our theater seats to no profit that we could identify or pleasure we could be sure of. The operation had been successful. Now what of the patient?

Donald Freed's *Inquest* was unpersuasive even when it cheated, and to my mind it finally called into question—and perhaps threw out of court altogether—the whole possibility of a Theater of Fact. This fragmented reconstruction of the trial of Julius and Ethel Rosenberg of course intended to plead the Rosenbergs' innocence of the charge of conspiring to steal atomic secrets. That was understood and accepted before we entered the theater. But it did not mean to make a stump speech or to use fiction, rhetoric, or stage melodrama to do the job. It purported to base its plea upon the record and upon nothing but the record so that, listening to the evidence offered, we might be able to arrive at a valid judgment out front. It was here that the occasion exploded in our faces.

We could arrive at no judgment at all. We did not even know

when we were in or out of the theater, when we were in or out of
the truth. When the play was produced in New York, the problem
presented itself before we had quite got through the lobby. There,
on the wall near the ticket-taker's door, was a placard that read,
rather too gravely, THERE WILL BE NO CURTAIN CALLS. Oh? Why
not? Was what we were to be seeing too real for that sort of
pleasant acknowledgment of artifice? Naturally, electrocuted persons, whether they are villains or victims, do not take curtain calls.
But actors do. Were we, then, not to be seeing actors tonight?

The problem was subtly compounded as we took our seats.
Before us, lettered in typescript on eighteen varicolored glass
panels, was a message: EVERY WORD YOU WILL SEE OR HEAR ON THIS
STAGE IS A DOCUMENTED QUOTATION OR RECONSTRUCTION FROM
EVENTS. Authenticity was guaranteed us.

We did notice the word "reconstruction," though. Reconstructed from what? From the testimony of witnesses, from
circumstance, from probability? We turned the pages of our programs to see if further explanation was offered. It was. The
reconstructions, we were told, "draw on letters and verbal reports
but they are inventions in the service of truth rather than facts."
In the service of whose truth? If they are admittedly inventions,
can you invent *the* truth? And if they are admittedly inventions
"rather than facts," why did the opening message so urge docu-
mentation, factuality upon us?

No matter. Some linking up, some bridging, no doubt was
thought necessary for clarity and a degree of coherence. We sat
up attentively as the stage lights rose, ready to have our memories
jogged and our store of information expanded. But the lobby card
and the insistence upon fact had already had a peculiar effect upon
portions of the audience. On opening night, when the clerk of the
court strode onstage to request the jury to stand and pledge
allegiance to the flag, perhaps a third of the main-floor audience
straggled to its feet, unevenly and uncertainly, as though it were
truly in court and obliged to respond as ordered. The balance of
the audience remained seated and tittered audibly. The event was
split, shattered in its essence, torn between treating the stage as a
courtroom or as a stage, the play as fact or artifice.

Still, the tittering subsided and close attention was paid as actor-
attorney James Whitmore moved forward to make an opening

statement for the defense. Now there were interesting things to focus upon. Mr. Whitmore was a fascinating performer, carved out of shale, square and tight-lipped and constantly hunching his shoulders in pain as though some unshakeable burden pressed hard on his neck. His passion, and, more than that, his fiercely imposed self-restraint, were instantly enormously believable—not evidence, but believable.

The evidence, as it began to trickle out, was not so much unbelievable (it was sometimes that, it was hard to believe Ethel Rosenberg's brother intelligent enough to know an atomic secret when he saw one, hard to believe that a court would ever think him so) as it was unfocused, incomplete, elusive. Mr. Freed had chosen to excerpt it in very small bits and pieces, out of sequence; he had constantly interrupted and cut across it with flashbacks, interpolations, News-of-the-Day photographs on those panels overhead. We were never long enough with a witness to feel that we had got close to the story, or even to the personality involved; we simply could not piece the probabilities, or even the accusations, together for ourselves. We constantly felt we had missed the vital question and that somewhere in all the transcripts there must have been material the author overlooked.

What we did occupy ourselves with as the shards of evidence flew off into space were the faces of George Grizzard and Anne Jackson as the accused couple. They are two of our most sensitive and reliable performers, and though they had little to do in the courtroom they were presences to keep an eye on. Mr. Grizzard had only to let his mouth drop open in astonishment at a statement made on the stand to persuade us that he had truly not anticipated such a falsehood. Miss Jackson accomplished precisely the same thing by letting her fingers move to her mouth as her eyes widened; there was innocent agony in the gesture.

Then, following the merely listening performers so closely, you brought yourself up short. "I am beginning to believe Julius Rosenberg innocent because George Grizzard is a fine actor" is what you were saying to yourself, wondering whether your conduct was proper. The faces, the dropped jaws, the hesitant fingers that were persuading you were not those of the Rosenbergs. They belonged to George Grizzard and Anne Jackson, who were not on trial.

Strangest of all, however, was what happened during the "re-constructions." These were not at all slender bridges, small neces-sary patches. They occurred quite frequently, they "invented" passages of lovemaking and quarreling and family estrangements, they were substantial. But it was in them that we seriously began to doubt the figures before us, whether they were to be taken as Rosenbergs or as actors. Belief paled because the scenes were in some sense empty, drained of genuine psychology, without the little catch of life that makes you say, "Oh! Yes, of course."

What was it that created this negative effect and turned the sequences directly against the intentions of the playwright? After a good bit of memory scratching, I think I know. The purpose of the passages was to let us see the principals in private, and as innocent. (If we could see them as innocent when they were alone together, we should believe them innocent in public.) Thus, natu-rally, they never said anything even remotely incriminating when they were being casual and candid together. But they also never said anything about the trial, the accusations against them, their attitudes toward what was happening or about to happen, about communism or politics or McCarthyism or acquaintances who might or might not be involved.

They were *so* silent, in private, on the central issues of the play that the silence came to seem deliberate, as though they felt their rooms were being bugged and they had best be inordinately care-ful. Ready to believe them innocent, we could not believe their imperviousness, their placidity, the narrowness and caution of their conversational range. Almost any one of us living at the time might have said, in private if not in public, most unflattering things about the atomic bomb or about McCarthy; they seemed never to have heard of such matters and to be living on another, impossibly pure, planet. They were too remote, too unaware, too *uninterested* to be true; and it was here, away from the issues, that the strongest seed of doubt was sown.

The "reconstructions" were not evidence; since the acted-out evidence of the trimmed transcripts was inadequate—one way or the other—the invented intimate scenes tended to take over. And because they felt so unreal, they became prejudicial. The method of the Theater of Fact had backfired both ways.

Nudity

I

I wonder if Robert Anderson ever wants to take it all back. It was Robert Anderson, really, who got us into this whole thing. He was the very first person to suggest, however whimsically, that a theatrical producer just *might* want to send an actor out on stage in the nude, and, what is more, he hinted that when producers and playwrights did become brave enough to do plays in the buff they would have no difficulty finding actors braver than they.

In *You Know I Can't Hear You When the Water's Running*, which most of us laughed at such a short time ago without the least intimation that we were looking at prophecy and not comedy, Mr. Anderson presented us with a very young, very earnest playwright who'd decided, in his integrity, that his new work required a performer to enter from the bathroom stark naked. He also presented us with an actor zealous enough and hungry enough to do just that, tossing away his clothes at an audition with the most commendable good cheer. In the play *we* saw, the stripping stopped at the actor's shorts. Mr. Anderson dropped his curtain before the actor could drop everything, no doubt in the belief that that was the real end of the joke and that no one would, honest to God, go any further. He was posing something preposterous, wasn't he? That's why we were all laughing, wasn't it? Actors couldn't truly be persuaded to saunter into view jaunty as jaybirds without help from the costume designer, could they?

So much for suppositions, so much for laughter, so much for actors. Scarcely before Mr. Anderson had made his joke, the old solidities on which we thought the world—and comedy—had rested had vanished. Somebody had been listening. Somebody hadn't thought the notion was farout at all. Somebody had stopped laughing, or never laughed in the first place, and simply taken up the dare. Come on naked? What an interesting, original, provocative, courageous, *serious* idea! In a trice, and in very little more than that, on came the gauze-draped Davids and Junos of the somewhat skittish *Tom Paine*, on came the dimly lighted real nudes of *Hair*, on came the briefly seen but brightly lighted nudes of *Massachusetts Trust* at Brandeis University, on came the heroine of *Sweet Eros*, in full view for forty minutes, downstage where binoculars weren't needed. These and more. Today the preposterous is simply commonplace, and if Mr. Anderson's little conceit is still playing anywhere it must seem quaint indeed, fuddyduddyish even. All that fuss about no feathers? Silly.

Correct as he was in sensing the wave of the future and in giving it the one gentle push it apparently needed, Mr. Anderson was slightly wrong about one thing. He overestimated the ardor of actors. Some actors are perfectly willing to let the fig leaves fall, but not all, and in a short-lived musical called *The Fig Leaves Are Falling* everyone was satisfied to sing a good game ("People dressed in fig leaves can't raise Cain or Abel") while keeping their own neckties tied tight and their miniskirts at full mast. When the original leading lady in a recent Broadway comedy by Jerome Weidman was told that she would be expected to do a sequence sequinless, she promptly took a walk, fully clothed, and even Sally Kirkland, the off-Broadway girl who has tended to specialize in not dressing (*Tom Paine, Massachusetts Trust, Sweet Eros*) was not long ago heard complaining to interviewer Frances Herridge about the difficulties inherent in the new dispensation.

For instance, it was virtually impossible to hire an understudy for Miss Kirkland. Miss Kirkland had no hangups about getting out there exactly as her mother bore her, but when it came time to cast a standby for her in *Sweet Eros,* no dice. The job wasn't wanted, somehow, and for as long as *Sweet Eros* ran there was never anyone backstage in that dressing room waiting for a glorious opportunity to go on. The place was deserted except for the star— and, of course, her co-star, the male of the play who kidnaped her, strapped her to a chair and promptly stripped her—and the burden of responsibility was heavy. Any time Miss Kirkland didn't show, the show didn't show. The girl couldn't even risk getting a cold. Now when you consider that, of all the people in New York City, she was the one most likely to get a cold, given her circumstances, you can see how the problems of the new dramaturgy multiply. In the case of *Sweet Eros* Miss Kirkland was able to demand that the management install additional heaters—what could the management do but acquiesce, lacking a backstop?—to keep her toasty warm, and she did look toasty warm the night I saw her. Toasty warm and rather wistful, whether from loneliness or the fact that she had no lines in the play (she just had to be nude and be there), I can't say.

You may possibly think that the issue of colds and no under-studies is a trivial one, not worth our serious concern. You'd have thought twice if you'd been at the American Place Theater the night I saw Werner Liepolt's *The Young Master Dante.* In this case, there *was* an understudy and the leading player *had* caught cold. A severe bronchitis, I was told. The leading player here was male, being named Dante, and it was his duty (as a performer) to let himself be seduced by a wicked-witch type who lolled about on a vast bed under a canopy composed of cows' udders, after which, and being naked anyway, he was castrated. As I say, some-where along the line he developed bronchitis.

His understudy was going on for the very first time. It was early, very early, in the run, and the understudy hadn't learned all of his lines yet. He was going to have to carry the book. Good enough. If an actor reads lines well, no audience is going to care that he's actually *reading* them. Theatrical illusion is such that spectators can quickly wave that book away, render it invisible, if it pleases them to do so. And reviewers may be readier to adapt than most people. There was just one catch. As tension mounted and passion flared, as young Dante found himself deeply, deeply stirred by the invitation to bed, as he clutched at his tight clothing to tear it hotly from his body, he was forced to undress himself with the book in his hand.

It is highly probable that you have never tried to disrobe in a hurry while holding—*and reading from*—a large leatherbound manuscript. Things do not work out very well. Held in one hand only, while the other fumbles feverishly at a belt buckle, the manuscript tends to flop about like a frightened bird, slip out of balance, threaten to glide away. Only a quick fast grab with both hands will retrieve it, wherever the gesture may leave the belt buckle. And to untie one's shoes, kneeling, while peering closely at a text held open on the floor with one's elbow is to risk all sorts of catastrophes: knotted shoelaces, scraped elbows, astigmatism. But above and beyond all else, the entire process tends to reduce passion. By the time young master Dante finally made it to bed, he was plainly exhausted and ready for a good night's sleep (which, I am sorry to say, he did not get). He really seemed rather relieved when they got around to castrating him, mainly, I think, because he was given nothing to read during the operation.

Simply getting someone to play or to understudy these new and challenging roles isn't the whole of the story. Even where applicants are limited, not all applicants will do. I don't propose to make a detailed inventory here of all the possible flaws that may keep a perfectly good performer from being entirely majestic in the altogether, but I will mention one. Flat feet. A nude actor cannot have flat feet. Dressed actors can have flat feet, John Barrymore may have had flat feet and got away with it for all I know, flat feet are scarcely detectable, what with lifts and arch supports and long trailing robes. But the minute a naked actor thumps out onto the stage, putting each foot down as though he were depositing suitcases at the flight counter, glory dribbles away. The whole world seems to have settled unaccountably, the earth seems in process of reclaiming its own, spirit no longer soars. It doesn't matter that naked actors have dirty feet—all of them do, there's no way out of it—but when the dirt is seen to be absolutely evenly distributed, we know we're in real trouble. Old Leadhead is here again, grinding his spine into the dirt. Somehow or other *everything* slumps over visible flat feet—shoulders, ears, hipbones, the works.

Casting directors, then, must look for more than good voice projection and skill at fencing. The concept of talent takes on new overtones. If a girl is going to go topless during the big Dionysian revel, or if a boy is going to have his loincloth snatched away while he is in the process of strangling himself (as did indeed happen in Rochelle Owens' *Beclch*), bone formation and unsuitable fatty deposits become every bit as important as the ability to pronounce words. More important, perhaps. At least I think *Beclch* was cast on that principle. *Beclch* was a play more or less in praise of depravity, a celebration of the flesh not only in its pleasanter, but in its more gangrenous aspects, a wide-open welcome to blood, bone marrow, and pus ("I hope I drool like an animal"). One of the celebrants said of the play's high priestess, "She can't help her depravity." Only she pronounced it "de-*pray*-vity," with the "a" long as in "ale," not short as in "add." I forget to what degree this particular actress stripped—it varied from tease to total in *Beclch* —but I assume her nonverbal contribution was substantial.

There is a further problem of finding actors who can keep straight faces. Any play in which one or all of the actors are nude is bound to turn up a certain number of perfectly ordinary lines of dialogue, routine observations, casual remarks, that simply can no longer be said. Not until everybody gets back into clothes. One of these occurred, for instance, in *Sweet Eros*. The hero had long since stripped his captive, looked her over thoroughly (even to the point of examining her with a magnifying glass for blackheads), and begun to order her into his bed nights. Twenty minutes, thirty minutes, forty minutes—the girl wholly nude the whole time, the boy talking, talking, talking as he stared. After approximately forty minutes, he said, "You know, I sometimes look across the room and feel I almost know you." It is terribly important at such a point that you have players who can keep themselves from falling off their chairs, laughing hysterically, and beating the floorboards with their fists.

On the whole, actors control themselves pretty well, at least while they are on stage. The male lead in *Sweet Eros*, for instance, didn't crack at all as he reached for a red-and-black checkered bib and ever so carefully tied it about the neck and upper shoulders of his otherwise unprotected prisoner. He was about to feed her, you see, and apparently didn't want jam all over her collarbone.

Offstage, however, I suspect the actors give vent to the hilarity
that must sometimes overtake them in the course of their sworn
sober duty. Most evenings that go in for nudity and/or sex also
tend to place a stress on body functions in general—in *The Fig
Leaves Are Falling* there were not only songs about the delights of
infidelity, there were also lively lyrics about the children's toilet
training—and in the course of one recent bill at the American
Place Theater a character who was being denied access to an
onstage bathroom rather ostentatiously carried a tin can about for
emergency use, placing it directly under any chair in which she
happened to be sitting. This was all done straight, very straight.
But anyone who had occasion to use the downstairs men's room
during intermission quickly discovered one of the city's more
interesting bits of graffiti. DON'T FLUSH—WE NEED THE PROPS the
simple inscription said. And it was clear that the actors had been
holding their sides all along, if in silence.

The only person who really failed to hold his sides in silence that
I've come across lately was a member of the audience, an over-
weight fellow who'd have had difficulty holding his sides in any
case, at a Saturday night performance of *Beclch*. He was seated in
the very first row—there were only about twenty of us there that
night, down among the sweltering palms—and as *Beclch* plowed its
way through its catalogue of calculated horrors, he became shrill,
tearful, and at last utterly helpless with laughter.

"Oh, my God! Oh, my *God!*" he kept repeating to himself as he
rocked back and forth, endangering the entire row of swaying
seats and gradually catching us all up in his unseemly merriment.
He was never able to say anything more as *Beclch* pursued its
deadpan course, showing us a nude island queen being massaged
before she chopped a lamb in half and ate its entrails, showing us
her lover being made the victim of a cockfight before he could
bring his bloodied body to her bed, showing us one of her subjects
being deliberately infected with elephantiasis so that his leg might
become a mass of "green pus and purple gore" before he was
issued an invitation to "Strangle yourself—nobilize yourself."
(Language *does* become a bit odd when the off-Broadway moon is
full.) Our portly customer was simply left stunned, gasping, and
repeating himself as his eyes popped in disbelief and his funnybone
splintered in awe.

What he was actually saying, of course, if he could only have got it out, was, "What in heaven's name will they do next, what *can* they do next, what's left?", a series of questions—or sputters —much on everyone's mind at the time. Actually, the questions were a bit disingenuous, if not downright insincere. Everyone knew perfectly well what they could do next if they wished to put their talents to it, because everyone knew exactly what was left.

If, say, they'd so far only stripped the girl in a two-character play, they could strip the boy. This might bring the audience to a point of total distraction—if the naked girl now distracted from the boy's lines, which she did, the naked boy would no doubt distract from the girl's lines, if she had any—but it would at least go All the Way. We could, in fact, arrive at that sublime, and more or less absolute, state of theatrical affairs reported by Anita Loos in her memoirs. Miss Loos tells us that during her childhood in San Francisco there were entirely nude companies steadily engaged in performing the works of Sir Arthur Wing Pinero.

And that brings me to the only question *I* want to ask. The notion of doing Pinero without a stitch on seems to me utterly engaging, irreverent to a purpose. It may even be good dramatic criticism. I like whoever thought of it because the scoundrel had a sense of humor.

But why are we, in our new visual and psychic freedoms on the stage, so dreadfully, laboriously humorless? Why are we so serious about sex and why do we dislike it so much? The last thing any of these plays is is playful. The act of disrobing is most often approached as portentously as though it were the Lincoln Memorial being unveiled. Hush, reverence, apprehension. Or anger. My most vivid image of The Living Theater, now that some performance details have receded in memory, is of many near-naked bodies seething with rage. The actors began by being furious at not being allowed to take their clothes off. They then took them off and were *more* furious.

In virtually all of our uninhibited plays sex and nudity are associated with dirt, disease, bloodshed, and death. "What I'm trying to tell you is that this is nature," says the young master Dante as he insists, before copulating, that in nature "there's a lot of nasty stuff underneath," a lot of "raw, rotten meat." Beclch, the island queen, would agree with him, would then insist on eating the meat. In

Dionysus in 69 the revelers who stripped, stomped, and claimed the license of the orgy moved forward to a bloodbath: abandon ended in violence. Elsewhere it ends in castration. The loincloth that is snatched away to reveal a man's sexual organs is snatched away only while he is in the process of killing himself.

The message, if it is one, is odd indeed, and it corresponds to our current infatuation with four-letter words, all of which, I think, have now been spoken. And spoken and spoken. Four-letter words are not direct or precise terms, as some of their champions have maintained. They are reverse euphemisms. An ordinary euphemism is a deliberately soft word meant to make sex, or any other natural activity, prettier than it is. A reverse euphemism is a deliberately harsh word meant to make it uglier than it is, to show contempt for it. Most phrases scrawled on latrine walls sneer at the body. They do not celebrate it. Most graffiti having to do with the sex act mock it. There is neither joy nor casual acceptance of fact in four-letterdom. There is something closer to resentment, even hatred.

A trace of that hatred seems to be coming along with the words as they march into the theater and breed visual images. Our new-found stage freedoms seem to offer very little in the way of release; they are more nearly constructed to frighten. I keep asking myself, what can this be? The last Puritanism? The ultimate utterly candid exposure of sex for the ghastly thing it is? Cotton Mather would not really disapprove the conclusions reached by the plays that seem to us most liberated. Indeed, he could take his text for the day from *Beclch*: "People like us must be careful—all the evil in the world might get to us and give us the jitters."

What I hope they do next is relax and rediscover the fun of it all, even if they must dress to do it.

2

And Puppy Dog Tails was a foolish little primitive designed, I concluded, as a striptease for the homosexual trade. Each of the play's two acts was constructed in exactly the same way.

The act began with everybody's clothes on. In Act One the hero of the occasion, a deceptively straightish-looking chap named John Hendrix, opened the door to welcome an old school buddy, just out of the Navy and with nowhere to lay his head nights. In Act Two he opened it to his regular and thoroughly gay roommate, just back from vacation.

In both acts the two sat down, mixed drinks, and chattered for a while. In both acts the conversationalists were interrupted by the arrival in full flight of a Gypsy Moth (male) who lived below, was lonely, and was most noticeably on the make. This fellow's name was Tommy; he wore star-spangled shirts and rings on most fingers, and he didn't so much lift his eyebrows as lift the rest of him to get up where they were. Eventually he was got rid of, at which point one of the remaining two noticed that it was dinner time. They got up and went out the door, leaving the stage lights nothing to do but go down.

When the lights came up again (it happened in both acts), they were back and had had their dinner, though they were otherwise little changed. Now, however, one of the men was weary and in need of a shower before tucking himself away for the night. He possibly did take a shower, since he reappeared in a moment either stark naked (Act One) or in jockey shorts (Act Two), swinging a towel about his singularly dry but otherwise glistening form. In both acts one or the other well-structured male was now to be seen draping himself lengthwise over the sofa top or breadthwise on the bed, shifting postures in a *Playboy*-centerfold kind of way, waiting for his companion to leap or to snuggle into his loving embrace. Lights down again slowly, both acts.

That is to say, twice in the course of the evening we waited through drinks, dinner, and a shower for a glimpse of male musculature and—briefly—male genitals, which we got. It was an economical way to put a play together.

There was a narrative thread of sorts to alter matters slightly between eight-thirty and ten-tired. The old school buddy of the hero who turned up in Act One didn't know that his friend and host was a homosexual. His friend and host didn't *want* him to know he was a homosexual. And so they just talked about old times, especially old times running "bare-assed" through the wild-wood and going swimming with all the other fellows and snug-gling together in sleeping bags at Boy Scout Camp.

But there was that acquaintance from below to come popping up and spoiling things with his ivy-climbing gestures, his fingered necklaces, and his outright passes. After about twenty minutes of this in Act One our host became a bit worried, drew the interloper aside, and whispered, "Tommy, will you get out of here before he starts suspecting something?" This was the biggest laugh of the evening. It had to be, inasmuch as it had practically been necessary to pluck Tommy off the top of a lampshade to get through to him at all, and because the old school buddy would have had to be just a wee bit obtuse not to have noticed something pretty odd about Tommy.

But, you see, he was obtuse, very obtuse. At the end of the first act it was he (old school buddy) who went to bed with the host-hero. In the second act he was shocked to learn that the man he had just been to bed with was a homosexual. You heard me. Don't ask me to clear it up, just believe me. And now it was all out in the open, the other members of the company were bitchily suggesting to old buddy that he, too, was a faggot, old buddy was stoutly and sincerely and I am afraid rather stupidly insisting that he wasn't, and everyone was deeply hurt because old buddy kept telling them that faggotry was *wrong*.

Obviously a distinction was being forged here between a homosexual and someone who enjoys having sex with other men, but it was a fine point that was not quite worked out by playwright David Gaard. At the end the old school friends could only separate, clinging to their separate convictions. Besides, it was now time for that shower again and the hero was pretty happy to have his regular roomie at last back from vacation. You could tell that by the way he pulled off his roomie's shorts.

Lest you think that the enterprise might have had something of the psychological interest and emotional force of *The Boys in the Band* let me quickly say that it was all written at a cribbed-camp level (Tommy made one entrance in a floppy black hat and caracul jacket, carrying a can of Pepsi-Cola in his hand and announcing "I'm Joan Crawford") and performed with that hollow languor and hideously self-conscious naturalness that marks "sincere" television commercials or, worse still, educational films of sociological import.

3

WHEN I was a young man and altogether inexperienced, I read a borrowed sex manual (I was too shy to buy one) which began its instructions with a small, kindly caution. The caution went something like this: "You may, as you turn these pages, find your fingers trembling a bit, your heart starting to race. Don't be worried about this, it is quite naturally so, the very subject of sex is apt to set the whole man a-quiver." I remember being a bit skeptical about the fatherly warning. I don't think my own fingers began to tremble until I was told that they should. But I do begin to wonder, now that I have seen *Oh! Calcutta!*, whether that wasn't a wise little manual, after all, to have wished to alert us to the possibly unsteady hand. Certainly something happened to Kenneth Tynan's hand as he approached the tricky wonderland of sex.

Mr. Tynan's hand is normally an exemplary one, cool, restrained, meticulous in motion and suave in repose. When he is using it to write, he is a most admirable critic, an impeccable stylist. When he is using it to select plays for the repertory of the British National Theatre, he is a judicious adviser, idealist and realist at once. Coming to *Oh! Calcutta!*, though, a revue of his own devising designed to play with sex on the stage without robe or reservation, he was suddenly a fevered butterfingers, so agog with a promised glee that he had entirely neglected to notice what was *on* the pages he had, with a racing heart, handed his director and his so willing actors.

Taste, an ear for wit, an eye for form, a heart that usually insists upon being pleased only in the highlands, had all vanished. The clumsiest, most labored of jokes were permitted to succeed one another in obsessive monotony. Language no longer mattered, structure no longer mattered, inspiration no longer mattered. Anything would do so long as it met two requirements: that the actors undress and that they engage in simulated sexplay.

The evening was so entranced at having discovered the fact of masturbation that it included *two* sketches displaying the act.

Children were recognized as sexual beings: Jack raped Jill on a pile
of translucent building blocks. Victorian or Edwardian ladies were
revealed—the astonishment of it!—as less than virgins, as pos-
sessors of very real backsides. A wide-eyed wife stuffed Fritos into
her mouth while watching her husband copulate with a swinging
acquaintance, then dived into the melee herself, top girl on a
phallic totem pole. A man cried out, "Role-reversal time!" as he
slipped into his paramour's panties and leaped for the bed.

Words were pressed upon us, repeatedly, in lieu of humor: "I
will be removed from my position at the head of society and
placed directly in its crotch!" cried an upper-class wench about to
be ravished. Lines did not have to be funny or ideas in any way
fresh to pass muster. The people on stage were not engaged in
being amusing or pertinent or impertinent or imaginative. They
were engaged in being naked. It was an exclusive occupation.

The matter was important because it swept straight across the
board. If Mr. Tynan's vision had been blurred in every other way
by its absolute focus upon sex, the authors from whom he had
drawn material had lost all steadiness as well. They had, in fact,
lost character. Samuel Beckett, Jules Feiffer, John Lennon,
Leonard Melfi, Sam Shepard, and Mr. Tynan himself were among
the writers credited with sketches. The program did not choose to
say which writer had written which sketch. The significant thing
was that *we* could not say. Though the writers were all men whose
work we knew, whose personalities and stylistic habits were real to
us, there was no way at all of distinguishing one from another by
the activity or the language on stage. We could make guesses. We
could seek out inside information. But there was never any little
leap of recognition in the theater that said, on the spot, that we had
found our man. All plodded to the same beat and in the plodding
all blurred. The preoccupation with visual, literal, immediate sex
had wiped out not only quality, but identity.

We should pause to notice how odd it was that this should have
been so. *Oh! Calcutta!* was really a very good test case for the
validity, or the inadvisability, of extensive nudity and intimate
sexplay on stage. The show wasn't the work of a clumsy and
probably untalented amateur, as *Che!* had been. It wasn't a mere
bid for money put together by opportunistic flesh peddlers. It was

the work of intelligent and gifted professionals, the work of men who should have been able to make the materials work if they can be made to work. The evening also, most carefully, removed some of the objections regularly made to nude performing: the bodies of the company were good bodies, in the case of Margo Sapping-ton—who first danced the event's only truly erotic passage—genu-inely beautiful. An attempt at quality had been made, in writing and performing both. In which case the overall failure, and it was a disastrous failure, must mean something. What I think it means is that the stage as such is hostile to the effort being made.

Most people who arrive at this conclusion arrive at it on the grounds that sex is essentially a private act whereas the theater is a public place. "*Why* need sex be a private act?" is the immediate and obvious rejoinder, and, to tell the truth, we haven't yet found an absolute answer to that. Sex is public for animals; it might be, with some inhibitions shed, for men. I'm inclined to come at the matter in another way. Literal sex is wrong for the theater, I suspect, because it is an exclusive act.

Sex, as I believe Sophocles once said, is a tyrant. It does not brook interference, it does not acknowledge equals. There are many things we do in life that we find it possible to do in tandem. We read a newspaper while we are eating our breakfast. We carry on coherent conversations while we are driving cars. We smoke while we talk on the telephone (how many times have you taken pains to light up before dialing?), dance with one girl while keep-ing an eye on another. Actors can count houses while they are actually saying their lines; most of us are ambidextrous most hours of the day.

Not with sex. Sex belongs to another kingdom, really to no kingdom except its own. We don't read and have sex, don't smoke and have sex, don't drive and have sex (not safely, surely), don't converse intelligently and have sex (converse, yes; God forbid intelligently). Sex is a total act, rather as my sex manual suggested, absorbing and obliterating, standing jealous guard over its rites. No foreigners need apply. Sex, for its little time, takes full possession of the flesh and the psyche, is a law unto itself, solitary in its splendor, single-minded, uncompanioned. Thinking ruins it. *Any* companion, any intrusion, ruins it. (I rather imagine it became private because of its autonomous quality, not the other way around.) Sex cannot be had inattentively, or part-time. It is its own unity.

Taken into the theater, where it must instantly acquire a thousand collaborators, it tends to behave as it always has: ruthlessly and unilaterally. It is not going to care much about a writer's words; it will dominate them and maybe discard them. It is not going to care much about actors' temperaments or personalities; where all are nude, a great effort must be made to keep them from becoming interchangeable. It does not ask questions of Mr. Tynan's taste, or of yours or mine; it rejects the concept of taste as being irrelevant to its goals. This is not to say that it becomes tasteless, merely that it *is* autonomous. Where theatrical sex is actual rather than described or intimated or formally imitated, it tends to usurp all other roles, to put down any counterclaims, whether they be claims to wit or style or structure. These things are puny beside it, easily broken. Sex is simply too powerful a presence to be so conveniently tamed.

Now at the same time that literal sex is tending to ride roughshod over values which might impede or modify it, another perverse thing is happening. The erotica on stage is becoming anti-erotic. The phenomenon has been commented on before. So much onstage sex seems not to praise sex but to disparage it, to be harsh with it. Audiences are not much embarrassed by what they see, but they are often repelled by it, as I think you would probably have been repelled by a sketch in *Oh! Calcutta!* in which we were almost savagely forced to look at a girl's backside while we were just as savagely—venomously, really—told that the girl was exposing herself by her own choice.

What is less often mentioned is that the experience is clearly antierotic for the actors too. In the original production of *Che!* the exposed genitals of two men were subjected to every conceivable stimulus over the course of two and one-half hours. Neither man ever become potent. Nor did anyone become potent, even when engaging in the actions of intercourse, in *Oh! Calcutta!* Some male performer must have been aroused somewhere, sometime; I have been in fairly faithful attendance at these experiments and I have never seen it happen.

I suppose that, medically and psychologically, various reasons can be advanced for the sustained impotence. (We must take note of the fact that impotence is what is finally celebrated in all of these ventures.) I find myself wondering if it is not the result of simply being *in* a theater, in a place where the exclusiveness of sex cannot be honored because the actors are doing something else at the same time (acting). The actors are working, adopting mental sets that relate them to an audience, to a stage, to a building, to a script. Is sex so wrecked again?

I am of course not speaking of sex as material but of sex as a physical presence. It is possible for *Portnoy's Complaint* to be some kind of masterpiece, which I think it is, because in it sex is robbed of its exclusiveness by not being directly present at all. It is represented only by words, permitting words to retain control. *I Am Curious* (*Yellow*) seems to me no masterpiece at all, though its playful sex sequences are occasionally touching in a funny-dumb way. But in film the idea of form is still protected: by the fact that the players are not present when we are, by the fact that everything we see is subject to the management of an editor. The theater, however, is an open and total confrontation; that is its distinguishing mark and chief glory. Sex, introduced into this arena without any disguise of form or reduction to metaphor, asserts itself for what it is, exclusive, and thereby ruptures the nature of the event.

Or so it seems to me at present inventory.

4

A REVIEWER's problems are his own. They're his to solve and he has no business passing them along to the general public. But there is one problem that has cropped up for almost all reviewers in recent seasons that may take a bit of talking about, if only because of the multiple cries of outrage that filled the Drama Mailbag of *The New York Times* one memorable Sunday.

The issue at hand was an article a guest writer, Margaret Croyden, had done for the newspaper's drama pages describing the premiere of Arrabal's *The Architect and the Emperor of Assyria* at the Stratford, Ontario, summer festival. The Arrabal play had been, most deliberately, gamy—if that is a word that continues to serve any definable function. It had dealt, freely and insistently, with perversions of various sorts (it ran the gamut, rather) and Miss Croyden called considerable attention to these precisely because it had been playwright Arrabal's intention (honorable or otherwise) that they be stressed, forced forward, grotesquely ballooned. (Mr. Arrabal belongs, after all, to the Theater of the Absurd.)

I wouldn't take up the subject at all if it weren't for the fact that *all* of the letters mailed off in response to the piece struck pretty much the same tone, stood on the same attitude. The attitude: Whatever Arrabal may have been saying aloud on stage, Miss Croyden ought to have kept silent, at least in the pages of *The New York Times.* Perhaps the uniform attitude is best summed up by a short outburst that served as a tag to the collection: "Not only should such actions be forbidden on stage, you should not lower yourself to report on such muck. Why give dignity to such actions? For shame!"

Well, that question about "giving dignity" to material that simply may not deserve serious discussion is one that almost every reviewer must have asked himself as he walked away from, say, a play like Lennox Rafael's *Che!* Did *Che!* display any evidence of a genuinely creative mind at work? No. Was *Che!* patently the work of a pretentious amateur, a novice at language with no capacity at all for turning combinations of words into even minimally poetic images? Yes. Would I be in this theater at all, every reviewer must have asked himself, if it weren't for the "scandal" of the sexual deportment displayed? Would I bother to write a review or a paragraph or so much as a line about the event if it didn't violate, coarsely, such conventions of taste as had obtained until that time? No and no. The evening was without merit. It simply existed as an event.

What exists as an event, however, may very well be attended by audiences; almost certainly it will be attended if there is something "scandalously" newsworthy about it. (Various such productions have carefully postponed inviting reviewers, hoping that gossip would attract enough customers to pay off production costs before reviewers could get at the quality of the work done.) And whatever is going to be attended, or *may* be attended, requires comment in a newspaper if a newspaper reviewer is going to behave responsibly to his readers.

What kind of comment? It seems to me that a reviewer has not only a right but an obligation to describe accurately, and more or less fully, what is actually being done on the stage. I don't mean to make a case here for a particular article, Miss Croyden's or any other, or for the playwright under discussion, whose work has always seemed to me giddy, posturing, and unformed even in Absurdist terms.

But, in general, the obligation is there if only because the reader has a need to know what he may be getting himself into. Reviewers can always write around material that they find, or think others will find, distasteful. It's possible to discuss *Portnoy's Complaint* without mentioning masturbation (and the book isn't *about* masturbation, though skipping reference to the act would be somewhat like discussing *King Lear* without bothering to mention that the man had daughters) and it *might* be possible to talk about the Arrabal play or *Che!* or Michael McClure's *The Beard* by concentrating exclusively upon the intellectual notions that are meant to lie behind, and be symbolized by, the words and acts in the foreground. You can, for instance, talk about *The Beard* entirely in terms of hostility, of male-female duality, of passion that is masked by—and to a great degree made up of—hate.

If you did, though, you might seem to be talking about *Who's Afraid of Virginia Woolf?*, shocking enough in its own now superseded moment, or, for that matter, and if you're really evasive, *Getting Gertie's Garter*. The abstract background may be there and may be duly reported. But the reader who is told that and nothing more than that, and then goes into the playhouse to discover the actors relentlessly poking at one another's zippers, is apt to feel betrayed. (He may, of course, like this kind of theater, but, considering what he's read, it isn't what he's come for.) *His* cry of outrage—at not having been told, at having been lured into a kind of theater he may detest because it has been described as another kind of theater altogether—may now soar higher and sear more harshly than that of the reader who's been shocked by a description before he's gone anywhere at all.

For the reviewer, it's a bit of a bind. (I remember a flurry of canceled subscriptions because I'd mentioned, in reviewing Le Roi

Jones's *The Toilet* for the New York *Herald Tribune*, that one of the principal characters died with his head in a urinal. Ah, days of innocence!) It's a bind because a reader who is thinking of going to the theater deserves some *sense* of what the occasion is like, not just its rational underpinnings, and giving him a sense of the occasion means being more or less graphic about some of the things that occur during it.

In fact, it becomes increasingly impossible to evade the contemporary theater's sensuality with a carefully disinfected prose because a new sensuality, an open sensuality, a candid sensuality is one of the things the contemporary theater has in mind as content. This is no odder than that there should have been a Kinsey report or a Masters report or a bestseller purporting to tell you what you didn't know and were afraid to ask and really knew all the time. It's a social phenomenon, not a purely literary or dramatic one, and, for good or ill, it's here. (Keep looking; you'll find some good in it.) It can lead to disastrous evenings, it can lead to delightful ones. There is little difference between the impulses, nervous or philosophical, that set in motion a callow, campy, self-indulgent exercise like *The Dirtiest Show in Town* (its attractive bodies apart) and a thoroughly charming, because much better written, evening like *The Last Sweet Days of Isaac*. The latter, too, is about the need people have—boys and girls particularly—to *touch* each other. The contemporary theater, with its excesses and its gross failures allowed for, doesn't only mean to open our eyes wider; it means to put out a hand.

That is the urge, the command and demand, of the moment, and it's not going to go away because reviewers decide not to write about it. Some of it will soon go away, no doubt; the stage has retreated from nudity before, discovering gradually that its surprises are limited and that by comparison psychological values seem both infinite and more interesting. But while we are making what seems to the whole of society a necessary investigation, asking for a kind of visual and verbal information long sealed away, the nature of the investigation ought not to be falsified, or even underplayed, in print. Those who want no part of it, good or bad, need to know where it is in order to head in other directions. Those who want the good of it need to know where the good is. And those who are merely curious about the phenomenon of man need to know, amply and accurately, what the creature is up to. A reviewer, it seems to me, should be as precise as possible. And description is one of precision's best tools.

One caveat, perhaps. A reviewer shouldn't take underhanded advantage of his materials. One of those Mailbag letters suggested that a certain number of "nastyisms" had lately been creeping into print in the course of reviewing. I think this has been true on occasion, though of course one man's nastyism may be another's firmly called spade. Certainly a reviewer ought not to connive—to use an old term of François Mauriac's—in the material he is attacking. If he likes something, he is honor-bound to say so and to try to describe it in a way that will make its attractions intelligible. If he doesn't like it, he's not entitled to introduce for sheer shock value items he is deriding as having nothing more than shock value. That's to say, he can't liven up his own copy with a license he is busy deploring. He's got to live within his own stated canons of taste.

Otherwise, though, the information had better be there—with candor and without prejudice.

PART TWO

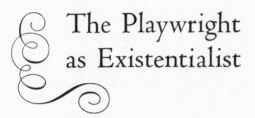

The Playwright
as Existentialist

MUCH of the experimental work we have been discussing, certainly the most radical portions of it, have been indifferent or actively hostile to the "literary" tradition of drama, the concept of a play as something written. "Faced with this literature," if I may repeat Grotowski, "we can take up one of two positions: either, we can illustrate the text through the interpretation of the actors, the *mise en scène*, the scenery, the play situation. . . . In that case, the result is not theater, and the only living element in such a performance is the literature. Or, we can virtually ignore the text, treating it solely as a pretext. . . ."

It has become a pretext for Schechner, for O'Horgan, even to some degree for van Itallie. In the process of reforming the theater, the playwright is looked upon with considerable suspicion. He is, perhaps, too tied by habit to tradition, too skilled at old tricks, too much a part of a *history* that is being superseded. He is. also an autocrat, a man who will impose limitations upon discovery before directors and actors have discovered enough that is new. Newness, in this view, must come spontaneously, freely, through uninhibited improvisation. The playwright belongs to the old dis-

trusted and failed order of things; his concern with shape is both
out of date and premature; let him dictate no longer—or at least
not for the time being.

In point of fact, however, innovations quite as radical as those
proposed by a Peter Brook have been made, and are being made,
within the "literary," or written, or master-minding tradition. The
playwright, too, is capable of altering, perhaps renewing, the face
of the world; with a controlled hand he can alter the habits of his
hand, so much so that the new play he produces would scarcely be
recognized as a play by someone born a few years earlier under a
different philosophical sky. I should like to speak of one such
playwright at some length because what he is doing *is* new, *is*
radically different from what has gone before, *is* as much a reflection of the changed condition of our lives as the loosest of current
experiments—and *is* written.

Harold Pinter seems to me the only man working in the theater
today who writes existential plays existentially. By this I mean that
he does not simply content himself with restating a handful of
existentialist themes inside familiar forms of playmaking. He re-
makes the play altogether so that it will function according to
existentialist principle.

To show this it will be necessary to recapitulate briefly, and at
the expense of some subtlety, the premises on which existentialist
philosophy rests. At root, existentialism rejects the ancient Platonic
principle that essence precedes existence.

What does this mean, practically speaking? Platonic theory,
made more explicit by Aristotle and then accepted as a habit of
thought by Western society in succeeding generations, proposed
that before any one man, say, came into being, there had to exist,
somewhere in the mind of the universe, an idea of man—an immaterial essence which contained, bounded, dictated the nature of the
species.

In this view, the essence Man exists before any one individual
man. Individual men are, in effect, derived from it. They take their
physical, mental, and moral capacities from it. Because individual
men are concrete, idiosyncratic, and limited by having been incorporated in matter, no one of them perfectly expresses or
realizes the abstract universal from which he has taken his name
and shape. Pure being—including the pure essence Man—is a sort

of fountainhead, a reservoir, a pool of unadulterated spirit from which isolated individuals siphon off so much spirit as they have. Aristotle located this immaterial and universalized source in the mind of God. God thereafter, as it were, made man by die-stamp. From the concept Man, men took their existence. Existence became a hand-me-down. Men, as they walked the earth, were predefined. They conformed to an essence prior to themselves.

Viewed in a Platonic light, man was both inhibited and most helpfully guided. He was inhibited in the sense that he could not escape the boundaries set for him by his essential nature. Though he was obviously in some measure free, he was not free to behave as other than a man—and what a man was could be explicitly determined. Man was made to perform in a certain way, to pursue certain goals, to expect certain natural and logical rewards and punishments depending upon how well or ill he played out his assigned role.

The inhibition had its comforts. If man was predefined, he did have an identity. He was this, not that. He had a name, an address, a secure position in the universe. He was not altogether footloose in a void; he had instincts, a conscience, and an intelligence to tell him what steps to take. These tools were trustworthy precisely because they belonged to, or were drawn from, the essence Man. Listened to, or used properly, they could not very well lie. What was Of The Essence was bound to return to the essence, to echo it, to reflect it as a mirror reflects. Man could know himself by drawing deductions from the equipment he had been given.

Existentialist philosophy, moving from troubled speculation in the nineteenth century to aggressive assertion in the twentieth, reverses the Platonic order. It insists that existence precedes essence. That is to say, the notion of an original immaterial archetype is jettisoned. There is no matrix from which individual men in the concrete are drawn. There are only individual men, born undefined. It is not even possible to say what a "man" is until we have seen how this man or that man actually behaves, until we see what this man or that man has done. Man does not come to the planet with an identity; he spends his time on the planet arriving at an identity.

As with the Platonic view, this new insistence has its comforts and its cruelties. Its principal comfort, which may in the first stages of discovery seem small comfort, lies in the unprecedented freedom now granted to man. Man is no longer to regard himself as confined by a "nature," by a given set of behavior patterns which are inbred and fundamentally inviolable. He is open, an experiment, a reaching, an adventure. There are no known limits to his possible activity. Man has no absolute face to be worn daily and Sunday; he can make as many faces as he likes, in something of the manner that Albert Camus' Caligula does.

At the same time he must walk through the world alone, without instructions from a central computer, without friends who share his nature, without confidence that his intelligence reflects anything absolute, without assurance that he fits into any discernible scheme. He is nameless, as yet featureless; he *is* footloose in a void; and his task, if he can be said to have one, is to create his identity by exercising his freedom to act. When he has done all that he can do, he may be able to say what *he* is. He may achieve his essence. Until the ultimate moment of actualization comes, however, he must move, with some vertigo, through a silent universe. Man is "condemned" to be free, Sartre says.

From these various corollaries of the proposition that existence precedes essence have come the characteristic dramatic themes of our time. Who am I? the man asks as he discovers that he has lost the wallet that contained his identity cards. Why can't we communicate? the stranger on the park bench snarls. Why has man no home? the vast, vacant settings on a hundred stages inquire. What are reasoning, logic, intelligence worth? demand the professors who contradict themselves word by word, line by line. What are we waiting for? wonder the nonentities who have been waiting so long for Godot. Is anything real or is everything illusion? anguish all of the people who cannot find themselves in mirrors. How silly conformity is when there is no essence to conform to!

Dozens of playwrights have made use of existentialist themes. What is surprising is that none of them—none but Harold Pinter, I think—has taken the fundamental proposition seriously enough to *present* his plays in the new existentialist sequence. In the current philosophical climate, the matter of sequence should be important. If existence does indeed precede essence, if an actual thing precedes an abstract concept of that thing, then it should also do so on the stage. Exploratory movement in the void, without preconception or precommitment, should come first. Conceptualization should come later, if at all.

But Samuel Beckett, for instance, does not really work that way. Mr. Beckett has been most influential in imposing upon contemporary theatergoers an awareness of existential loneliness, homelessness, facelessness; our strongest image of the void comes from the careful emptiness of his plays. Yet Mr. Beckett takes his curtain up upon a woman buried waist deep in sand. Or upon an aged couple confined to ashbins. Or upon Didi and Gogo immobilized, already waiting.

The fact that Mr. Beckett does not make much use of the existentialist freedom to act is not the point here. A playwright is free to use one strand of available material to the exclusion of others; he is a temperament, not necessarily a doctor of philosophy. The point is that in each case—in all cases where Beckett is concerned, I would say—we are first offered a concept, a statement of essence. What the opening image of *Happy Days* says to us, immediately, is that man is essentially earthbound. Nagg and Nell in *Endgame*, lifting the lids of their ashbins occasionally but never leaving them, are essentially discards. Whatever Mr. Beckett's philosophical disposition may be, he builds plays as a Platonist. He forms an abstract concept of man's nature and role and presents it to us in its original conceptual form, individualizing it only very slightly. We are not concerned with persons forming themselves; we are concerned with persons inhabiting set forms they cannot escape.

Our habits of thought are so strong—after several thousand years of being trained in Greek method—that even when we wish to make an anticonceptual statement, even when we wish to say that man has not been and cannot be defined, we do it by conceptualization, by starting from a definition. First we reach a conclusion. Then we arrange a stage situation to illustrate it, precisely as an earlier playwright might at any time have begun with the essential quality of Ambition and manufactured a character to conform to it. Though Samuel Beckett holds very little in common with the medieval world-view of things, his actual method of composition is not radically different from that of the author of *Everyman*. A symbol—which is the sign of an essence—is hung up in plain view; later, some individualizing detail is added to it, though not so much as to obscure its continuing function as an abstract, almost immaterialized, concept.

Thus, though the drained-out and disjointed worlds which Beckett, Ionesco, and other contemporary playwrights place upon the stage may at first sight seem very strange indeed, the strangeness consists almost entirely in what is being said, in the inverted value system that is carefully organized into an image. There is very little that is strange in the organizing process itself. The Platonic sequence keeps its grip on us: a concept precedes, and dominates, whatever we see existing on the stage.

"I don't conceptualize in any way," Pinter has said in an interview given to Lawrence M. Bensky for *Paris Review,* a statement which may well be taken at face value and which may help to explain why Pinter's plays seem strange to us through and through.

Watching a Beckett play, we immediately engage in a little game of "Concept, concept, who's got the concept?", no doubt because we sense that, beyond the play's opaque surface, there lies a conceptual nub. We want to get at this, to abstract it. We know that it was abstract to begin with.

Watching a Pinter play, we give over the scramble to stick pins in ideas and fix them forever to a drawing board. We feel that the drawing board isn't there and that our eager thumbs would only go through it. Instead of trying to bring matters to a halt by defining them, we permit them to move at will, understanding that we have been promised no terminal point. We give existence free rein, accept it as primary, refrain from demanding that it answer our questions, grant it the mystery of not yet having named itself.

To have drawn us into so complete a surrender of our ordinary long-standing expectations and demands is a considerable achievement, and Mr. Pinter has taught us to follow the sequence his way by being strict in his presentation of it.

To begin with the matter of place. In his very first play, *The Room,* the existentialist challenge is formidable—and, within the limited confines of the piece, absolutely met.

Existentialism imagines man living in a void. At the same time it asks that we refrain from conceptualizing this void. How shall it be defined when it has not yet been fully explored? In short, we are asked to enter a void that is not an *abstract* void.

The Room completely satisfies this difficult—one would have thought impossible—requirement. Everything in "a room in a large house" is entirely tangible, concrete, present not as idea but as actuality. There is a gas fire, a perfectly real one. A gas stove and sink. A window. Table and chairs. A rocking chair. The foot of a double bed protruding from an alcove. The walls are solid, the dirty wallpaper has been firmly pasted up, the objects handled by a slatternly housewife as she moves in and about the aggressively dimensional furniture all have weight, texture, the density of experienced life.

These objects, and the actions involved in handling them, are given blunt importance in the stage directions—not as symbols of other values, but in and for themselves. They are important because they are there, because they exist. Handling them is important because they are there to be handled and because hands exist.

> Rose is at the stove. . . . She places bacon and eggs on a plate, turns off the gas and takes the plate to the table. . . . She returns to the stove and pours water from the kettle into the teapot, turns off the gas and brings the teapot to the table, pours salt and sauce on the plate and cuts two slices of bread. . . . She butters the bread. . . . She goes to the sink, wipes a cup and saucer and brings them to the table. . . . She pours milk into the cup. . . . Sits in the rocking-chair.

There is no comment in all of this, no suggestion that plate or teapot, salt or sauce, contains a meaning that will serve as metaphor for some larger value. The salt does not represent savor, or the loss of it; it is salt. The sauce is not poisoned, nor does the housewife's action in serving it signify the slavery of Woman. The rocking chair does not mean to suggest that Rose has retired from life, or is a lulled prisoner of it. We are to attend to these things as things. The deliberateness, the patience, the concentration with which these companions in existence are listed and then handled breeds a kind of awed respect for them. Audiences tend to stare with an unfamiliar intensity at the cup, at the stove, at the chair. Each object seems more important than it would in another kind of play precisely because it is not a minor sign, a diminutive stand-in, for something of greater significance than itself, but because all of the significance it has is its own. Everything that exists is self-contained. It does not derive from something prior to it, nor is it a marker indicating something to come. It *is* now. Handle with care.

Objects observed in a Pinter play tend to generate something like awe. They may be utterly commonplace, they usually are; yet they seem uncommon here because they have not been absorbed into a pattern that explains them away as mere tools of a narrative or as looming symbols of conceptual value. Sometimes these objects acquire such self-importance as to seem ominous, though that is not their initial function in a Pinter play. If we feel faintly startled to see how solid a cup is, or how shaped, we feel so—in the beginning—only because we are used to ignoring the solidity and shape of cups in our absent-minded lives. Normally we think of a cup as a means to an end, as an indifferent utility making a passing contribution to another, much more identifiable, purpose: our tea, our pleasure, our life-roles as wife, husband, host. Thinking of a cup in this way, we render it more or less invisible. In effect, we make it absent.

By suppressing the past and future of the cup, by refusing to name its origin or its destiny, Pinter increases its presence. It catches, and for the moment wholly occupies, our eye.

Whatever exists in the room is made to exist at its maximum intensity. Nothing within our view is in any way abstract, as, say, the landscape of *Waiting for Godot* is abstract. *Waiting for Godot* takes place Nowhere, or Anywhere. But in *The Room* we are Somewhere. Environment is utterly explicit; every piece on the premises could be sold at auction, the place as a whole could be rented.

At the same time that the tangible is insisted upon, literally thrust into our faces, the surrounding void is implied. The void is outside the room, upstairs, downstairs, everywhere beyond the walls. The real is real. The void envelops it. It is all rather as though a cyclone had picked up a still intact shed—as we used to see cyclones do in the movies—and were carrying it, still intact, through unknown air to an unknown end.

The outlying void is rhythmically described as Rose rocks. Does anyone live in the basement below Rose and her husband? "I don't know who lives down there now. . . . I think there was one first, before he moved out. Maybe they've got two now."

Perhaps there's no one below. No matter. "If they ever ask you, Bert, I'm quite happy where I am. We're quiet, all right. You're happy up here. It's not far up either, when you come in from outside. And we're not bothered. And nobody bothers us."

Upstairs may be empty too. When Mr. Kidd, the landlord, drops by, Rose asks him, "Anyone live up there?"

"Up there?" Mr. Kidd ponders. "There was. Gone now."

"How many floors you got in this house?"

"Floors. . . . Ah, we had a good few of them in the old days."

"How many have you got now?"

"Well, to tell you the truth, I don't count them now."

"Oh."

"No, not now."

Though the immediate room, the direct experience of life, is entirely dimensional, the universe in which it exists is unstructured. There is not even any knowing where Mr. Kidd lives once he leaves these tight tangible four walls. A prospective tenant asks Rose where the landlord might be:

"Well, say I wanted to get hold of him, where would I find him?"

"Well, — I'm not sure."

"He lives here, does he?"

"Yes, but I don't know—"

"You don't know exactly where he hangs out?"

"No, not exactly."

"But he does live here, doesn't he?"

". . . As a matter of fact, I don't know him at all. We're very quiet. We keep ourselves to ourselves. I never interfere. I mean, why should I? We've got our room. We don't bother anyone else. That's the way it should be."

Rose, who is only Rose and not Everyman, knows only what she experiences: her husband drives a van and enters and leaves the room at regular hours; a landlord drops in, but lives no defined existence once he has left; it is dark outside; it is cold inside; sitting down and getting up are important matters because they are events which truly happen as opposed to the mere rumor of events beyond the room; cups and saucepans can be touched.

Whatever impinges directly upon the consciousness is the sum total of what can be known. We share Rose's consciousness, knowing exactly as much as she does and no more.

Let alone, Rose would be content simply to exist.

Rose is not let alone, any more than the two hired killers in *The Dumb Waiter* are let alone. Quite soon Rose is disturbed by two discoveries. Apparently it is her room that is to let. Though the rest of the "building" may very well be unoccupied, the prospective tenants may be in the act of displacing her. And it would seem that someone does indeed live in the basement, someone who may intrude upon her at any moment.

As we move from the solid-inside-a-void environment of a Pinter play toward what we shall have to call the narrative movement of the people who have their being in that environment, we are instantly embroiled in threat. "Menacing" is the adjective most often used to describe the events in a Pinter play; "suspense" is considered one of the playwright's most satisfying effects.

It is almost shocking that this should be so. For narrative suspense in the past has almost always been derived from one clear source: known danger. Oedipus' fears are absolutely defined: the tyrant lives in dread that somewhere, somehow, it shall be proved that he has killed his father and married his mother. If Oedipus tries to blot these things from his mind, it is because they are so terribly present to his mind. Macbeth knows that it is Macduff he has to fear; no matter how much certain prophecies seem to support the notion that Macduff cannot be the man to best him, Macbeth trembles in apprehension. Willy Loman worries that he will not be liked. Charlie Chaplin worries that the cabin in which he is trapped will tumble over a precipice before he can get out of it. Watching these figures, we are frightened for them because we see—we are able to name and describe—the shape of the terror advancing upon them.

Yet the one thing Mr. Pinter steadfastly refuses to do is to offer his audience—or his characters—any information whatsoever about the forces they come to feel as hostile. We see no precipice; we are not told what may happen at the stroke of midnight; no oracle spells out, not even in ambiguous terms, the doom to be looked for. Ordinarily, danger is conceived in the future tense:

this is what will happen if steps are not taken to avoid it. Apprehension rises as the future comes closer—while still remaining the future. Mr. Pinter writes exclusively in the present tense.

In *The Dumb Waiter* two minor-league thugs are uneasily whiling away the time in a basement room. Presumably they have been sent there to do a killing. They do not know, however, who is to be killed. Neither do they seem to know who has hired them. This is simply the situation in which they find themselves: it is without an explicit beginning, it looks forward to no explicit end. Once again the situation itself—everything that belongs to the experienced moment—is concrete. There are newspapers to be read, lavatories to be flushed, biscuits to be parceled out, gas ranges to be lighted.

After they have waited a while, sometimes quarreling over football matches and tea, an overlooked dumbwaiter in the wall gives off a sudden clatter. Opening the slot, the two men discover that an order for food has been sent down. "Two braised steaks and chips. Two sago puddings. Two teas without sugar," the order reads. But though the order itself is once again explicit, there is no telling who sent it down, or why. Was the building formerly a restaurant and this the kitchen? Inside the basement flat, which is real, this sort of realistic speculation can be indulged. But it cannot continue to have meaning once it is applied to the world outside the flat: there can really be no restaurant which would send down orders to a "former" kitchen. Speculation is cut off in mid-breath, is plainly useless.

Yet orders continue to come down and the two men find themselves under immediate compulsion to fill them, however inadequately. Biscuits, crisps, a bar of chocolate, half a pint of milk—whatever catch-as-catch-can provisions they have brought to the flat with them—are loaded onto the dumbwaiter box and sent up. Still greater demands are returned and, in a frenzy of placation, the gunmen part with everything in their packs. In their inadequacy they are humble. Discovering a speaking tube on the wall, one of them sends a message above "with great deference":

"Good evening. I'm sorry to—bother you, but we just thought we'd better let you know that we haven't got anything left. We sent up all we had. There's no more food down here."

They are not above resenting the sacrifice they have so will-ingly, so feverishly, made:

We sent him up all we've got and he's not satisfied. No, honest, it's enough to make the cat laugh. Why did you send him up all that stuff? (*Thoughtfully*) Why did I send it up? (*Pause*) Who knows what he's got upstairs? He's probably got a salad bowl. They must have something up there. They won't get much from down here. You notice they didn't ask for any salads? They've probably got a salad bowl up there. Cold meat, radishes, cucumbers. Watercress. Roll mops.

But the sacrifice was swiftly and unquestioningly made at the time. Only when the moment has passed and the men have begun to exist in a succeeding moment can one of them ask his "thought-ful" question: "Why did I send it up?"

The question is central to the problem of Pinter's curious narra-tive power. For during all of the time that the gunmen have been desperately trying to meet the demands of the wholly mysterious dumbwaiter, suspense on the stage has grown in proportion to their ignorance of what they were doing. The suspense of *The Dumb Waiter* is in very small part due to our awareness that the two men are possibly waiting to kill someone. We are only half certain that that is their function, their edginess is much more directly concerned with tea kettles than with potential victims, we cannot fear very greatly for an unspecified victim in any case. The existence of the dumbwaiter is, in addition, apparently irrelevant to the task on which they are engaged; its commands are not necessarily the commands of the unnamed "he" who has hired them, indeed there seems no patterned relationship between the one kind of command and the other. Yet the intrusive, unlooked-for, in a narrative sense distracting activity of the dumbwaiter not only occupies the center of the play but markedly increases its tension.

The command "now" actually agitates the men more than the command "when." When a visitor taps at the door and enters, they are probably going to kill him. About such a matter they can be relatively casual. When a command, any command, is issued in the present tense—even though it has no recognizable source and even though they have no understood obligation—they are terrified.

Mr. Pinter exploits a contemporary form of terror. He sets his plays in motion on a track that runs directly parallel to—or perhaps coincides entirely with—the track on which twentieth-century man feels himself running. It is a track quite different, in its tensions and apprehensions, from any most previous societies have found themselves pressed along.

All societies have found themselves driven by guilt. We find ourselves much more driven by what has been called angst, which the dictionary defines as "a feeling of dread, anxiety, or anguish." W. H. Auden has labeled our time "The Age of Anxiety," and the descriptive term has stuck; it was partly out of an effort to explain the prevalence of the sensation that existentialist philosophy came to birth.

There is a simple distinction to be made between the sensation of guilt and that of anxiety. The two are by no means identical. Guilt is felt for a specific crime or sin or failing; apprehension follows because man expects to be punished, in some way, for having permitted himself a particular well-defined lapse. A man knows what he has done and lives in fear because he has done it.

Anxiety, on the other hand, rises from no single guilty act and fears no clearly spelled-out retribution. It is a *general* state of mind, a diffused sensation of spiritual and psychological unease which may have its roots in one or twenty of a thousand possible causes but which has no root in any one cause we can name. Anxiety lacks a clear origin. Lacking a clear origin, it lacks a clear ending. We cannot imagine atonement, or any means of freeing ourselves from the sensation, when we cannot say what initiated the sensation, or motivated our fear, to begin with. To use the dictionary again, anxiety—in its psychoanalytical reference—is "the expectancy of evil or danger, without adequate ground." A man who feels guilty always feels guilty about *something*. But a man in a state of anxiety is anxious about *everything*—his dread is not confined to responsibility for an act but is distributed throughout his environment and becomes his environment.

Pinter earns his special suspense by constructing his plays in such a way that we are forced to enter this state of mind in the theater. We have not always done so in the theater. When we watch Macbeth grow fearful, even to the point of hallucination, we can make a clear and objective judgment about his fear: he feels as he does because he is guilty of having killed Duncan. We are linking an observed effect to a known cause. We are not undefinably disturbed.

Even during the recent years of our mounting and thoroughly recognized angst we have not been accustomed to experiencing in the theater what we have experienced on the streets or at our desks. We may have felt a vague terror at the office, and not known where the animus was coming from. We then went to the theater, observed a man in terror, and saw plainly where *his* terror came from. The two experiences—one of life, one of art—have not generally coincided. We have felt anxiety on the subway, but seen guilt on the stage. Willy Loman is guilty of having bartered his soul for a smile and a shoeshine. His distress can be diagnosed. Blanche DuBois is to a serious degree guilty of misrepresenting her own nature. Simple exposure to the light will bring her screaming to heel. Such plays look for blame and find it, though the blame may not be confined to a single individual and may indeed attach to an entire social system; wherever it is lodged, the blame can be located. We stand outside the pattern and know what to expect of it.

Pinter deprives us of our detachment—and our security—by taking us into the pattern. He does so by refusing to say what the pattern is or by hinting very strongly that there is no pattern. Bewildered, we look about us for points of reference. Finding none, we begin to share the anxiety of the characters whose lives we can observe but cannot chart. We no longer judge their collective state of mind. We inhabit it.

The act of unpatterning is therefore of great importance in the working out of any Pinter scenario. Whatever action is taking place must have no clear beginning, which is to say it must not have originated in a guilty act. In this way the past is eliminated as a conscious source of worry and the two men of *The Dumb Waiter* are bound to the tense "now" of commands which are without cause or precedent. The two men become tense on the instant because the position in which they find themselves is, to them as to us, unintelligible. Instead of passing from past crime to future punishment, they stand trembling before *all* possibility.

Similarly, whatever action is taking place must have no foreseeable future, which is to say that there are no logical, deducible consequences coming from an earlier crime or event. The earlier crime or event has not been specified and therefore cannot have preordained consequences. Thus the future is also eliminated as a reasonable source of worry. There are no *reasons* why Rose should be dispossessed of her room—she has done nothing to deserve uprooting—or why she should expect a visitor from downstairs. A reasonable worry is, in a way, a comfort. It is only the altogether unreasonable, perched on the shoulder of the "now," that is altogether terrifying.

With the past gone from the pattern because no prior guilty act can be attributed to anyone, and with the future gone from the pattern because no deserved and identified threat looms ahead, the pattern itself disintegrates into a shapeless immediacy, a fearful moving about among objects and persons that are directly present but are without histories or discoverable essences. All persons, all objects are now to be feared—and revered, in the sense that they produce awe—because no one of them can be isolated as a single source of apprehension. A major part of Pinter's suspense, then, derives from his drawing us into the unpatterned angst which we know well enough in the dusty uncertainty of our days but which we normally keep at arm's length in the playhouse by insisting that the playwright show us cause and effect, crime and punishment. "Step into my parlor," Mr. Pinter says. We do so, feeling like so many flies, wondering where the spider is.

Perhaps it is easy enough to understand why we should feel effectively dislocated in rooms which may or may not have floors above or below them, or why we should feel a nameless anxiety in the face of commands being issued from wholly invisible sources in a restaurant above. These things are rumors, and rumors are always unsettling precisely because their origins cannot be traced or their effects anticipated.

But how is this faceless menace to be sustained as an effect in the theater when it acquires an actual face, when it is clearly and physically embodied in a character who walks in at the door to confront another, quickly quailing, character? If the threat is no longer a matter of hearsay, or of mysteriously delivered messages from nowhere, but an actual, breathing, talking, even obviously violent human being, hasn't the threat now been made concrete, tangible, defined on the spot? And aren't we back to regulation playmaking in which protagonist and antagonist face one another in broad daylight to thrash matters out?

In Pinter's first full-length play, *The Birthday Party*, perfectly tangible confrontations of this sort are arranged. In outline, the play would seem to contain all of the standard paraphernalia of old-fashioned stage melodrama, or of the suspense film. We are concerned with a victim, Stanley, who is being hemmed in by apparent gangsters, Goldberg and McCann, who mean to "take him for a ride." The hemming-in is done openly on the stage. How shall this sort of danger remain nameless and faceless?

The confrontation is so direct and sustained that it is almost as though Rose had met her man from the basement early in the play, or as though the thugs of *The Dumb Waiter* were face to face, from the beginning, with the man they were hired to kill. We seem close to a play in which fear is reasonably motivated and in which the parties to the struggle are clearly identified. We are dealing with beginnings and ends, with patterns, again.

But are we? As it happens, no one in the play understands the pattern through which he is moving. Presumably, Stanley is being repaid for something he has done in the past, for some betrayal or other. But Stanley cannot quite remember his past, not even his father's address. Of one thing he feels certain: he's not the "sort of bloke to—cause any trouble." In the last place he lived, the place in which he might be thought to have done whatever it is Goldberg and McCann think he has done, he "never stepped outside the door."

Goldberg and McCann, though they seem to have a clear duty to carry out now, are no clearer about the impulses that have propelled them into motion. They are not personal enemies of Stanley, though they personally—and very viciously—rough him up. There is vague talk of an "organization" which Stanley has betrayed, but Goldberg and McCann give no indication of being insiders to that organization. They are emissaries, set on a certain course by an irresistible force outside them, but they are not intimates of the force at work nor are they even capable of thinking about it coherently. When Goldberg attempts to state his beliefs about the world and its patterning, his mind stammers to a halt, becoming first "vacant," then "desperate," then "lost."

This is a blind collision. Existentially, it reports an experience we have not yet dealt with. Though each man exists uniquely in the void, straining to discover his identity and unable to relate intelligibly to other creatures like him, he is not the sole inhabitant of the void. The void is like the vault of heaven in which shooting stars may, without warning and for no immediately discernible reason, cross paths and even crash into one another. Each shooting star follows its own orbit. It cannot help doing so. It is following the laws of the "organization." But two separate courses, initiated by two separate impulses, may come into conjunction at any time, and most tangibly.

Any man who is in the process of achieving his identity is bound to meet, bump into, recoil from, affect, and be affected by other men engaged in the same process that occupies him. It is a historical accident that any two such orbits should coincide, since the overlapping paths are separately initiated and not logically related. But the overlapping, the collision, has consequences.

One man sets one foot into space, to see what it does. Another does the same thing at the same time. The two meet, and the meeting may be disastrous for one or the other or both. One thrust foot may prove stronger than another thrust foot. Each foot will contend for the space with the equipment it actually has, will struggle for what seems power but is actually definition. The encounter will end in some way or other. But it has not been a planned encounter and it will not have an effect-from-cause ending. Only the encounter is recorded, in its suddenness, in its blindness, in its mystery. Yes, the encounter has a result. But the result is a fact, not an explanation or an interpretation. *Pinter does not invite interpretation.*

This blind encounter is dramatized in a simpler and more literal way in *The Caretaker*. Here a homeless, shiftless, scrofulous, exceedingly self-righteous old man encounters a younger man who voluntarily offers him living space in his quarters. The generous act is not logically motivated; the old man cannot grasp why he has been taken in—though he is quick to come in, and quick to demand more than he has been offered—nor can he in any other way fathom the mind of his benefactor. His benefactor's mind is in fact unfathomable: he has earlier been subjected to a frontal lobotomy.

The old man next encounters his host's brother. This brother is sly, taunting, hostile—though again for no cause the old man can discover. The two encounters coincide in time but are not organically linked in the sense that they can explain each other; they are wholly baffling to the mind enduring them, and they are actual. The old man is given an actual pair of shoes, an actual bag is handed to him by one brother and snatched away by the other.

The play confines us to the sensations of the man to whom these things happen and for just so long as they are happening. At the end of the play they cease happening. The old man continues talking, but he is talking now to silence.

He has had the experience of colliding with two other forces which exist precisely as he does: as self-determining isolates whose "natures" have not yet been resolved. There has been a meeting, a bumping, an abrasion. The meeting has been suspenseful because anything at all *could* happen. The three men in the room do not come from a common matrix which might enable them to predict one another. They go on finding themselves through what they cannot find in others.

Pinter maintains his mystery, even when his menacing forces are perfectly visible and in head-on confrontation, by carefully denying them psychological access to one another. They are face to face and still impenetrable. They have not yet acquired essences that can be detected.

Though there is a degree of violence, or of sensed menace, in every Pinter play, the plays are not straightforward melodramas. Comedy is the constant companion of threat, and sometimes the threat itself contains an elusive comic edge. The messages from the dumbwaiter make the gunmen who are receiving them apprehensive; they also make us laugh, sometimes openly, sometimes nervously.

Apart from the fact that the playwright himself has a knack for the curtly phrased retort that, read blandly, has an air of amusing insult about it—he has, in fact, written a number of revue sketches —the very methods he employs, and the shifting-sands vision of man's precarious existence which these methods record, tend naturally toward one kind of comedy.

Comedy has always made capital of mistaken identity. When one man is taken for another, or one thing taken for another, we are invariably surprised and most often delighted that such easy interchanges should prove to be so possible, that the universe should turn out so slippery. *The Comedy of Errors* is a root comic design: one looks into a face and cannot say whose face it is.

Existentialist uncertainty is, of course, not so blithe in tone as a mere tumbling about of twins. Not being able to tell one twin from another has a clear logic inside it to guide and comfort us: we know the "natural" cause of our confusion and can readily respond to it without any admixture of dismay. The Pinter approach is necessarily darker than this, for we look into a face and find ourselves unable to name it without being able to explain, on the spot, our bafflement. We are disturbed; our equipment for detecting reality is not all that it might be. Yet there is no getting away from the laughter that follows and was inherent in the situation all the time: we have used our eyes and been made fools of. In two medium-length plays originally written for television, Mr. Pinter has deliberately explored what is lightly amusing in the ambiguity of his premises. *The Collection* and *The Lover* are both a great deal more than revue sketches, but here the scales are tipped to favor what is funny in our inability to define one another, or ourselves.

The Collection takes place in two simultaneously visible flats. One is shared by Harry and Bill, both dress designers; though there are no explicit homosexual gestures, Harry is jealous of Bill. The other flat houses James and Stella, husband and wife, operators of a boutique. There has been a fashion display in Leeds the week before; both Stella, from the one flat, and Bill, from the other, have gone to it. Stella and Bill may have met in a hotel corridor, just outside an elevator, kissed on impulse, and spent the night together. Stella's husband thinks she has slept with Bill and he calls, unannounced, on Bill to get at the truth. Harry is equally concerned that Bill has slept with Stella; he calls upon Stella to urge her to break off the relationship.

But there is nothing to say—for certain—that there has been any relationship. Stella may be lying (boasting? teasing? tormenting?) when she seems to admit the affair to her husband. Bill, pressed to confess by James, may confess simply because he is expected to or because it amuses him to do so. All parties are sparring. No party knows the other well enough to say what he might or might not do. Around musical chairs the four contestants go; in a fashion reminiscent of Pirandello, each makes the other into the image he has of him.

There is no violent pressure here, simply an anxious—though generally polite—need to define. All are poised, self-controlled, in cool command of a situation that is endlessly open. James, intruding upon Bill, behaves as though he were in his own flat, not Bill's; he asks Bill what he would like to drink. Bill, at first dismissing the night in Leeds as a bit of pure fantasy Stella has invented ("Really rather naughty of her"), pauses to ask her husband, "Do you know her well?"

If neither of them can know Stella absolutely—is she a whore or is she putting it all on?—neither can they quite know themselves. James and Bill spend a moment, side by side, looking into a mirror, though James expects nothing to come of mirrors: "They're deceptive."

A degree of violence does obtrude before this psychological parlor game has run its course. Bill, backing away from James, tumbles over a piece of furniture and suddenly finds himself wondering whether James will permit him to rise again or whether he is about to lash out at him with his feet. During a subsequent meeting, James and Bill contemplate a duel with fruit knives, and there is in fact some minor bloodshed. But the comic emphasis is maintained even at knife's edge. Bill, ready to shrug the contest off, announces that he is putting his knife down.

JAMES: Well, I'll pick it up.
James does so and faces him with two knives.
BILL: Now you've got two.
JAMES: I've got another one in my hip pocket.

Pause.
BILL: What do you do, swallow them?

Ignorance has a preposterous side to it, and it is possible to be flippant about it. In the end, the play refuses to perspire over the problem of identity. James returns home to Stella, who is playing with her kitten. He has decided for himself, or rather he wishes to decide for himself, that Stella and Bill didn't really "do anything" in Leeds. If they met, they merely sat in the hotel lounge and chatted. If they discussed going to Stella's room, the discussion was hypothetical, the projected act unrealized.

JAMES: . . . That's the truth, isn't it?
Pause.
You just sat and talked about what you would do, if you went to your room. That's what you did.
Pause.
Didn't you?
Pause.
That's the truth . . . isn't it?

End of play, with Stella looking at James, "neither confirming nor denying," her face "friendly and sympathetic." Uncertainty may be a tolerable condition of life if one has the patient good sense to cock an eye at it whimsically.

The Lover is even lighter, very close to extended vaudeville, though, in its existential playfulness, it opens the door to yet another aspect of the continuing proposition that existence precedes essence.

"Is your lover coming today?" Richard asks his wife Sarah, as the curtain rises. Richard is leaving for his office, where he is pictured as slaving over ledgers all day, but he is concerned with Sarah's happiness and he wishes to be sure that she'll have a "pleasant afternoon." Returning in the evening, he solicitously inquires how the afternoon went. Sarah, equally considerate, supposes that Richard has a mistress. This, as it turns out, is not quite the case.

RICHARD: But I haven't got a mistress. I'm very well acquainted with a whore, but I haven't got a mistress. There's a world of difference.

SARAH: A whore?

RICHARD: (*Taking an olive*) Yes. Just a common or garden slut. Not worth talking about. Handy between trains, nothing more.

Though Richard and Sarah pride themselves on "frankness at all costs," because frankness is "essential to a healthy marriage," Sarah confesses that she is surprised by the news that Richard has a whore. "Why?" Richard asks. "I wasn't looking for your double, was I?"

At this point—it is one of the few instances in which Pinter's surprises are not so surprising—we begin to leap ahead of the playwright. Yes, the lover who comes to visit Sarah in the afternoons is Richard. And Sarah is Richard's whore, her own double and not her double. Such a visit is dramatized and the two behave entirely differently to each other. Indeed, when Richard the lover speculates on whether or not he'd hit it off with Richard the husband, supposing their paths ever crossed, Sarah thinks not. "You've got very little in common," she points out.

What makes this relatively brief conceit more interesting than a simple and fairly obvious vaudeville "switch" is its introduction of the notion that both Richard and Sarah truly possess the two separate identities they assume. They are not children playing bawdyhouse. They are adults who are other adults than themselves, unconfined by one or another social role. Looked at conventionally, *The Lover* might simply seem to be saying that married couples need to pretend a bit now and then in order to refresh their relationship. Or, conceivably, it might seem to be saying that in a highly structured society sexual impulses are rarely given free play and that some subterfuge is needed to release such impulses even in marriage. Looked at existentially, it says another thing altogether: no woman is essentially wife or essentially whore, she is potentially either or both at once; the same duality, or multiplicity, holds true for the husband-lover. Personality is not something given; it is fluid.

In *The Collection* no character could say what another was; but there was always the lingering assumption that, if only one could see clearly enough or probe persistently enough, a firm fixed identity—a "truth"—might be uncovered. Here, in *The Lover*, we do see clearly enough, we walk directly into the situation as though we had walked into that hotel room in Leeds. And what we see, now that we see clearly, is that nothing human is fixed, everything human is mobile. The same woman can be a whore in a hotel room and an innocent playing with her kitten at home while remaining the same woman, without contradiction.

If existence precedes essence, and if plays are to be written in such a way as to reveal this sequence, then no character on a stage dares be essentially anything: husband, wife, lover, whore, brother, father, beggar, host. Instead, character is potency, possibility, movement.

We are touching now on that freedom of movement, without prior direction or definition, to which Sartre says man is "condemned" and which constitutes man's exploration of the void in search of his realized, until now unknown, self. Categories and traditional roles contain no man unless he lets himself be contained by them, choosing to conform to a pattern that does not actually express his potency. Man cannot be described except in terms of motion: he is what he does next. And there may be another "next" after that, which means that there will then be a new, and still unfinished, "is."

In two thematically related plays, *A Slight Ache* and *The Homecoming*, Pinter has gone on to examine identity as movement, not as category. In *The Homecoming* the issue is made most explicit, set forth in a single speech. The men about Ruth are debating intellectual categories. A table is a table, just as a wife is a wife.

> RUTH: Don't be too sure though. You've forgotten something. Look at me. I . . . move my leg. That's all it is. But I wear . . . underwear . . . which moves with me . . . it . . . captures your attention. Perhaps you misinterpret. The action is simple. It's a leg . . . moving. My lips move. Why don't you restrict . . . your observations to that? Perhaps the fact that they move is more significant . . . than the words which come through them. You must bear that . . . possibility . . . in mind.

The possibility is going to have consequences a few scenes later. But it may be best to glance at *A Slight Ache* first, not so much

because it was written four years earlier, but because in it the
contrast between category and movement is more simply and
swiftly outlined.

A man—and for Pinter the male now tends to become the
categorist—is baffled by the presence of a filthy old matchseller
who stands at the bottom of the lane near his house daily. There
are very few passersby. The old man never sells any matches.
Why does he come? The householder cannot let the question
alone; he becomes feverish in his anxiety to know the answer. He
invites the ragged presence into the house, offers him a drink,
cajoles him, coaxes him, finally commands him to say who he is
and what he is doing. The matchseller never utters a word. His
inquisitor is now half mad with frustration, distressed by his inability to define.

The householder's wife enters and takes over. She asks no questions. She simply embraces the visitor. She is, that is to say, open to
him and to his possibility. Shortly she installs him in the house.
The husband goes out to sell matches.

The woman here is readily seen as catalyst, as the agent of
change. And she is. Through her the husband drops his "role" as
husband and as categorist and finds himself assuming another role
he could not have anticipated, cannot even now define. Through
her the matchseller, still silent, becomes partner. But she is not
merely an agent of action in the play, mistress of shifting possibilities. She is herself in motion, and it is her own assumption of a
second identity—wife-mother to the matchseller—that is the central event of the play. She has been one thing; without hesitation,
she moves forward to become another. Questions of identity—her
own, or anyone else's—do not concern her, as they have so concerned her husband. She is what she finds it within herself to be,
she is the movement she finds herself making.

This situation, with its altering relationships, is repeated in the
climactic sequence of *The Homecoming*. Ruth is Teddy's wife
and has come, after some years of marriage, to visit her husband's
family. Teddy, her husband, is the categorist par excellence. He is
a Doctor of Philosophy at an American university. For him, everything is fixed. He has seen stability. "To see, to be able to *see!*" he
exclaims. "I'm the one who can see. That's why I can write my
critical works." He is proud of his "intellectual equilibrium" and a

shade contemptuous of those who move uncertainly about him.
"You're just objects. You just . . . move about. I can observe it. I
can see what you do. . . . But you're lost in it. . . . I won't be
lost in it."

Teddy is rigid and detached, wedded to essences, a Platonist.
Once more there are intruders with whom he cannot be comfortable: his father and two brothers. The father and two brothers,
observing Ruth and her presence as motion, make Ruth a proposition. Let Teddy go back to America, let her remain with them as
their "whore." They will give her a flat and furnishings, they will
enable her to pay for these by leasing her out some nights to other
men, they will take turns being with her and being whatever they
can be to her. She will be whatever she can be to them. Ruth,
having embraced one brother in a dance and the other in a copula-
tive roll-about on the couch, accepts the proposition.

Teddy accepts Ruth's acceptance of the proposition. He is not
so anxious about identities as the husband of *A Slight Ache;* he is
certain that he has arrived at them, he is beyond becoming involved; he does, however, go into exile as surely as his predecessor
does. As he leaves, there is no sign of animus, rejection, or even
finality in Ruth. "Don't become a stranger" is the last thing she
says to him.

The woman, Ruth, is the center of the play because she is the
existential suppleness of the play. She continues to become her
identity. She has been wife, mother, daughter-in-law, sister-in-law.
But these roles are not terminal, they are not permitted to become
absolutes. "Whore" is a part of her possibility too. Neither is
"whore" to be regarded as terminal, as defining. Who is to say
what movement lies beyond, before the self comes to be the self?
When does the movement of lips, legs, underwear cease, saying, in
sum, "This is I"?

Pinter uses the "whore" image repeatedly—it has appeared in
three out of the last four plays we've mentioned—precisely because the whore, by definition, lacks definition. The whore performs no single social role, she is what each new man wishes to
make of her. She is available to experience, and she is an available
experience. She is eternally "between trains," she is known in passing and as something passing. In fact, she is simply unknown.
Existentially speaking, we are all life's whores to the degree that

we are in motion and have not arbitrarily codified and thereby stilled ourselves.

Rich man, poor man, beggar man, thief—the picaresque hero, who is generally something of a whore, is all of these in turn, which is no doubt why the picaresque hero has enjoyed a considerable revival under existentialist pressure. Viewed in an existentialist light, each of us is picaresque-hero-whore: permanently subject to unpredictable intrusion, to the unlooked-for event and the unthinkable proposition. Until we have actually responded to these things, actually moved and behaved in the circumstances they create, we cannot say what our response, or our very selves, might be. It is only when responsive movement has been exhausted that we can lay claim to knowing essence.

In the contemporary theater Pinter's work is original in method and unique in its effect upon the stage. An Arnold Wesker and a John Arden can be related in intention and style. Beckett and Ionesco have sunspots in common. It is possible to put John Osborne and Edward Albee side by side and see that they raise their disturbances with much the same lift of voice. But Pinter's territory is very private territory. True, he has drawn upon a philosophical disposition that is very much in the air and available to everyone. But he is the one man who has fought essence to a standstill, refused it houseroom until he has finished moving freely about.

"I don't know what kind of characters my plays will have until they . . . well, until they *are*," he has said. "Until they indicate to me what they are. . . . Once I've got the clues, I follow them—that's my job, really, to follow clues. . . . I follow what I see on the paper in front of me—one sentence after another. That doesn't mean I don't have a dim, possible overall idea—the image that starts off doesn't just engender what happens immediately, it engenders the possibility of an overall happening, which carries me through. I've got an idea of what *might* happen—sometimes I'm absolutely right, but on many occasions I've been proved wrong by what does actually happen."

The play is discovery in the way that personality, under existentialism, is discovery. It has not been fashioned to fit a hard and fast idea about man, or society, or the nature of things. "I distrust ideological statements of any kind," the playwright adds.

He has been remarkably successful in constructing a series of felt realities that do not depend upon conceptual underpinning: the experience of entirely tangible places unmoored in a void; the experience of living and fearing and even laughing in the present tense without knowledge of past or future; the experience of encountering other objects just as impenetrable as we are as we jockey for position in a swarming footloose universe; the experience of never being certain what gesture any man may make next because everyman is, at the present writing, incomplete.

These are not statements made in the plays. They are the movement of the plays. The play is only an event, not a logical demonstration; the event must speak, illogically but persuasively, for itself. The play persuades by existing, and in no other way. If it failed to persuade in this way, no theory—however correct, however contemporary—could save it. Pinter takes his uncertainty seriously.

Perfectly? Of course not. Playwrights have a habit of not being perfect, and in this case a writer is attempting a break not only with recently conventional modes of playmaking but with a kind of thinking that has simply been reflexive with us since Plato. It's not surprising that he doesn't entirely escape conceptualization, try as he may.

Clearly there is something schematic and preformed in his recurring use of the male as conceptualist, the female as existentialist, the male as rigid, the female as flexible. Such an observation may, of course, be true enough; it is even a very old one, echoing the ancient contrast between the male as rational, the female as intuitive. But it does suggest a return to a belief in essential natures—the mind of the universe has made men this way, women that way—which tends to contradict the author's own insistence that the moving lip is more important than the word it forms.

The schematic pursues him in other ways. The frontal lobotomy which has been performed upon the benevolent brother in *The Caretaker*, for instance, very literally freezes that character into an essential position. This man is fixed, his patterns are determined, he cannot be further altered by any free forward movement of his own. The use of the lobotomy is, I think, a vulgarization in Pinter's terms: it is too easy, too expedient a way of saying that communication has been cut off. Instead of the mysteriously impenetrable we have here the symbolically impenetrable; the figure becomes a concept rather than an unpredictable fluid force.

Actually, *The Caretaker* is a kind of battleground of styles, an unresolved tug-of-war between older methods of characterization and the newer method Pinter is reaching for. The play really functions in three degrees of perspective: we look at it as we might a toy theater in which three cut-out figures had been placed in different slots in the floor, at different distances from us. The caretaker himself, the garrulous and tenacious old man, is nearest to us, full-bodied in a familiar way, as rounded out and complete as an ebullient whiner out of Dickens. We know him utterly. There is nothing unfinished or elusive about him. He is perfectly realized. But he is realized, in his wrapped-up complexity, in what here must be called an old-fashioned way.

The benevolent brother occupies the middle distance. He is symbolic man, two-dimensional, forever representing the same value, as he might in Beckett or certainly would in *Everyman*. He stands for an impasse, and has no other qualities, unless he can be said to have the quality of hinting that only the mentally destroyed are given to kindness in a violent universe intent upon exercising power to determine identity. He is a morality-play figure.

The inexplicably hostile brother, threatening even in his sporadic geniality, is placed in the far distance, nearest the shadows. He is the man Pinter's hand is most often after, all change and motion and indeterminateness, perpetual mocker of proposed stabilities. The others in the play have plans. So does he, in a whimsical and obviously untrustworthy way. But all plans dissolve as he touches them. His very presence destroys plan, exposes it for the mirage it is. He is the unfinished, the unascertainable, the existentialist man.

We are apt to like the caretaker most, simply because we are accustomed, in our theatergoing, to his sort of complex but firmly defined being. But the hostile brother, the taunting one who refuses us access to himself because the self is not ready to be named, is the presence in the play that leads us most directly into the Pinter landscape as a whole. He is, indeed, the only figure in the play to do the new thing most persistently and characteristically pursued by the playwright: behave before he has been pigeon-holed. Strictly speaking, the three men probably do not belong in the same play: each comes from a separate and somewhat isolated literary world; none can really move from one slot, one dimension, to another. This difficulty does keep the lines of communication down, which is an existentialist requirement. But it achieves that particular effect by a mixing of modes, at some cost to stylistic unity.

Curiously, explicit violence is also a troubling, and not quite assimilated, element in the playwright's work. So long as violence is threatened, intimated, promised, the chill in the air is actual and the atmosphere of the play uncorrupted. But whenever the sinuous seeking movement of the play breaks open into concrete deed, into physical definiteness, an aura of the stage trick, the artificial climax, the merely surprising act-curtain intrudes. The sudden death at the end of *The Dumb Waiter* is surprising, and in that sense theatrically effective; but it also leaves us with a feeling of having been taken in by mere Grand Guignol. The entrance of the Negro, the savage assault upon him, and the instant blindness of Rose at the end of *The Room* have a similar flavor of the startling for its own sake, or for the sake of getting the curtain down on a sufficiently defiant and baffling note.

Why is the deed sometimes less persuasive than the rumor of deeds to come? I suspect precisely because it is a defined act, which means that it terminates the groping forward that is the whole environment in an existentialist view of things. To kill someone is to put a name, a meaning, an identity upon the situation before us. The condition being dramatized has come to an end. But the end must be arbitrary because no existentialist is yet ready to say that he knows ends, that he can announce essences.

Pinter confesses that he likes "a good curtain," and some of his eruptions may simply come from a craftsman's passion for good stage rigging. The stylistic problem remains unresolved, however. If existence is endlessly open, where is it to be closed? If movement is all, who dares stop it?

One last qualification. I find myself preferring the shorter plays—plays which may run anywhere from thirty minutes to an hour and a half—to the full-length extensions of Pinter's highly individual vision. *A Slight Ache,* for instance, seems to me to do the work of *The Homecoming,* or a very great deal of it, with a succinctness and a sustained tension that are distributed and seriously dissipated in the longer play.

Why should the longer plays delay, or circle, a situation that can be accounted for quite satisfactorily in a tight forty minutes? I suspect that it has not quite occurred to Mr. Pinter that it is possible to display more than a single altering step into the void, a single transposition of personality, a single throw of the existentialist dice, in any one play. There is nothing, really, to prevent him from moving forward again once the initial elision has taken place. Having moved from wife-mother to whore, Ruth may very well move to yet another extension of being. Since she is not predefined, she is free to go on taking steps without worrying about the kind of footprints she leaves or what prying detectives may make of them. One gesture is not definition, is not the end of things. A play might very well take us through three or four persons in one, as *Hamlet* does, before it chooses to curtail its possibly endless investigation of possibility. There is nothing in the method to say that we must stop at Stage Two. Thus far Mr. Pinter tends to confine himself to a first change of state, a practice which makes many of the shorter plays perfect but which attenuates and makes repetitive the longer ones.

I've mentioned *Hamlet.* Mr. Pinter has described himself, and not necessarily baitingly, as a "traditional playwright." The fact of the matter is that there is a theatrical tradition of pursuing existence without being certain of essence—it came into being long before any philosopher elected to challenge Plato in so many words—and it has given us some of our most cherished, if hotly debated, masterpieces. It would seem very likely that Shakespeare traced Hamlet's course without any dead-certain concept in his head of where Hamlet's quest was to end. Death, yes, most likely, though in Shakespeare's source-legend Hamlet doesn't die. But precisely how the tangle of personality was to unravel itself, when and where it was to assert itself as defined, seems bafflingly open throughout Shakespeare's play. Now cruel, now kind, now dedicated, now dilatory, now—but we have gone over these unpredictable alterations in Hamlet forever. It is the very lack of a sensed master plan, or a conceptual program for the play, that has led to the sort of exasperation with *Hamlet* for lacking "an objective correlative" that T. S. Eliot felt. In the end, Mr. Eliot controlled his exasperation and took his criticism back. Why? Because, "objective correlative" or no, Hamlet existed. Critics may quarrel about Hamlet's essential nature to the end of time. But Hamlet stirred first, and still does.

Thus, in a sense, Pinter is returning us to a "tradition" at the same time that he insists upon destroying what we call tradition. The stage has always been open, in spite of the rigors philosophers have imposed upon thought, to the tasting of experience experimentally. Its very nature tempts it to do so. The stage is an arena, a bear pit, a bullring, an empty space until challengers enter it. Who is to say what all challengers are to do on the spur of the moment, in the heat of passion, under the pressure of the contest? Bear pits and bullrings breed surprises. Claw and cape behave differently on different days, in different winds. An arena is an open, initially empty, space not because it is a place for fighting but because it is a place for finding, for discovery, for realization. It first gapes at us as though it were a great question mark. Then movement fills it and—perhaps—makes a shape.

We tend to forget that this is a possible theatrical tradition or a possible playwriting method because we have lately lived so long under another dispensation: that of the "well-made play," the play built of bricks selected to shore up a thesis, the play dominated by a writer's logic. This later, neater, more predictable method has wearied us for a considerable time. We have understood its virtues, its enclosed intellectual systems and its clear time-and-thought sequences well enough; but we have intuited, all along, that drama had something less reasonable and more impulsive to say to us, given its other voice.

Pinter might be called "traditional" in the sense that he has begun to restore, under the fresh questioning of a twentieth-century philosophical method, an old and neglected urge to enter the arena naked, without the support of tried-and-true tricks or proved propositions but with a firm determination to move as much as a man may move against whatever can be made to yield to him. When Euripides entered such an arena in *The Bacchae* it was probably without hope of fully resolving the contest between Dionysiac excess and Dionysiac rectitude. But in he went, all the way, giving every god and devil his due, to see what an uninhibited probing, an unrestricted invasion of the Greeks' very own void, might uncover. Conceptualization, prior commitment, would surely have stopped him short of the play's boundless frontier, its resolute pressing forward into the infinite. Asking only how extensively any one force might assert itself, he made—out of such a reaching—an ambiguous, deeply mystifying, bloodcurdling masterpiece. He did not seek to devise or support a system, as Aeschylus had done in *The Eumenides*. Focusing his eyes beyond system, he sought instead to see all that was.

PART THREE

Remembrance
of Things Past

I

IT SEEMS to have become psychologically necessary, in this time of theatrical transition and theatrical breakage, for the theater to renew its lines to the immediate past. During the past few seasons in New York an unprecedented number of revivals has turned up, quite a few of them surprisingly successful. We have not been in the habit of reviving relatively recent plays. I suppose we were afraid of being embarrassed by them; what we had thought good twenty years ago might make poor prophets of us now. They also had, when they were tried, rather discouraging box-office records; a fine revival of *The Rose Tattoo* five years ago could manage a run of only a few months. This is still to some extent true; the old plays that will summon audiences to them remain unpredictable. A recent mounting of Clifford Odets' *Awake and Sing* drew excellent notices and played to appallingly skimpy houses.

But the urge to revive is there, stronger than we have known it in our time. It may be there because, as our newer experiments gallop off into twilights that are now unfathomable, we wish to pause for a moment to see where we have been. It may be there because, being so frequently disoriented in our more adventurous playgoing, we are simply nostalgic for a past that was easier to grasp. It may be there because we are wondering whether we have a national character at all, what it may be like if we do have one, whether or not it is one capable of justifying a National Theater devoted to displaying it. All three reasons may converge, spurred on a bit by a desperate need to be entertained before we return again to the barricades.

Our responses are not simply open-armed; they are complex. For instance, we bring a curious intensity to our visits to *Our Town* these days, going to each successive revival in a strangely mixed hope and fear that the work will at last seem tarnished. I think we hope it will tarnish so that it will stop affecting us; it *does* affect us, it does make us cry, and we dislike being thought subject to such emotional impress. We are embarrassed to be found fond. At the same time we are fearful it will turn up tarnished because it is one of our remembered pleasures and, while we have just about decided to give up all present pleasure, we hate surrendering those few we thought we had locked away in the trunk. We still like to think that dawn, at least, was decent.

But the fact of the matter is that *Our Town* doesn't change at all. It functions in the theater exactly as it always has. Our own changing responses and awarenesses muddle us, make us ask questions of ourselves, invite us to doubt ourselves, put the tremulous "What *should* I think?" at the forefront of our minds, trying to bar the way. The play is indifferent to all that. In its most recent revival, from the time that Henry Fonda, as the sweatered, pipe-smoking, confiding but not overly solicitous stage manager, strolled onto the stage to pick up a chair and efficiently set it down with some definiteness where it could best be used by other actors, the evening went its own way, quietly, sparely, firmly, without interior fuss. Here, it would make us laugh. Here, it would make us apprehensive, sorry. Here, it would show us itself, nothing more. When it was done, it would walk away briskly, scarcely a word spent foolishly. It had been stripped down long ago, by its author; there was little that could be taken from it now.

Its effect had always been in its economy. There is, for instance, a little girl in the play—you won't remember her name, she is George Gibbs's sister—and not much time is ever spent on her. She climbs a ladder in the moonlight once to bother George. She comes downstairs to fill out the breakfast table. But, across the breakfast table on the play's first morning, she bursts out with sudden shrill ardor, earnest joy. "Mama," she asks as her eyes glow, "Do you know what I love best in the world? Do you? *Money!*"

She doesn't really ever have to say anything again because, laughing, you have seen in her the cold blood of innocence, the delightfully transparent greed and unselfconscious candor of the species and the sex before society (Grover's Corners or any other) has got at it. Out of your own experience you may be able to offer a thousand variations on the line; can you write *one* that will stand in as well for all the thousands?

Sometimes Thornton Wilder has adopted the mandatory cliché to get his work done: when Emily Webb badgers her mother to tell her if she is really pretty, Mrs. Webb, awkward and exasperated, replies, "Pretty enough for all normal purposes." More often he has gone about his task of making a simple thing out of multiples by distilling and refining memories until they seem to lie quiet in the hand, as quiet as Emily's unbothered assurance that she was born bright, as final as George's holding his breath until he can hear the night train reach Contoocook.

When the play was last seen, a lovely company listened carefully to the author, spoke what was set down for it, sternly resisted embellishment. That was enough.

Is it possible you've never seen *Our Town?* Then look for it. Or haven't seen it in ten years? Then seek it out again. You'll be surprised at how much younger it is than you are.

2

FUNNY, how we remember it wrong. No, we don't even remember it wrong. We get it wrong in the first place.

What do we think of William Saroyan, author of that celebrated and now once again revived comedy *The Time of Your Life,* Saroyan the Armenian, Saroyan the humanist, Saroyan the Hollywood writer of films about boys on bicycles, Saroyan the lofty lover of all the beautiful people and the man who wouldn't take a Pulitzer Prize when he was handed one? Why, of course we think

of him fondly, as though sometime or other we had forgiven him
for something; we think of him with amusement because he has so
often in his swarthy catlike laziness amused us; we think him
rather a spoiled writer because nothing else was ever as good as
those first stunning short stories; we think him a bit of a poseur
perhaps; but above all—above all—we think him a sentimentalist.

We even know what he was sentimental about. Those beautiful
people. Their goodness, their lostness, their dreaminess. How
sweet Joe is, sitting in that barroom and dispensing all that money
for free, ready to declare his love within minutes for the latest
forlorn lady to occupy the next table, ready to take Kitty Duval,
adorable whore that she is, out of her shabby quarters where
sailors interrupt her weeping and her sleep and to install her
grandly at a hotel reserved for ladies of quality. How kind they all
are to one another, these bartenders and hoofers and piano players
and idling cops, just so long as no alien principle of evil happens to
move among them. When one does move among them, in the
person of a particularly brutal fellow from the Vice Squad, his
crime is quickly made plain: "He hurts little people."

Indeed, indeed. And it was all there recently on the Vivian
Beaumont stage, mellow and moonshiny and tied together with the
tinkle of "When Irish Eyes Are Smiling," "The Missouri Waltz,"
and a cupful of Salvation Army hymns. When Priscilla Pointer
tugged her feet beneath a chair into a tight little knot, as though
they were ashamed of her drinking and her unhappiness and her
willingness to tell a total stranger that she loved him, there was a
little catch at the throat, somebody's throat, hers or yours. When
Biff McGuire, naïve as Abel before Cain had got at him, squinted
intensely at the whore *he* loved, his mouth cut open in strangled
adoration, his chewing gum silenced for as long as the lyric moment lasted ("I love you." "Do you want to come to my room?"
"Yes." "Have you got two dollars?" "I've got five dollars, but I
love you"), the old peculiar pleasure of hearing worldliness rearranged for use in a fifth-grade reader returned.

When Joe reminisced about just missing getting married and
having all those imagined children ("My favorite was the third
one"), the grin in the playhouse came up broad and warm. When a
drunk offered a solemn toast to "reforestation" or Joe urged his
runner to get rid of a gun by giving it to "some worthy holdup

man," the laugh was quick, indulgent, genuine. Actually, John Hirsch's production was *too* mellow, *too* musical, *too* self-consciously atmospheric, but let's put that aside for a moment. Inside its studied booziness the soft charms, the expected charms, lurked and worked.

Why, though, are these charms all we ever remember about the play and why do we persist in thinking of it as fundamentally cheerful, as fundamentally (and maybe spuriously) an act of faith? It's nothing of the sort, nothing at all.

I confess that I may have been influenced in my last visit to the piece by the dinner I had, or rather by the reading I was doing with the dinner I had. I was alone on this particular evening. I passed the dinner hour reading Kurt Vonnegut's *Cat's Cradle* and it thus so happened that with my first oyster the world began to come to an end.

Cat's Cradle is a bizarre—and brilliant—novel about several thousand things, one of which is a scientific discovery known as Ice-nine. Ice-nine, when unleashed, instantly and progressively locks the particles of water together, so that a filled washbasin becomes an unbreakable frozen block, an ocean becomes a rockhard mass. Let the stuff loose at shore's edge and all life must vanish from the face of the earth. Naturally one assumes that mankind, having come into possession of such an instrument, will not be dumb enough to use it. One's assumption proves false. Mankind was being exactly that dumb as I reached for a lemon.

Any hope, in Mr. Vonnegut's blunt and bumpy, funny and frightening view? His principal character has been poring over a certain prophetic text, the Fourteenth Book of which is entitled: "What Can a Thoughtful Man Hope for Mankind on Earth, Given the Experience of the Past Million Years?"

Vonnegut: "It doesn't take long to read *The Fourteenth Book*. It consists of one word and a period.

"This is it:

"Nothing."

So. Mr. Vonnegut is a persuasive fantasist and I can't say he lightened my meal. I looked at the coffee as though it might lock. I did think, however, as I rose and headed for the Beaumont, that Saroyan would lighten it, retroactively. And what did I find as I watched the 1939 play? The Fourteenth Book all over again.

There isn't a shred of hope in *The Time of Your Life*. Central
passage of the play, carried by a cop named Krupp:

> They're all guys who are trying to be happy; trying to make a
> living; support a family; bring up children; enjoy sleep. Go to a
> movie; take a drive on Sunday. They're all good guys, so out of
> nowhere comes trouble. . . . I been thinking everything over,
> Nick, and you know what I think? . . . I think we're all
> crazy. . . . We're crazy. We're nuts. We've got everything,
> but we always feel lousy and dissatisfied just the same. . . .
> There's no hope. I don't suppose it's right for an officer of the
> law to feel the way I feel, but, by God, right or not right, that's
> how I feel. . . . We're no good any more. All the corruption
> everywhere. The poor kids selling themselves. A couple of years
> ago they were in grammar school. Everybody trying to get a lot
> of money in a hurry. . . . Nobody going quietly for a little
> walk to the ocean. Nobody taking things easy and not wanting
> to make some kind of a killing. Nick, I'm going to quit being a
> cop. . . . I'm going to quit. That's all. Quit. Out. I'm going to
> give them back the uniform and the gadgets that go with it. I
> don't want any part of it. . . ."

Through this is threaded the one desolate line we *do* remember
from the play, "No foundation—all the way down the line," repeatedly intoned by an Arab who sits alone at the bar. Somehow
or other we seem to remember that line as funny, perhaps because
it's a catch-phrase and is repeated so often. But in fact it's not
funny: the bitterest explosion of the evening comes from this Arab
when he is finally prodded into sustained speech.

And as we take a new look at the play now, attending to it as
something less than affirmative, we're a bit surprised by what we
see. Joe is, at his own evaluation, worthless: he detests money, he is
certain that making money is invariably a matter of hurting
people, he goes on making money. The one vigorous act he
attempts to perform—shooting the Vice Squad man—he bungles.
The girl at the table who has accepted the idea of Joe's love is a
woman who should be happy. She has a husband and children and
nothing in particular to be sad about. "Then why are you sad?"
Joe wants to know. "I was always sad," she replies. "It's just that
after I was married I was allowed to drink."

If Joe hates himself and the cop hates his job and the girl hates having grown up to drinking, no one else on the premises is really any better off. The dancing comedian cannot, by his own admission, get a laugh. The intelligent longshoreman cannot avoid becoming involved in a strike. The piano player is beat up, the society slummers are embarrassingly routed, Kit Carson is a fraud until he becomes something better than that, a murderer. Maybe there's some hope for the young innocent and his nice whore, running off to take a job driving a truck together. On the evidence offered, it would be a surprise if they survived the first turnpike.

Sounds almost like Artaud, doesn't it? It's not, naturally. An outline has no tone, whereas Saroyan's tone is omnipresent, and it is soft and friendly. In fact, you could say that if Saroyan is sentimental about the likeableness of people he is equally sentimental about the doom they are headed for. Even pessimism can be sentimental, since sentimentality is simply an excess of emotion in relation to the evidence offered. Pity can be too much as a pat on the head can be too much. Perhaps there's a shade too much of both here, for this slightly later and more ascetic age. But always remember: the author himself turned down at least one of the prizes he was offered. Maybe he was the realist.

Never mind. My point is that we think of Saroyan as incorruptibly sunny, whereas *The Time of Your Life* is really all about the day the last sun went down. There isn't any tomorrow in it for anybody—maybe the bartender, but will he have customers?—and instead of being a poem in praise of the green lawns of MGM and the high hopes of Mickey Rooney, it is much more nearly the matrix for all of the doomsday plays that have followed.

It is more fun than most of them. But it does not promise more than most of them. We probably should remind ourselves, now that we are in the business of reminding, that Mr. Saroyan's earlier and quite beautiful play, *My Heart's in the Highlands,* ended with everybody either dead or dispossessed, and with a small boy—nothing like Mickey Rooney—wandering homeless down the street while he says to his despairing father, "I'm not mentioning any names, Pa, but something's wrong somewhere."

3

NEVER mind marijuana. Should Harvey be legalized? In the twenty-eight years since Mary Chase wrote *Harvey* some men have been to the moon, some men have been to psychiatrists, and all men, wherever they've been, have had their knowledge increased, their frontiers expanded, their inhibitions freed. But that rabbit is still around.

It's been good to see him again. And don't think we weren't seeing him. In the delicate, respectful, hilarious, and finally very moving revival of the play at the Anta, it was actually Helen Hayes who saw him first. I know Harvey wasn't supposed to come on until Jimmy Stewart brought him on (it said James Stewart on the program, but the audience was thinking Jimmy and I'm going to leave it at that), gently urging his large white friend through a doorway.

But Miss Hayes happened to appear first, conducting a Wednesday Afternoon Forum in her home (which she described to a newspaper reporter as "festooned with smilax"), seriously taking thought for a moment to consider whether or not some of her elderly guests might in fact be dead, and hoping against hope that her brother would not arrive with his embarrassing companion until after the neighbors had all gone home.

The thing was, right off, that Miss Hayes was embarrassed not because her brother drank or because he tended to introduce people to his invisible friend. It was the *rabbit* that embarrassed her, his size, his silence, the space he occupied, his tenacity, his being or not being there when you didn't know whether he was or not. Harvey rattled this lady because he was real, and that's what Miss Hayes was communicating—fearful eyes darting, fourth and fifth fingers flexing in her outstretched, warding-off hand—all the while she was denying his existence and worrying for her brother's sanity and pretending to all the world that pookas didn't come to parties. Miss Hayes's denial described; her protestations made pictures as incontrovertible as photographs; her alarums had the force of a footman's loudly announcing that Harvey was descending the royal staircase. Miss Hayes brought him to life backwards.

Then, having made the invisible visible simply by looking over her shoulder too often, the actress gave way for a moment and Mr. Stewart took over. For a few minutes now the rabbit was just a bit less real, because he was supposed to be there. Mr. Stewart had to make room for him to waddle past obtrusive chairs (chairs are never that obtrusive, we were being a shade less honest here), he had to urge him to sit, offer him a drink, ask if he was comfortable. Mr. Stewart, shaggier than ever before now that age had tucked in his chins and untidied his hair, was doing all of this very nicely, mind you. But a pooka, it seems, exerts more displacement when he is being doubted than when he is being catered to; looking at him in an empty chair we had to squint harder than when we knew he was waiting just outside the door.

In not too long a time, though—there was a scuffle in a mental home to which Miss Hayes was vainly trying to have Mr. Stewart committed—Harvey, the real Harvey, got lost. He had left his coat and hat behind (the hat made allowance for his alert and rather long ears), but no one knew which local bar he might have wandered off to or why no one could lay eyes on him just now. It was at this point in the play that he joined the cast of characters irrevocably and forever, thick as a church door, heavier than night air, sound as a bell. In everyone's anxiety to find him in order to get rid of him, he became eternally present, the production's third fixed star.

It is necessary to stress the brilliance with which this feat had been accomplished. No one wants to talk about popular comedies, or immensely successful comedies, or comedies so familiar that you feel you could flick them off your overcoat like cigarette ash, as being in any way brilliant. They're just good hack work, aren't they? Lucky strikes, triumphant tricks? *Harvey*, my friends, is no trick. As hack work, it wouldn't even be very good: too sloppy in its entrances and exits, too fussed and footloose in its aimless, though inspired, design. What accomplishes *Harvey* and Harvey both is not dexterity, not deviousness, not surprise, not chicanery, but—of all things, of all things—simplicity. That is the play's personal, particular genius.

Look. While Harvey was wandering off on his own, Mr. Stewart was being asked (by various doctors, reasonable as cream) to talk about him. Mr. Stewart was happy, in a cooperative and very thoughtful way, to do so. How had he met him? Well, Harvey, late one night, leaning against a lamppost, had called out to him by name. Hadn't this surprised Mr. Stewart? No, not really. You see, he'd lived a long time in this town, and when you've lived a long time in a town, almost everybody gets to know your name.

Mr. Stewart looked up, having answered the question to his, and I must say to my, satisfaction. I am going to suggest that that is one of the great lines of the American theater and that its greatness stems from its effortlessness, its quiet, its utterly logical escape from the logical. It cannot be faulted, as it could never have been faked. It doesn't depend on a set-up, it's no mere inversion of words. It is an inversion of mind, one man's natural way of thinking about things and accepting them because they fit into his method of grasping reality. There's nothing wrong with it as a means of grasping reality. You just pick the end of a question that strikes you as needing answering, that's all.

The line is perfect and it's not alone. When Mr. Stewart explained that Einstein managed to overcome time and space but that Harvey had managed to overcome time and space and any objections, he (courtesy of Mrs. Chase and her intractably Irish waywardness) had come upon another such. He had also, in those few words, effectively described the way the play works. The play can be as patchy as it likes, it can tread water when it wants, you can raise any objection to it you care to and you can be as right as your wrongheadedness lets you be. Nothing of this will ever matter because Harvey, who just walked through, *has* overcome.

I don't want to go on quoting lines, not even to point out how blissfully superior some of them are. There is, however, one kind of line that acquired a new emphasis in this particular revival and it should be mentioned in order to do full justice to Mr. Stewart. A psychiatrist, probing for a prior association that would explain Mr. Stewart's choice of Harvey as a name for his six-foot crony, asked for the names of his father, his closest childhood playmates, etcetera, etcetera. It turned out—I can feel you're beginning to remember this one—that none of them had been named Harvey. It turned out, in fact, that Mr. Stewart had never known *anyone* named Harvey. "Perhaps," he added reflectively, "that's why I had such hopes for him."

I am not going to tell you that this is Mrs. Chase's best or most characteristic line; it is warm and ironically sentimental and just a bit reminiscent, reminiscent of Saroyan perhaps. But as Mr. Stewart read it, and thought it, and began to use it against what was coming, it took on a very special tone. For the actor was himself neither sentimentalizing the role nor the rabbit, he was not being whimsical or nostalgic or wry or, for God's sake, cute.

He was being serious. Almost everything Mr. Stewart did as the evening gathered its wits together for a climax was intensely attentive, listening, relaxed and waiting for the spheres to speak. He meant his engagement with the human race, with the pretty nurse who kissed him without flustering him, with the people who sold him magazine subscriptions on the telephone, with the doctors' wives he hoped to meet at cocktail parties to which he'd never been invited.

He took his own solution, his pal, his pooka, with no grain of salt and no grain of sugar, just with a complete and open earnestness. He had no shield; prove to him that Harvey was hurting someone or something and he would give him up; Harvey wasn't a defense, he was the human imagination honoring itself, enjoying itself, and then surrendering itself when the hard edge of the world so required. In his uncluttered, unidealized, plain ordinary decency, Mr. Stewart made the play's last act astonishingly moving. (Had Frank Fay been funnier? Who can honestly say now? Perhaps. He was nowhere near so touching.)

Being at the Anta became an occasion during the nights of *Harvey*, an odd sort of occasion for what might have been a routine revival of a familiar play, done for a few weeks to kill time by two stars going gray. The audience had come, delight ready in its eyes, not just to see Helen Hayes (you can see Helen Hayes any week of the year, she works all the time) or just to see Jimmy Stewart (stay home and watch television, he's there) but for the most specific purpose of seeing Miss Hayes and Mr. Stewart *together*.

It was a meeting. People came because they thought it was going to be fun to be in on it. They glued those hopeful eyes to each star with each entrance, mouths open in a beginning smile. They didn't overreact or laugh too soon. They waited for the stars to be as good as they should have been. Then, when they were—and that's a kind of miracle, isn't it?—they expanded with joy. They gave

the theater their satisfaction. The house filled with assent, with
judgment, with a massive gratified relationship. And, because they
had come for and were giving such complete concentration to the
stars, they could be silently surprised by the play.

Not even the standees left before the last rites, including the
curtain call for Harvey, were done. When I got to the parking lot,
there was no one ahead of me.

4

KILROY was not here. Amanda Wingfield was, but not Kilroy.
Blanche DuBois was, but not Kilroy. Kilroy was not here because
Tennessee Williams forgot to invent him. He just named him, and
put the Name on the stage.

So it goes all through the sad and sorry way of *Camino Real,* the
one play of Tennessee Williams that must surely have come from
his college trunk and belonged to the days when a Platonic
idealism—names for things, concepts of things, never the things
themselves—occupied a young man's mind. It is strange how our
early habit of imagining that abstract types exist and actually walk
around persists in us, deep into what is in some respects our
maturity, luring us back now and then into a simple schematic
unreal world where Man and Heart and Truth and The Dreamer
constitute the whole cast of noncharacters.

Camino Real is almost the essence of this sort of thing, a tabula-
tion of its sleepy and limitless and unaffecting possibilities. Don
Quixote—a name again, the character is not there, not Cervantes',
not Williams'—stumbles down the aisle, staff in hand, to go
drowsy and begin to dream. He dreams of the Camino Real, that
place "where there are no birds but wild ones and they are caged
and tamed." It is a police state. The inhabitants, hoping for escape
in a plane called the Fugitivo, are more nearly certain of being
picked up by trashmen, dumped into carts and hauled away. The
inhabitants are indeed Wild Birds, "captive hawks trapped together" as Camille says to Casanova, creatures of extremes now
condemned to their extremes and seeking solace in their common

pain, common exclusion, common dreaming, common despair: Quixote, Camille, Casanova, Lord Byron, Kilroy who won the Golden Gloves, the earringed Baron de Charlus thinking of using chains tonight because he has been so wicked lately, gypsies, cowled monks, a figure listed on the program as A. Ratt. When they have all played out optional scenes together—scenes that do not demand to be played—a hitherto sterile fountain spurts a cleansing water, the advice "Do not pity yourself" is given to one and all, Don Quixote leads the way up a staircase into new light, crying that "The violets in the mountains have broken the rocks!"

It is perfectly possible to play games with this play, thought games, and one is always tempted to do so out of respect and affection for Tennessee Williams. But the understandable impulse to indulge Mr. Williams, to give him this play in gratitude and exchange for all the plays he has given us, should not be permitted to obscure the plain fact that *Camino Real* doesn't happen. The poem doesn't rise. Because no true people are there, no true event takes place, inside us or outside us, a circumstance that couldn't be clearer or more harrowing than in the passionate outlines of Jessica Tandy's performance in the play's revival at the Vivian Beaumont.

Miss Tandy, a fine actress, was Camille. She described herself as "the ghost of a kiss" and she seemed that, with her gray lyric voice pressing steadily upward though always with a little catch in the cords just halfway up the scale. When Miss Tandy heard the offstage motors of the Fugitivo, she summoned up a savage determination to board it, with or without permit, with or without lover, with or without knowledge of where one more journey might take her. She raged the stage down, battering it with her feet, trying to grasp its air with her fists, ready to take the world in her teeth. All the power that was in her came out in her fury, in the clutch of her claws upon shoulders, in her flinging aside all the forces that would say her nay. It was as though she had taken the deepest breath ever recorded, perhaps on a seismograph, and then exhaled sheer will. The effort to attack the moment was spectacular, the skill employed was breathtaking.

And all, all of it, accomplished exactly nothing. For we had no sense of this woman except by the remotest hearsay left over from Dumas, we were not acquainted with a *person* who wished to board an airplane, we knew that the plane itself was not a plane but an idea and that ideas can't be boarded, we knew that we were here only making empty gestures, without human consequence. We could not give ourselves over to the passion of a gummed label, a sticker, a baggage tag.

Later, Jean-Pierre Aumont came to the edge of the apron, shook his harried head, sat with one shoulder hunched forward, let anguish dictate the slant of his head. He had been as good a Casanova as one could wish for in the unfleshed circumstances; as we looked at him now we admired the posture of pain; we were also conscious of the fact that we were looking at a posture and that no one was feeling pain inside it. Emotion was play-acted; it was never communicated.

It could not be, because there was neither bone nor blood at the base of the dream. There was almost, once. Casanova and Camille were sitting at a table; a waiter discreetly moved forward to unfold a screen about them, making them private; they now began a fearful little fuss about something practical, about whether or not his remittance check had come through. For a few seconds the players seemed joined in mutual concern, they were agitated about a specific envelope whose contents might affect them both. Then the moment dissolved, Casanova was walking among shrouds and giant rooster heads, Camille had gone off to—where? We shrugged, turned our attention to the newest but not inevitable Dreamer or Ratt the playwright had plucked from the abstract stockpile, we doggedly went on, perhaps taking some small satisfaction in Sylvia Syms' amusing Gypsy or in the bronzed marble sky Peter Wexler had thrown against the rear wall. But having shrugged now, we couldn't arrange to weep later.

And so with Kilroy. He came on riding the hook of a giant crane—we wanted to ask why, but we suppressed that sort of question—and wearing, over his faded dungarees, the ruby-and-emerald-studded belt that proclaimed him Champion. He was no sooner there than he was transformed by police into Patsy, clown and symbol, with a streamered skirt, an orange wig, and a long red nose that lighted up. When he went under this costume, we didn't miss him. He might just as well have disappeared under it, for all we cared, because we hadn't met him, he was no familiar of ours, one or another disguise would do. Instead of conceiving an identifiable fellow who might thereafter have expanded to become as omnipresent as Kilroy, Mr. Williams had only borrowed him from a wall, and left him chalk.

Would any of this have mattered if the poem did rise, if the fragments we perceived through drifting blue smoke came somehow, suddenly, emphatically together to make a mysterious impact? Perhaps not. But, strangely, *Camino Real* is the least poetic of all of Mr. Williams' plays. When the effort at poetry is left naked and abstract, as it is here, it loses the glint of passing life, of turned light; it becomes bald and even platitudinous. "The most dangerous word in any human tongue is the word for brother"; " 'Used to be' is the past tense, meaning useless"; "I came from a place where the money wasn't legal tender—I mean, it was legal, but it wasn't tender"; "That is the real—not the royal—truth"; and so on. All of these are arbitrary constructs, unevocative, without grace or bite or teasing humor. They simply cannot stand beside the quotations from various other of Mr. Williams' plays that had been sprinkled over the revival program, though even these were not the best of Williams, having apparently been chosen by the same hand that had elected to remount *Camino Real*. For Williams, you must go to your memories, which will take you quickly to the texts. This is how a creature named Blanche Du-Bois talks, coming home late with an escort, coy and schoolteacherish and yearning and terrible:

> Eureka! Honey, you open the door while I take a last look at the sky. I'm looking for the Pleiades, the Seven Sisters, but these girls are not out tonight. Oh, yes they are, there they are! God bless them! All in a bunch going home from their little bridge party. . . . Y'get the door open? Good boy! . . . Honey, it wasn't the kiss I objected to. I liked the kiss very much. It was the other little—familiarity—that I—felt obliged to—discourage. . . . I didn't resent it! Not a bit in the world! In fact, I was somewhat flattered that you—desired me! But, honey, you know as well as I do that a single girl, a girl alone in the world, has got to keep a firm hold on her emotions or she'll be lost!

There are a great many "heart" images in *Camino Real*. But what breaks *my* heart is the painful playfulness of "Good boy!" in the middle of that speech, or the arch and yet not altogether unimaginative image of the Seven Sisters going home from their little bridge party. Listening to the false ladylike discretion of a fading woman in a shabby doorway, so entirely present that you can feel her weight against the doorframe, you know that a woman once talked like that. It is the difference between life and thought, between creation and speculation, and I would, at this point, rather see Mr. Williams honored than indulged, rather have him encouraged to go back to the mining of men and women which is no doubt harder to do but which stands solid as rock alongside the vapors, the drifting insubstantial Naming, of *Camino Real.*

5

O ADMIRABLE *Front Page!*

Plays that perfectly represent their own times never have to worry about what time it is. I don't mean the time that *The Front Page* is ostensibly about, those early twenties in a slightly post-tintype Chicago when newspaper men still wore salt-and-pepper suits and straw boaters and played "By the Light of the Silvery Moon" on soft banjos. All of that had been devoutly, sweetly reconstructed for the revival of the play at the Ethel Barrymore, forty-one years after it was written. The light bulbs not only had no shades on them, their quivering filaments were exposed. Under the light bulbs, the sport shoes were brown and white, the louvred blinds were pre-Venetian, the skirts were undecided about whether to grip the knees or allow them their soon-to-be-Charlestoning freedom. Loving hands had been at work giving a dingy press room and its lively amoral denizens the innocence of the Bobbsey Twins at their favorite summer camp; the cigarette-littered atmosphere had so much of springtime about it that you felt everyone visible had begun smoking at five.

But it wasn't this sort of fidelity that made the play such a treasure or the occasion so enchanting. *The Front Page* isn't really faithful to the early twenties or the later twenties or to anything in particular. Its authors, Ben Hecht and Charles MacArthur, admitted that at the time. Having begun to write a hard-headed exposé of what hard-hearted newspaperdom was really like, they wound up writing a "romantic and rather doting tale" of all the larcenous reporters they'd loved. What had begun as vitriol turned effortlessly into a valentine (their word for it) and all the "inequities, double-dealings, chicaneries and immoralities" which constituted the clattering plot coalesced into an ambiance called The Good Old Days. They knew they were indicting no one when they were having such uncontrollable fun.

What the play actually represents is not historical time but playwriting time, which is a kind of Evening Saving Time and has—ever so often—saved an evening. This is the kind of playwriting that was thought to be a good kind of playwriting when the playwrights first sat down to write the play, and because the play lives right smack up to its aspirations and meets all of its own demands, it is beautiful. Broad farce, gamy farce, hollering farce, exquisitely mechanized farce, and therefore beautiful.

A play was held to be something of a machine in those days, something that could be intelligibly put together and made to serve a specific function. It wasn't a machine for making money or scoring points or demonstrating the efficiency of the authors, though it might in passing (one hoped) do those things too. It was a machine for surprising and delighting the audience, regularly, logically, insanely, but accountably. A play was like a watch that laughed.

Just notice two tiny bits of technique in the making of this sunny, heartless, unaged marvel. We're in the second act. We've heard about Walter Burns, the suavely ruthless managing editor, for some time. But we haven't met him. We know that he is scheming to make certain that Hildy Johnson, his ace reporter, never leaves him for another job or for the girl of his dreams. We *have* met Hildy, have met the girl, have met the murderer who has broken jail on the eve of his hanging, have met the prostitute who is helping Hildy to keep the murderer out of the hands of the police.

In the process of helping, now, the prostitute not only takes on a roomful of savage reporters, cracking a chair over their heads, but, in a last desperate distracting gesture, leaps suicidally from a window to the prison courtyard far below. The stunned reporters rush to the window, guilty, panic-stricken, and knowing that there's a story in it. Reports are shouted up from the courtyard, the girl is hurt but not dead, the reporters curve baying out of the room—terrified and exhilarated—like the last crackling snap of a whip. Walter Burns passes them on his way in.

That's all, and it is immaculate. Walter Burns has been so built up that finding him an adequate entrance is next to impossible. He can't just come on and declare himself. Furthermore, he's two of a kind. He's mean and he's funny. He's got to walk into a tough situation in order to be brutally nonchalant, which is what we think is funny about him. The machinery has not only given him and the play the right punctuation, the change of pace that refreshes even as it moves on. It has also covered him, kept him from being obvious while exploiting the one most obvious thing about him. You might say that the machinery has covered *itself*, perfectly squared itself. We are delighted to have the man on, we are delighted to have him on at this time, we are aware that it is sleight-of-hand that has got him on, and we are as delighted by the sleight-of-hand as by the man.

One other instance. The murderer is finally located, stashed away in a rolltop desk. Hildy and Walter Burns have stashed him there, hoping to spirit him away from the other reporters. Burns has sent a loyal thug into the streets to gather up men, any old men he can find, to lug the desk away. But it's too late. The others—sheriff, mayor, reporters, bit players—have all caught on; they are now standing with drawn guns facing the desk, roaring at the criminal to come out. Suspense is up, the countdown is on, the smog of the room is overheated with expectation. Directly into the melee, cleaving it with a bursting open of doors, at last comes the thug. He has two Boy Scouts in tow. (In the revival he had two Boy Scouts in tow; the script specifies one boy in short pants, a sailor and a seedy old Trader Horn type. No matter, same principle.)

Conceivably this entrance drew the new production's biggest laugh; there were a great many big laughs, so it's a bit hard to say. It was over in a few seconds. The intruders were hustled right out again, doors slammed, guns raised. But let's pay attention to what has happened. The play is, from first to last, a meticulously careful combination of vigorous melodrama and cynical comedy. It must take great pains at all times never to separate the styles; they've got to feed each other, and on each other. *If* the flushing out of the criminal were to be followed straight through as suspense stuff, the tones might fall apart. We rather like the criminal, feel somewhat sorry for him already, his capture as such isn't going to cheer us any. We could be riding for a letdown, a collapse of high spirits. And so the high spirits are hurled right into the center of the storm (at the count of "two" from the gunmen, in fact), ridiculing the capture before we have time to grasp it seriously, reducing the melodrama to the farce that all melodrama is. To get an enormous laugh when things are at their toughest requires enormous skill. In *The Front Page* that skill is on tap from first to last, proud of itself, almost showing off.

6

I THINK we must take some pains to develop a nostalgia for the present.

In 1969 the old Burns Mantle yearbooks celebrated their fiftieth anniversary. Going back over all forty-nine earlier volumes in the Best Play series—and I have now reread all forty-nine descriptions of seasons past, if not all four hundred and ninety shining plays—is illuminating in at least one way. The seasons we admire most are those we never saw.

Pick up almost any volume between 1919 and 1930 and you will be staggered not perhaps by the absolute quality of the plays selected, but by a feeling of theatrical robustness that seems to leap from the Table of Contents page. The New York theater had almost too much energy. In 1921 alone it managed to produce 196 plays, *Anna Christie*, *A Bill of Divorcement*, *Dulcy*, *He Who Gets Slapped*, and *The Circle* among them.

How do you think you'd have felt about being in on a season that led off with *What Price Glory?*, *They Knew What They Wanted*, and *Desire Under the Elms*, and found time thereafter for Philip Barry's first play? There's a vigor in those first three titles that may simply come from the sound of the words (you need only hear the phrase "What Price Glory?" to imagine an uproar in the playhouse) or that may suggest to us the exuberant freedoms that were being born, willy-nilly, in 1924, but a vigor it is and its bristle is contagious.

What of a season that included *Broadway*, *Chicago*, *The Constant Wife*, *The Play's the Thing*, *The Road to Rome*, *The Silver Cord*, and *Cradle Song?* Doesn't that sound a tumble of treasures—of legends, even? *The Silver Cord*, after all, was definitive with us, a watershed play that meant mother-love would never be the same again while Freud would become a casual playgoing companion.

But notice that, for all its "modernity" and its introspection, *The Silver Cord* comes directly alongside a couple of blockbusting melodramas, *Broadway* and *Chicago*, with hoofers and gangsters and acquitted murderesses everywhere. The very existence of such melodrama cheers us as we look back on it. Too bad we were born so late, too bad we're no longer innocent enough to enjoy unabashed melodrama's special pleasures. Melodrama could be even more unabashed than *Broadway* and *Chicago* and still find a place in Burns Mantle's early lists: think of *On Trial*, *Seven Keys to Baldpate*, *The Green Goddess*, and *The Bad Man*. Editing the series, Mr. Mantle could be charmingly unruffled in dealing with such plays. Making no particular claim for literary merit, not even supposing the issue entirely relevant, he could drop something like Channing Pollock's *The Sign on the Door* into the hallowed ten with the offhand remark that it was to be "accepted as the most stirring of the season's melodramas." "Stirring" is the evocative word here. As late as 1926, the *Silver Cord–Chicago* year, playgoers could go to the theater to be both harried *and* stirred. Our consciences hadn't narrowed yet, we hadn't thrown out the lively in our search for the literary, there was a range to what was going on on Broadway that still seems attractively animated. The theater had an appetite.

I'll mention one more season and then stop tormenting you. The season that began in 1927 included *Strange Interlude*, *The Royal Family*, *Burlesque*, *Coquette*, *Porgy*, *Paris Bound*, John Galsworthy's *Escape* (I mention the author because I think you may have forgotten that one), and *The Plough and the Stars*. The fact of the matter is that for quite a long while in the twenties Mr. Mantle had such an embarrassment of apparent riches on his hands when he came to selection time that he was unable to fit either *Saint Joan* or *Juno and the Paycock* into his lists. We really don't seem to be faced with such hard choices any more.

As *I* run my finger down the Burns Mantle years the very type

seems to dance until—well, about 1930–31. There my hand hesitates a little, I go back to see if I have really read aright, my heart
grows a shade heavy. Glamor and yearning seem suddenly to have
dimmed, as though some of the light bulbs in the marquee had
burnt out and not been replaced. A creative pressure has weak-
ened; I find myself less jealous. True, there were plays that are still
remembered: *Elizabeth the Queen, Once in a Lifetime, The Bar-
retts of Wimpole Street.* There is even a single melodrama, just for
old time's sake, a yellow-journalism exposé called *Five Star Final.*
Add a big showpiece, *Grand Hotel.* But in and around these still
teasing titles on the Ten Best list are softer, less assertive inclu-
sions: *Alison's House, As Husbands Go, Overture.* What, in
heaven's name, can *Overture* have been? During the following
season, and in spite of *Mourning Becomes Electra,* there are more:
Another Language, The Devil Passes, Cynara. Not bad plays—just
quieter ones, tamer ones. The theater had been jumping up and
down. In the two seasons 1930–32 it sat down and sighed, rather.

Historically speaking, things had been happening to it. The
matter can be explained, or explained away, rationally, objectively.
A depression had happened. Fewer theaters were open, fewer plays
being produced. Talking pictures had happened. A great many
stars who had formerly kept vehicles alive on the strength of their
personal followings had gone to speak in Hollywood. Worse,
many, many playwrights had gone, in dire need of the money
available there. A part of the playwriting range had been usurped
by Hollywood; certainly melodrama, and *Grand Hotel* show-
pieces, were now the property of Warner Brothers and MGM.
The theater lost some crackle because a soundtrack could crackle
louder. It became more reflective, having little else to do. And it
had, along with the country, lost the brash confidence that had
sustained it joyfully, jazzily, since the end of World War I. The
go-getting American of the twenties was dead, killed by what he
had got. The go-getting theater of the twenties, the theater of
appetite and ardor, of course had to leave the scene with him.

Ah, yes. Ah, yes. If that were all. But it wasn't all, not really.
Something else had intervened to halt my urgent finger and delay
my racing heart. In 1931 or 1932 nostalgia had lost its force, I
realized with a start, because it was approximately at that time that
I began seeing the plays.

This sounds as though I were going to say that the theater's magic is essentially spurious and cannot survive direct acquaintance, that it only functions by hearsay or at discreet distances. I am going to try to say something else, though of course we must take a moment to admit that *some* of the yearning we all feel for glories past is mightily helped along by our imaginations. I had always loved George S. Kaufman's *The Butter and Egg Man* until I saw it off-Broadway not long ago. There are funny things in it, but not enough of them to warrant continuing the affair. I don't know what *What Price Glory?* would look like now. I have an idea that I'd like to see it—in fact, I have an idea that I'd like to see it in a repertory house with Moses Gunn and Godfrey Cambridge in the principal roles—but I haven't quite had the nerve to take it down off the shelf for a many-years-after reading. It might bite me. Has anyone seen *Elizabeth the Queen* lately? Don't.

Some few plays have kept their glow, some will keep it. *Anna Christie* will be done again, whether *Strange Interlude* is or not. *The Front Page* still has good skin tone. *The Constant Wife* has been successfully revived, as I'm sure *The Circle* could be. *The Plough and the Stars* has by no means vanished—no more than the slighted *Juno and the Paycock* has—and *Liliom* and *Saint Joan* do seem to be with us. Occasionally, with a sufficiently sensitive production, a work felt to be lost can be made to display its special virtues, as the A.P.A.'s tender production of *The Show-Off*—one of the Ten Best Plays of 1923–24—emphatically demonstrated. With skill and patience, the colors of a time can be renewed.

But most will not be. We know that we must surrender the halos that hover, ever so faintly now, over a thousand plays we never saw. The age did not belong to Pericles, or to Elizabeth the Queen. It belonged to Harding and Coolidge and to the playwrights they begat. All right. We can stifle our sniffles and become cagier about the unremembered memories we revere.

But what about the thousand plays we actually saw? Need we be so very, very cagey about them?

We are cagier about them. We are *sure* they are destined for oblivion, certain they represent a falling-off from some vague earlier excellence, ever ready to proclaim the new season we have just sat through as "undoubtedly the worst within the memory of living man." Why are we so sure?

Of course our conviction is part common sense: Pericles and his writers didn't put in an appearance in 1931, or 1969 either. We live, generally speaking, in a time of second-rank theater, theater at less than masterpiece heat, and we know it. Truly great periods come infrequently and it just hasn't been our luck to have stumbled at birth into one of them. Our conviction is also, no doubt, part self-protection. It is always safest to say that the plays one is seeing aren't masterpieces, or aren't even likely to be recognized by the children we are presumably educating. (My children occasionally come to me with the news that they have just discovered a fascinating piece of material on television. As likely as not, they have just come upon an old movie version of *Arsenic and Old Lace*, or *The Petrified Forest*. They are invariably surprised to realize that I know the material and that it once had something to do with that alien and vanishing rumor, the theater.) One doesn't like to be caught overpraising something that falls to dust in a year or two, and overpraise can be avoided by maintaining a sufficiently skeptical attitude toward everything that happens between seven-thirty and ten on a postmidcentury evening. You can't go wrong saying no. Ninety-nine times out of a hundred no is prophetic.

But there is at least one more factor, I think, to be taken into account in accounting for the diminished enthusiasm we feel for the immediate. I started to say a few paragraphs ago that something of the tarnished luster that attaches to everything *I* saw beginning about 1931 or 1932 has less to do with the plays I saw than it has to do with me. I play a part in the changed attitude, the refusal to wax nostalgic, the reluctance to praise (and not because I happened to become a reviewer either; it is nothing so personal nor so accidental as that). The thing is, I belong to the play, I am in and of it because I happened to be there when it spoke, I participate in it directly—and nothing that I belong to or have participated in can ever be regarded as quite perfect.

You see, all of us bring *ourselves* into the act of judging any play we actually see and when we do we must necessarily be more severe. This play is our play because we literally helped to make it: sitting in the theater, we sent a response up to the actors and author, which means that we played a vital part in the shape it took, we played what was actually a determining part in its continued existence. The actors heard our laughter or silence, our applause or surly departures. Because of the way we behaved in the theater, they altered some of what they did. So, at least in his next play, did the author. We were more than the author's contemporaries. We lived as his collaborators.

Being on such intimate terms with the author, we were much more aware of him than we can ever hope to be, say, of Shakespeare. Above all, as play-watchers we are tremendously aware of possible danger, of the risk that the play may very well fall apart before it comes together, we can sense the holes in it. We are intensely aware of potential shortcomings because the author is there before us, alive, imperfect, vulnerable, never secure. He is a duplicate of each of us. We were born to the same lawns, grew up in the same apartment buildings, studied under the same teachers, went roller skating on the same sidewalks, stole into the same movies, suffered the same politicians, endured the same war (whichever it may have been), for all practical purposes married the same girl, and all had the same children. We know that playwright; we can check the truth of the report he is giving us. Indeed, we are in a contest with him—for truth. Has he got that inflection exactly right, has he misremembered the August weather of our adolescence, has he found out how we feel and shown it back to us exactly? Has he honored our self-knowledge, or is he in the business of making fakes? We do more than check. We challenge upon the instant, supposing a false note to have been sounded. Some notes are bound to be false. We won't miss a one of them. This play, however fine, however entertaining, however true, is honeycombed with minute error—or at least it may be. It may relax its grip upon exactness if we do not watch it with extremely critical eyes. We assume that it is not perfect and we spend a good bit of our time proving ourselves right.

There is nothing despicable in this, not even really anything captious in it. It is necessary and inevitable. A play is not only about a contest, it always *is* a contest between author and audience. Truth-seeking needs checks and balances, even delight needs a devil's advocate. Indeed, without just this sort of contention there would be no excitement in theater at all. Excitement is the result of risk, it comes of trying out the new knowing that the new may crash in flames, it thrives on the suspense of waiting to see whether this rather reckless dramatist will get away with all the chances he is taking. Opening nights are always cliffhangers. Who will surrender—the audience, or the poor fellow who's dared to put his eyesight on the line? At a good play there is a delicious moment when the audience finally gives in. At a bad play there is a shame-faced moment when the author does. Not to have this uncertainty would be fatal to the fun of theatergoing. Sitting only through secure plays, in which the worst could not possibly happen, would be like seeing *Macbeth* five times a week for the rest of our natural lives.

Awareness that the project before us, in which we are directly and vitally engaged, may very well be defective—will in all probability be to some degree defective—is perfectly natural in an audience when the audience is dealing with the new. It is the only responsible attitude an audience can take.

But it does destroy nostalgia, or whatever nostalgia might be called if it were ever applied to the here, now, and nervous. The apprehensively critical frame of mind that is essential to any experience of the immediate takes one color out of the spectrum. Rosiness, I suppose. A degree of glamor is forsworn, sentiment is suppressed for fear of sentimentality, we do not allow ourselves the luxury of loving unequivocally. We are hedgers, and it hurts a little. We do not take *all* of the pleasure we might take if our consciences were altogether clear.

Can we take a little more, can we permit ourselves to kick our heels *slightly* higher when we like something without confusing ourselves about what is actually there, without corrupting the standards we need to get home by? I would like to think so, if only to get us all past that faintly querulous tone that accompanies the enthusiasms we have. So often we apologize, and even temper an enthusiasm we actually feel, for fear of being caught out enjoying the ephemeral—as though the ephemeral weren't something that might be enjoyed. All too often we preface our praise with a waiver: "Of course, it's nothing, I know that," "Well, it's only trivia," "I suppose a lot of people aren't going to like it, but—" *But* constructions are commonplace enough in the theater to have become a joke; when we cannot do better, we cushion our praise of a play with an indictment of the season as a whole. With a little sigh of relaxation, Burns Mantle called the 1922–23 season "the first season in a generation not to have been described as the 'worst in years.' " The phrase is familiar to us, the exception to it is not.

Could we try it *this* way? Face the fact that most of what we see is certainly ephemeral. (The Ten Best Plays of 1941–42, to move up a little, were *In Time to Come, The Moon Is Down, Junior Miss, Candle in the Wind, Letters to Lucerne, Jason, Angel Street, Uncle Harry, Hope for a Harvest*, and *Blithe Spirit*.) Then consider that we are ephemeral too, and that if a man is going to have to dance with the girl he came with, he might as well take pleasure in the dance.

It is good to be strict where matters of quality are at stake. It is good to try to sharpen standards over those of a generation ago and to pass on to the next generation a select body of work for it to be mean about. But it is also good to exhale now and again, to embrace what is available because it and only it is available. You can put your arms around a girl you know to be less than perfect. In fact, you'd better.

Can we restore a little color to our pleasures by telling ourselves that they *are* our pleasures, that neither they nor we will happen this way again, that no matter how ill-made we think them they are in fact the fit for us, that a star danced and both of us were born? After all, sometime, somewhere, someone will be nostalgic about *A Streetcar Named Desire* and *The Waltz of the Toreadors* and *The Collection* and *Who's Afraid of Virginia Woolf?* and *The Odd Couple* and *America Hurrah*, wishing they'd been there on opening nights. Why not get the jump on them?

To speak for myself, I've decided to try. I know that *The Rose Tattoo* has faults. I'm sure the author thinks I've gone on endlessly about them. No matter. It's a nice thing, and I'm glad I was in New York to see Maureen Stapleton and Eli Wallach play it. I know that *The Tiger and the Typists* is slight. I would not have been happier if it had been heavier. I saw a lost Chekhov play salvaged (*A Country Scandal*); I am determined to be grateful. Joseph Chaikin and Jean-Claude van Itallie have not yet perfected their work at The Open Theater. It may in the end come to very little. I'm going to keep certain fragments of *The Serpent* tucked away in my head and take them out now and then for my remembered pleasure anyway. I'm happy to have heard George C.

Scott say, "I want to do it all over again" in *Plaza Suite*. It's not "Hey, Flagg, wait for baby!" perhaps; but it's a good line.

I could go on. I won't. Those are random choices and I'm not going to add to them because adding would make a list and making a list always seems to close the books. I suppose I'm trying to say that as long as the books are open, and our eyes are open, our arms might as well be open too. Think severely, as all living men must. But thank God and Tennessee Williams and Edward Albee and Jean Anouilh and Harold Pinter and Murray Schisgal between thoughts.

Dancing With the Girl
You Came With

I

WHILE the theater continues to try on new skins, it also continues to wear an old one. The old skin is partly composed of what is called commercial theater, not necessarily because it has only money in view but because it is produced in a regulation manner in Broadway houses for Broadway audiences. Every once in a while it displays an unexpected vitality, grinning rather shamelessly over its undestroyed power to please. The old skin can be seen too, in transition, sometimes on Broadway and sometimes off, absorbing colorations that are new—or are borrowed from the new—into textures that are substantially familiar. Few hard lines are drawn; you can see the theater that is coming and the theater that is going in the same piece of work quite often.

Paul Zindel's *The Effect of Gamma Rays on Man-in-the-Moon Marigolds*, for instance, sounded—when it announced its off-Broadway opening—as though it belonged to a school as far out as Sam Shepard's. Nearly every reviewer, once he'd seen it, remarked that what it really resembled was the early work of Tennessee Williams. Actually, it put out tendrils touching both; it was also,

very firmly and without worrying about its position in the scheme
of things, its own play.

When I think of it now, I think of three things, not one of them
the title (the title, by the way, made perfect sense and you remembered it readily once you had seen the play). The first was the
sound, the sheer weighted sound, of a load of old newspapers being
dumped from a balcony landing. Sada Thompson, slatternly
mother of two and savior of none, was at her housecleaning again,
which meant that she was picking up the accumulated refuse of
her life and hurling it to another, though no better, spot. The
bundle came down like a dead heart; the force of the drop was
shattering. And familiar. You seemed to have heard it before.

The second memory that keeps coming back is the tactile naked
terror with which Miss Thompson, at midnight during a thunder-
storm, brushed a prying flashlight away from her face. Her older
daughter had long ago had a breakdown, for very good reasons,
and was now desperately fearful of lightning; Miss Thompson had
crawled out of bed to console her, a motherly duty she was perfectly willing to perform. But in the dark the daughter had discovered a flashlight and she was using it to find the face that would
reassure her. Suddenly, to Miss Thompson, the probing, isolating,
totally revealing finger of light became a spider seeking out the
seams of failure in her face; without warning she was flailing at it,
attacking it as though the truth itself were something to be killed.

The moment continued, but in another vein altogether, arriving
at one of the most evocative conjunctions of performing, staging,
and writing that we have had in the theater, on Broadway or off,
in some years past. Miss Thompson was forced to suppress her
own terrors in order to help ease those of her daughter. To do it
she passed from her sharp alarm and irritation to making girlish
funny faces, conjuring up the child she once had been and the
way, perhaps, she once had made her father laugh.

From that she passed to telling stories of her father, of his vegetable wagon that she had sometimes ridden through the streets, of
the rhythmic cries he'd made to advertise his wares, of the sing-
song warmth that so long ago had promised her a golden life. As
she talked, the daughter became calm, pleased, half drugged with
delight, so much so that at last the two of them were musically

whispering "Apples—pears—cu*cum*bers!" into the night while the flashlight swung as lazily as the clapper of an old bell. The image was morose and singularly charming; it was also essential to the cruel body of the play.

The third thing I cannot shake from my head is the play's ending, a coming together of harshness and hope that exactly summarized, without preachment of any sort, the meanings Mr. Zindel wished his compressed and honest little play to carry. The brief lyricism of the wagon-bell-at-midnight passage was necessary if we were to endure, and understand, the venom that overtook Miss Thompson in her relationship with a younger daughter.

This daughter, played plainly and plaintively and very well indeed by Pamela Payton-Wright, was as bright as she was rumpled. We first met her alone, idly stroking a pet rabbit, staring at her hand, mouthing thoughts to herself about what the universe had had to go through—the tongues of fire, the explosions of suns—to produce her own five fingers. A knobby-kneed schoolchild with thin blond hair and a dress that bunched up in the back, she had a gift for scientific speculation; she was, at the moment, engaged in growing and studying marigolds that had been exposed to radiation and she might just possibly win a competition her teacher had urged her to enter at school. Precisely because she was intelligent, because others were interested in her, because some sort of future might open itself to her, her mother could not abide her. "I hate the world," Miss Thompson seethed as she stared at all the dreams that had emptied out before her. No one else was going to find it fascinating. Miss Payton-Wright was not even going to go to school all that often.

When a teacher phoned to ask why the child was not at school, Miss Thompson descended a cluttered staircase in a shapeless robe—toweling with the nap all gone—that contained both her despair and her cigarettes. She snatched up the ringing instrument with such brisk indifference that you knew she could only parody conversation, never truly enter it. Her eyes were wide, darting, expectant: they expected insult. Her body moved restlessly beneath the robe: it was a fencer's body, wary of attack and ready for evasion or assault. The woman was ordinary, recognizable and half mad.

On the phone, she was four or five persons at once. She was a plain bully: she would keep her daughter home when she pleased. She was a plausible, painful flirt: the teacher would either respond to her coy gestures or get himself classified a fag. She was all motherly concern: she cared so much for her children's studies that she "provided them with 75-watt light bulbs right there at their desks." Her eyes searched the room for the nonexistent desks as she prattled on: the room was almost nothing but empty cartons and sagging bureaus; she saw the desks.

She saw, when she wished, the carefree creature she might have become; she had, after all, been elected "Best dancer of the class of nineteen-bootle-de-doo." (No one alive could have managed this fey copout nearly as well as Miss Thompson.) She saw the husband who'd first got a divorce and then a coronary ("He deserved it," she parenthesized, swiftly, meanly). She saw her older daughter, tight sweater unbuttoned enticingly, turning into a fierce repetition of herself. She saw where they all were now, all except the gifted one. Their only source of income was a "fifty-dollar-a-week corpse," an abandoned crone for whom they cared, without caring. She saw "zero" wrapping its arms around her, and she repeated the word in a run-on babble that sounded like steam bubbling up from a lava bed. She was greedy, cynical, jealous, clever, irresponsible, vicious, and lost.

In the play's last sequence we were permitted to hear the schoolgirl's shy, halting, but determined brief lecture on the effects of radiation. Displaying her flowers in the high-school contest—some of them blighted, some richer through mutation, all the product of those first exploding suns—she voiced, tremulously but insistently, her own stubborn confidence that "man will some day thank God for the strange and beautiful energy of the atom."

That was half of the final stage image. The other half was of Miss Thompson, near mindless now, endlessly folding napkins for a tearoom she would never open, face to face with the half-paralyzed crone, silently watched by that other, older, sick and sensual daughter.

The play was thus framed. The mother was the wrong and right mother for these children, as the children were wrong and right sisters to each other. They all hurt one another simply by existing; the damage could never be repaired. But they constituted the situation as given, the human mutations thrown off; there was no dodging the gamma rays, there was only disaster for some and double blooms for some others.

The ending didn't press the point. It just expanded to it, and bitterly—but gently—left the matter there. The play itself was one of the lucky blooms; it survived and was beautiful. With it, Mr. Zindel became one of our most promising new writers. In it, Sada Thompson called clear attention—perhaps more emphatically than ever before—to the fact that she is one of the American theater's finest actresses.

2

Butterflies Are Free was an enormously entertaining light comedy which could always be called a commercial manufacture if you were persuaded that every time you enjoyed yourself in the theater someone was playing a dirty trick on you, but it could also be called something more interesting, and I'd like to take a moment to go into that.

There was a striking and exact sense in which it could be called a *stage* play, a *stage* comedy, an evening whose effects were very much *stage* effects. I'll have to wind around to why this was so.

The curtain went up on a delightfully improvised attic apartment—the bed, for instance, was some eight feet off the floor, just under the browning skylight, and could only be reached by a ladder without railings to crawl in by—and we learned that it had only recently been taken over by a young would-be musician, Keir Dullea. (One of the curious things about this enterprise was that the one song with which Mr. Dullea favored us was exactly the pretty good, just-about-possible song that a conceivably talented but still uncertain composer might really have written.)

He'd been there a month, eating his dinners off a wooden slab that could be slapped down over the bathtub, finding his freedom among the photos and posters that overlapped on the walls under the Tiffany lamp hung too high to do a reader much good. He had another month to go before his possessive mother would come to reclaim him or let him go forever. They'd arranged a two-month pact: he was out from under her eternally managing solicitude for just that long. He talked to her on the telephone, though, with excruciating patience, as he chafed and fidgeted, standing before the bureau that blocked the doorway—the locked doorway—to the apartment just beyond.

Now naturally as soon as we saw that blocked-locked doorway we knew that it was going to be unblocked and unlocked. A girl was going to come through it. We hadn't been seeing *The Seven Year Itch* and all its uncles, cousins, and aunts these many, many years for nothing. A girl did come through it, the girl of that particular theatrical year, Blythe Danner. Blond, leggily graceful in a random and wandering way, with a suspicious nose that seemed permanently aloft to make an isosceles triangle with the wry corners of her mouth, she was quickly everywhere and into everything. A new tenant herself, she had several thousand light bulbs but no coffee. She was a divorcee at nineteen, having been married for six days to a chap named Jack. Since her own name was Jill, she was forced to shudder prettily at her own utter thoughtlessness. She was a shallow, callow creature, possibly the shallow, callow creature of your better dreams, and she'd really meant to go to college (UCLA) but couldn't find a parking place.

The boy and girl rattled on, making acquaintance and making jokes, and you understood and accepted the kind of play you were listening to provided it could finally manage to be as funny as *Barefoot in the Park*. Except perhaps for one thing. The boy didn't ever seem to look precisely at the girl. Then, in the middle of the idle rush and prattle, while the girl was rather snootily remarking on the cigarette ashes he'd scattered on a table and he was asking, "Hey, did you move the ashtray?", she pointed out that of course she'd moved it, what was the matter with him, was he blind or something, and he said yes.

Yes. Without a pause or a skipped beat. Without inflection. No emotion attached to it. He was still smiling his customary smile and waiting for the next step in the conversation.

The stage stopped dead. The air emptied out of the auditorium. A single unstressed word and all our activities fell silent. We'd still been active, you see, in the way we'd been active before we came into the theater: our heads were full of today and yesterday and dinner and good gags tonight we might be able to repeat tomorrow. We weren't committed to anything new, to a change of attitude or altitude, a temporarily rearranged experience. It hadn't really seemed as though those two conventional kids on stage were, either. Suddenly we were all still, extraordinarily still. The girl had been halted, the boy was waiting, we did not move a muscle or dare shift the programs on our laps.

The theater had happened here, the stage had reached out and put a thumb down on us. We were now related to a play in a specifically theatrical way because a playwright—a careful and cunning and accomplished playwright named Leonard Gershe—had found a casually adroit way to snap all his partygoers awake, spectators and boy and girl alike, and pull them together into a shared breath.

The moment was extraordinary not because it cropped up in an unpretentious popular comedy but because it so rarely happens in the theater nowadays that we have almost forgotten what it feels like. We are inundated with plays that promise theatrical effects. We are dizzy from strobe lights and headachey from amplification and weighed down by the masses of revolving and dissolving and forward-leaping scenery which confront us. Yet all of these things constitute stage dressing, not a stage effect. They're expensive and overwhelming but they don't happen. This occurred. It couldn't have occurred in the same way at a movie, either, because at a movie the boy and girl wouldn't have been there to join our pause. In very modest circumstances, at the not very big Booth Theater, a reaching out and locking in took place in a matter of seconds, reminding you of why the Booth is called a Theater.

I should add two things about the moment before going on. It was not a sentimental moment. There was no pitch in it, its suddenness had nothing to do with a catch of emotion. The boy was perfectly tough about himself, his statement was only a statement of fact, in a minute he was going to be complaining that no dirty books are published in braille and in ten minutes he was going to be up in bed with that girl. The play *was* designed for some sentiment and would eventually become quite touching; right now it was doing its work fairly and sparely. The moment was made out of the deft movement of the playwright's fingers, nothing more.

And, very strangely, the effect was not made out of surprise either. The disclosure came very early in the play. Chances are most audiences had heard of it before they went to the box office. It you hadn't heard of it before you went to the box office, you were very likely apt to guess at the boy's blindness before it was announced, as I had. Knowing didn't alter the peculiar character of the sudden silence, the halt of habit and the shift of where-am-I gears. The whole thing came about, if there's any way of saying how it came about, by speaking a certain few words at a certain right moment in an auditorium where people were listening just attentively enough to be poleaxed into total attention. Crazy, but there it is.

Well, the play went on knowing what it was about, planning its strong laughs and paving the way for its near tears by shrewdly moving its little hometruths into place one hometruth at a time. It was a stylization, one of the many brands of stylization open to the theater at any given time. When Eileen Heckart, as the mother who came to claim her overprotected chick a whole month too soon, walked in to find the lovers scarcely dressed from their Adam-and-Eve idyll beneath the skylight (complete with apple), she was poised, pained, and headed straight for the point. Every time she opened her mournful mouth she was winding up for a haymaker. You knew that, you expected it, you delighted in it. Miss Heckart could say as little as "Oh, Jill," turning "Jill" into a three-syllable knifing done under cover of a cease-fire, and rock the house with it. Horrendous mothers are not that funny each time out in life. This was the stylization that said they ought to be if they are going to be around at all, and Miss Heckart offered the controlled statement superbly.

Mr. Dullea was just fine behind his permanently frosted smile, only hinting at the panic that might overtake him if he weren't so determined to be manly. Miss Danner was enchanting, in part because she was decently honest about her girl (the girl was constantly leaving all her men all too soon because she was terrified of staying long enough to discover how it felt to be left), partly because she moved like a trained fighter given the dream run of the prize ring.

Butterflies Are Free broke no new ground of any sort, it was the kind of domestic pleasantry we ought to have five or six times a season just for fun (and don't have), it had been honed to a practical perfection (nod to director Milton Katselas) that made you

distrust it a little simply because airtightness is proverbially suspect, it was engaging and warm and entertaining on purpose. It
had, perhaps, no loftier intention than keeping you from committing suicide in the lobby (it is strange there aren't more suicides
given the *real* run-of-the-mill of what we see), but it had something indispensable to theater if there is going to be any theater,
and that is a working knowledge of what makes a play play.

I'm making too much of it. But there's been too little play
lately.

3

1776 was, quite properly, the most independent new musical in
years. Look at what it was up to. It wouldn't budge on that title,
which could not be said to have a box-office ring to it. It really was
about the American Revolution, seriously, playfully, plainly, pre-
posterously. Wigs and all. In addition to having no title and no
stars, it hadn't got a chorus line. In fact, it hadn't even got an
intermission. And it was just dandy.

Just dandy precisely because it had a mind of its own. It would
not do things anybody else's way, even if everybody else had
always been right, and for a while you naturally thought it was
going to be just too young and green and naïve—rather like the
country that was being hatched between songs—for the sophisticated commerce of Broadway. Wasn't it going to fall into pag-
eantry, or patriotism, or something absolutely awful?

After all, there was John Adams again (William Daniels, fussed
as a partridge that had just been shot at), scowling and scuffing his
shoes and baiting everybody who wasn't from Massachusetts and
telling his wife she was pigeontoed when he had time for tenderer
matters. And Ben Franklin (Howard Da Silva, so happy with his
own jokes that he had to mop himself with a handkerchief to keep
from drooling every time he got off a good one), jabbing his
walking stick into the earth at his feet to make certain that his
points were rammed home somewhere. And the whole Continental
Congress, a deadlocked muddle a full year after Concord and Lex-
ington, badgered by whining letters from G. Washington ("the

gloomiest man on this continent"), doing its best to subsist on rum and rhetoric in the face of gout, toothache, heat, flies, and celibacy. How, pray, do you get a musical, rather than a Channel 13 television show, out of that?

By going about your business without compromise, apology, self-consciousness, piety, or fear, I guess. For instance, *1776* wasn't the least bit afraid to be clear about the whole technical matter of rounding up the necessary number of delegates to get the Declaration of Independence passed. It assumed that the process was interesting, it was willing to rip through an entire scene (Scene Three, in case you care to nail this down) without a musical number to interrupt the political needlework, and it was so successful in its assumption and its insistence that you found yourself grasping without effort the relative positions of *all thirteen colonies,* a triumph you probably hadn't been able to manage when you took American History in high school. The show made you feel smarter than you used to be, which was a gracious thing for librettist Peter Stone to have arranged, and smarter without having had to slave for it. Mr. Stone's book had the outline and energy of a hockey game: he'd convinced you it was fun to keep score.

As for the score—the musical score, I mean—it came and went when it pleased. There was never any sense of composer Sherman Edwards saying to himself, "It's time now for a thumping male chorus," or, "I'd better have something to push things here." The show moved at its natural pace, which might come now from the plot, now from the slapdash clanking of a seedy messenger's spurs, now from the universal male need for sex, now from the bullying intransigence of a diehard loyalist (Paul Hecht) who would speak the speech he had in mind. The music stole in most often as an afterthought, as a hint of grace following meals, as a bit of prying into the life that went on behind the law, sometimes as an exuberance that could not be capped if anyone dared let it loose for so much as a careless moment.

There was absolutely no need, let's say, for a delegate from Virginia (Ronald Holgate) to kick his heels high because he was being sent back home on a false-face mission. But he just happened to be a Lee, and Virginia is full of Lees, and all Lees are so wonderful that Virginia can't help being wonderful, and so there was simply no stopping Mr. Holgate as he exploded with the sheer happiness of having come to exist. In point of fact, they had to carry him off to get him to subside, and there was no real assurance that he had subsided even then; you could hear him congratulating himself, at the top of his lungs, half the way home.

There was perhaps some sense in having Adams, Franklin, and pretty Mrs. Thomas Jefferson (Betty Buckley) sing a song called "He Plays the Violin," though it was sense in retrospect, sense after the fact. The fact of the matter was that absolutely no one in the Congress had wanted to write the Declaration of Independence. Young Thomas Jefferson (lanky Ken Howard in a sunny red wig, looking just the man for Gutzon Borglum to sculpt after he'd put on another twenty pounds) had wanted to write it least of all because he was newly married and hadn't seen his wife in six months. Nonetheless, Jefferson, a most distressed Jefferson, had been stuck with it.

Jefferson's distress led to the evening's nicest bit of stage business: having scratched out one unsatisfactory paragraph, he crumpled the parchment and threw it away; he scratched something more, crumpled the parchment again; finally he was crumpling the parchment without having written anything at all on it—and meaning the gesture with his heart and soul.

In due time Adams, a not unintelligent man, had Mrs. Jefferson brought up from Virginia to Philadelphia, where, after a night or two, the trouble was tamed, the Declaration indited. There was now breathing space for the conspirator to relax and inquire of Mrs. Jefferson what sort of man her young husband was, which meant that she could at last sing about his expert management of the violin while Adams and Franklin whipped her, genteelly and then not so genteelly, through a friendly prideful gavotte. The entire sequence was easy, honest, foolish, and utterly charming.

Ultimately the score was willing to rush in and fulfill an urgent need, although it was willing—once again—only on its own terms. Near the end of the evening the Congress faced a near-fatal crisis over the issue of slavery. How did our composer contend with it? By permitting a fanatical gentleman, dressed in a passionate blue, to bare his teeth in virtually strangled song that was bound to go against the grain of the audience's readiest sympathies. The delegate from South Carolina (Clifford David) defended slavery by lashing out, hysterically, at the profiteers of the North who were thriving so piously on trade in "molasses, rum, and men." No drumbeats were wasted, you see, on shoring up positions we were eager to agree with; no one was permitted to congratulate himself in two-four time. Instead rhythm and melody were put to a more difficult task: that of helping us to understand the hatred—and the faint justification behind that hatred—that almost scuttled a nation before it could send out a calling card.

Otherwise, sometimes tellingly, sometimes lazily, the music suited itself. There was nothing more attractive in the evening, I think, than the plaintive white tones of a ragged soldier moaning a folk tune, a ballad about a Revolutionary lad who'd crawled off the common on which he'd been felled in order to die, unobtrusively, beneath a shadowing red maple ("Hey, Ma," the soldier sang, "I am done").

Book and music did what they wanted to do, not what musical-comedy custom dictated, and they did it so confidently and so well that you grinned and went along quietly. Jo Mielziner's compound setting was inviting in much the same way that the play was: it was relaxed, surprisingly dimensional, just an attractive shade off center. You sniffed irony in the wind everywhere, and when the excellent Mr. Hecht roared out "And is that how new nations are formed?", you laughed, thinking perhaps that at least this one was put together out of just such sass and such swapping. In fact, you rather hoped it was.

4

GOD takes care of babies, drunks, and good directors. If I speak of the stage direction of *Promises, Promises* first, it's not because Robert Moore had done his job any better than everyone else had done *his*. The musical was afloat with good jobs, filled to the Plimsoll line with good jobs, practically ready to capsize with good jobs. The thing about Mr. Moore, whose only previous directorial credit had been the considerable one of *The Boys in the Band*, was that he had understood exactly what everybody else's good job consisted of, and then made exact use of it. Never too much use, never too little, always exact use. That's why the evening, even if it was a smash, seemed so perfect.

Judiciousness may not be all, but it's a lot. Mr. Moore had noticed, for instance, how legitimately Neil Simon had developed the evening's libretto, living dangerously all the while. It would have been quite easy for Mr. Simon to go wrong; any talented man could have done it. For one thing, he was working from a film script, the one Billy Wilder and I. A. L. Diamond did for *The Apartment,* which had been superb to begin with. Just enough loving improvement might have wrecked it.

For another, the quality of the original had depended mightily on walking a very delicate line between hilarity and moral unease. With its impertinent and never altogether plausible story line asking us to feel sorry for a loser who managed to become an executive-type loser by lending his apartment nights to higher-ups with displaced girls on their hands, and with its very best sequence built to embrace attempted suicide and boozy farce in one and the same wild grope, it was good black comedy in constant danger of turning blue.

One joke too many, one laugh too loud, one extra little trace of enthusiasm, and the whole thing might have become comic pimping instead of a caustic, hard-headed, but fundamentally honest and therefore attractive pleasantry. To be kind to these people you had to take it easy with the jokes.

And so Mr. Simon, his intuitions in excellent working order, had come in gently, and from under. There were no lines marked as killers, no yocks built to black out on. The book was, if anything, on the shy side, cautious, grinning, hoping to be friends, candid, fond of kidding, *nice*. In fact, let's just say that Jerry Orbach was the book and go on from there.

Mr. Orbach had no confidence in himself. He let us know that early. He had a notion that he seemed a pretty limp type to anyone who noticed him, and the only saving grace in that was that practically no one ever noticed him. One of the first thoughts that occurred to him as he stood chatting with us—a cipher in silhouette against an amber-windowed New York sky—was that it might be a good idea if he could join us in the auditorium and watch the show. That way, possibly, he'd have been able to see what was so wrong with him.

He never did join us on our side of the house. He was not to be confused with The Living Theater. But his easy, open, *earnest* intimacies, his willingness to level with us, had already accomplished one thing. We'd joined him, moved over to his side. We appreciated his appreciation of us. When he developed a cold—having had to spend the night on a park bench in a snowstorm—he quickly waved us back as he entered. "Keep away from me," he said, terrified we'd pick up one of his germs. And he seemed to mean it. He wanted us to be comfortable, whether he was making overtures to a girl who couldn't have cared less or paying a visit to a company officer who might offer him insidious advancement. "Don't get nervous," he begged us. "If you get nervous, *I'll* get nervous." He calmed us, you see, by shifting the burden to himself: a polite thing to do.

When he deceived us, ever so briefly, he apologized at once. For instance, he met the girl he adored alongside the office elevator, and on the dot she made it plain that she was mad for him. Except, of course, she wasn't. The scene had been performed that way, and we had heard the girl say nice things to him, but he'd made the whole thing up, it was all his fault, he was simply not playing fair. With a shrug, he gave up his imagined scene and played it the way it really was: the girl couldn't even remember his name. "I'm sorry, I won't do it again," he promised us. (He was not to be trusted; he did it again, and it was winning again.)

He even gave us credit for thinking, and for wishing him well. Seated at a restaurant table, gloomily assessing his failures in love and his shilly-shallying about the uses to which that apartment was being put, he was about to be surrounded—from behind—by threatening executives. He glanced at us, his mournful eyes filling with gratitude. "I know," he said, "I see them," sure that we were right on the verge of giving him warning. By the time he finally told us, in despair over the way the whole world was going, "I don't want to talk to you any more, I'll call you next week," we couldn't possibly have been offended.

Mr. Orbach was superbly the Slob at Eve, superbly the whites of the eyes that everyone was supposed to fire at (his eyes were *all* whites, and all pleading), he was the sort of man who would have seemed well dressed if he hadn't somehow or other given the impression of wearing mittens. He was the fumbler par excellence,

and if you wanted him for a friend as much as he absolutely
needed *you*, it was because Mr. Simon had written him as a believable clod, not a clown, and because Mr. Moore had followed
through by keeping his blood pressure normal, his body tone
deferential. Ironically, Mr. Simon may have written his very
straightest comedy material for a *musical*, that normally broad and
brassy form. And, oddly and impossibly and happily, Mr. Moore
had then seen to it that the musical elements behaved themselves
responsibly too.

  Promises, Promises was all of a piece, all intimate, all conversational, all bright and chatty and fun and no fuss. The score clattered along like office typewriter keys, telling you something
swiftly, noncommittally, efficiently, making a certain percussive
music of its own. It was part new sound, part old, rock for over-
thirties with a parakeet insistence, a fingers-drumming-the-desk
impatience, a soft white wail coming up under an edgy beat. (If
you listened carefully to a duet, with guitar, called "I'll Never Fall
in Love Again," you knew what the phrase Having the Best of
Both Worlds meant.) Composer Burt Bacharach and lyricist Hal
David had, at least temporarily, solved the problem of what to do
about music in an age moving too fast for melody but yearning for
it.

  Michael Bennett's choreography knew just where to stop, too. I
mean that literally. One of the marks of the show was that it
wouldn't go splashy, wouldn't wave hands for a finale, wouldn't
scream, splatter, or beg. It avoided applause finishes, didn't bother
with rideouts, always seemed to take a tuck in the materials just
before anything could get noisy or demanding or otherwise out of
hand. Instead of socking home a song, it doubled back into book,
and instead of beating you to death with book, it caught its breath
and plucked a dance step out of nowhere. Then, having investigated just how far hips and arms could be swung with a discreet,
unhysterical, *tight* abandon, the dance would cut off, like lights in
an electrical storm, like a poem with a short last line.

  Something was always saved, reserved, so that the show could
slip forward slyly, gliding home on a private momentum that had
never been halted for incidental effect. *Promises, Promises* was an
untroubled, unhurried blend, and it went down so smoothly that
even those old implausibilities—you still *did* wonder why those

executives couldn't rent an apartment of their own—were cheerfully brushed aside. Who wanted to be captious when he'd been
made so incredibly comfortable? If the show was the smartest new
musical in town, it was also the simplest.

5

The Great White Hope was a play about a man who was afraid of
nothing written by a man who was not afraid of the theater. Two
kinds of boldness—eyes blinking, throat open for a cockcrow—
came together to create a bloodstained circus, the most unabashed
dramatic outburst we have had since *Long Day's Journey into
Night*. Eugene O'Neill—and no doubt his father before him—
would have recognized the play and stamped approval with both
feet.

The hero of Howard Sackler's restless, perpetually roaring rat-
race around the world did have something to be afraid of, if only
he'd been weak enough to pay attention to it. He had the insecurity of the white man to fear. He was Jack Jefferson, a Negro
boxer of 1913 closely resembling the Jack Johnson of legend, and
he had had the effrontery to whip a white champion in the ring.
He had had the additional impudence to take a white mistress,
operate his own cafe, run for his life to a more hospitable but
unprofitable Europe, refuse to take the obliging professional
"dive" that would bring him money and renewed approval of a
race waiting to be superior again. He was up against a vision, a
haunted look in the American eye: that of "millions of uneducated
Negroes massed." Massed and marching.

In James Earl Jones's tidal-wave performance, he was incapable
of imagining or measuring the intensity of the hatred that
reached out across continents to shred the black skin from his
back. He was a big man, glistening bald head thrown so far back in
triumph that he could not see—would not see—the dogs at his feet.
That head, after all, could always be lowered to butt anything in
sight out of sight. He was a trumpeting man, gargling water between workouts as though he were a geyser just tapped, grinning
and grinning as though insult and injury would forever ricochet

off his teeth. He was his own man, not the Negroes' ("What's my winnin' gonna do for you?" he asked a fellow black whose self-respect depended upon one more victory in the ring), not the whites', not his woman's, not the crowd's. He was a ready-made colossus, laughing and leering and devouring champagne, standing astride the battle, losing it. He was magnificent, and he was going to be maimed.

The process of maiming him, of turning him bitter and surly and bull-like until he was finally a bled animal at bay, was worked out by playwright Sackler as though he hadn't heard that drama had long ago turned polite. Polite in its structure, deferential in its scenes, discreet about noisiness.

The most striking, the most transparent, thing about Mr. Sackler was that he never wrote a scene for the play without throwing a hand grenade into it. An ordinary workout in a San Francisco training camp could not go by as simple visual exposition, fun with a punching bag; it had to be rent in two by a dagger-stroke entrance and a lacerating scream from a former black mistress (Marlene Warfield, in a stunning performance). A mother's funeral could not pass as chanted lament; it had to be violated by voodoo, by an unwelcome and blisteringly repulsed white man, by venom unleashed at the graveside. The happy, unselfconscious tenderness of a lovers' scene in bed (white Jane Alexander pulling the sheet over her head to hide her humiliation and her laughter because she had mistakenly supposed that her black paramour could not possibly suffer sunburn) was literally shattered by the breaking down of doors.

Each passage—and there were nineteen of them—came to its own violent punctuation: an uprising in a cafe, a thrashing with a towel, a direct lunge at the audience (the actors did not hesitate to play front, epically rather than intimately), the remarkable Miss Alexander fully unleashing her ladylike tongue. Mr. Sackler had paid no attention at all to the kind of caution that naturalism once forced upon us, uprooting an older habit of blasting out the back wall at five-minute intervals. Fearing that dramatic fireworks were obvious, we had given up the fireworks, scarcely noticing that we were often giving up the drama too. Mr. Sackler did not hesitate to be obvious so long as he could be dramatically obvious. The fireworks were thrilling.

The distinction of the play lay not in its language but in its reach and in its capacity for landing body blows that took an audience's breath away. Under Edwin Sherin's splendid, relentlessly hammering stage direction, it marched to a calliope bleat that became, in effect, its central nervous system. There were times when you began to fear that the sheer noise would defeat itself, times when you began to wonder whether drama itself could become coarse enough or robust enough to sustain this pitch. It invariably did. If there was hysteria in the air, hysteria, too, could become a kind of spine, a theme, a reflection of the white-black world as it was in 1913 and as it is now. The evening's final images—silent images inside the uproar—said all there was to be said about this kind of confrontation, said what we ourselves knew and were afraid to acknowledge that we knew. Mr. Jones, at last defeated because the odds were greater than his pride, was a bloody pulp. The white man who had beaten him was bloodier.

When the audience got to its feet for the curtain calls, as it did many times during the play's run, it did so out of nothing so simple as respect. The fearlessness onstage had infected it, lifted it into wishing to share a kind of theatrical experience that it had almost forgotten was possible. *The Great White Hope* was performed at black heat and the stage danced with an excitement that had to be joined rather than judiciously approved.

6

UNTIL quite recently most plays about Negroes have been written by whites. Today, a *Great White Hope* or a *Big Time Buck White*, both the work of white men, stand as exceptions. During the past few years blacks have taken matters into their own hands with an unbelievable swiftness, throwing up their own new dramatists writing on specifically black or black-white themes in numbers that could never have been anticipated. Sophistication has come suddenly, as though powers had been lying in wait for this precise moment in time; the black has been ready to speak and his tongue is on the instant rich.

In scarcely more than the blink of an eye Lorraine Hansberry,

Le Roi Jones, Douglas Turner Ward, Lonnie Elder III, Ed Bullins, Charles Gordone and at least half a dozen others have appeared as though the ground had opened to release them; released, they exhibit an energy and a capacity for free flight that constitute what is probably the single most exhilarating phenomenon in the American theater of this half-century. Who would have thought so much could be had so swiftly?

The results are not always likable. They are not always meant to be. And occasionally they are disastrous; a black can succeed in writing as falsely as whites so abundantly have done. Douglas Turner Ward's *Brotherhood*, for instance, may have been the most embarrassing forty minutes of theater I have ever managed to sit through, not so much because Mr. Ward had got his playmaking wrong as that he had got his hate wrong. Getting the hate wrong is worrisome, and is the reason I wish to pause to speak of the play.

Brotherhood was meant to fantasize a fairly simple black-white situation in which a casually dressed white couple entertained an impeccably dressed black couple in their home for an evening.

It was recognizable as fantasy on the instant because an otherwise perfectly ordinary living room was cluttered, and in fact overwhelmed, by a group of sheeted forms that appeared to be concealed statues, inexplicable on any realistic basis. The note of fantasy was immediately reinforced by the absence of ashtrays and the white couple's cheery insistence that the black couple simply scatter their cigarette ashes anywhere about the floor. So much for beginnings.

Fantasy is a form that has served many black playwrights well, for clear reasons. It is always possible, of course, to do naturalistic genre studies (*Raisin in the Sun*) that confine themselves to the harsh realities of black neighborhood life in an oppressively white society. But the vein is limited, the range of observation somewhat narrow, the mood an almost unrelieved ache. To escape this, as to escape a ghetto of feeling, and to leap into exhilaration, self-assertion, vaunting humor and dancing pride, it has been necessary to imagine an actual minority coming into a position of uncontested and immediate power—and only fantasy will accommodate that leap as yet.

Thus we have had Le Roi Jones's intellectual clubbing or

otherwise dominating the whites who fill a subway train while he gives a taunting girl her comeuppance. We have had, in other plays, blacks surrounding and commandeering the governors of southern states, black maidservants slaughtering entire families of fatuously trusting whites, blacks inheriting the family manse because the whites have all killed one another or dropped dead of apoplexy. This sort of imaginative projection, sometimes funny, sometimes savage, serves an obvious double purpose of promising blacks a future if they will wake up to their powers and threatening whites with no future if they don't stop abusing theirs.

It often works well in the theater. It worked reasonably well, for instance, during portions of Mr. Ward's own *Day of Absence*. In this play's first moments, deliberately sleepy ones, we did begin to believe that all Negroes had vanished, suddenly, mysteriously, from a small southern town. We believed the incredulity of the whites (performed in clown-white by blacks) and the exasperation of the whites. (Here Mr. Ward had got his white men right, particularly in the frantic outburst of a businessman who wasn't able to stay home and mind the baby because the damned greased pole of his office life, the competitive slipperiness and the professional despair, wouldn't let him.)

As the vacuum increased in size, we came to accept, with a smile and no argument at all, the notion that even the blacks who were in jail cells were unavailable because the cell doors just wouldn't open and that those who were in hospitals had simply frozen into place, unable to bleed or to die. We understood the complete, and silent, withdrawal that the fantasy meant to stand for, and we accepted it.

We accepted what we were seeing, too, in Ted Shine's *Contributions*, when Claudia McNeil looked out at the audience, fingered the friendly little packet of poison with which she had placidly settled many an argument with whites, and, lowering those slate-gray eyes of hers in slitted malice, suggested that any one of us might be next. We were, in fact, utterly delighted, partly because Miss McNeil herself is such an incontestable force of nature and fact of life, and partly because the fantastic image—that of a "yassuh" cook quietly doctoring the cornbread she served to her unbeloved sheriff—was perfectly proportioned to what the woman could be understood to feel. Both her patience and her hatred could be recognized as real. What would you do, in your dreams, if you had access to the cornbread and stood in her shoes?

But in Mr. Ward's *Brotherhood* nothing could be believed from beginning to end. This was not due solely to the playwright's present technical clumsiness, though he was clumsy indeed. We hadn't the faintest notion of what the white couple were scouring the floors for before the genteel blacks arrived. We did not understand, not satirically or in any other way, why the black couple or any couple should have been encouraged to scatter ashes on the floor. (Did it mean that the whites thought the blacks were accustomed to living this way? Absurd on the face of it, given the meticulous deportment of the blacks and the fact that they had been invited by whites who knew them.)

Shortly the white wife was breaking out drinks, only to realize with apparent shock that she had brought out a bottle of Old Crow and was forced to retrieve her error hurriedly by replacing it with a bottle of Black and White. (Funny? Does *anyone* think of Old Crow whisky as referring to blacks? Has any black ever supposed that Black and White Scotch symbolizes good racial relations?) Not so shortly, the black wife had to go to the bathroom. Now there was a scurry in which it developed that the bathroom was in the process of being painted and even the children's "potty" was unavailable. She had to go outside in the bushes, with the white wife accompanying her.

Yes, bathrooms have been segregated. But not by the kind of white liberals, fatuous or fake or whatever they might be, who receive black couples in their homes. The gestures were out of place, maddeningly; what we could have grasped as a clear reference in a southern railway station could not be grasped *as satire* here. The satirical thrust was irrelevant and we were disoriented. Did Mr. Ward mean to go after the comedy, and the perhaps submerged racism, inherent in the awkwardnesses, the painful eruptions of self-consciousness, that do sometimes overtake whites and blacks when they are trying to come together socially? Certainly that is a true and legitimate source of comedy, and of soberer comment. Dorothy Parker handled it beautifully many years ago, and Elaine May was getting at something like it more recently in *Adaptation*. The self-consciousness exists, and can be examined, regretted, made fun of.

But Mr. Ward wasn't doing that. Something larger and more extravagant loomed. When the couples had parted for the evening, the whites were finally, joyously free to whip from the statuary all those covering sheets—revealing enormous figures of coal-black Jemimas, jockeys, old retainers, boys eating watermelon. They ripped a concealing canvas from a painting to turn the whole back wall of the room into a bloody slaughtering of blacks. They popped into place pillows and doilies with black faces shining from them. They settled back onto the sofa, contented now.

And it was all as wrong as we'd *felt* it to be while we'd been sitting there, struggling with our bewilderment. It was wrong at a surface level on any count you could conceive. Whites who try to establish social relations with blacks do not secretly keep fetishes about to renew a subliminal hate. Suppose that they *do* feel the hate. What they do with it is suppress it, concealing it even from themselves. And whites who really hate and who are perfectly willing to acknowledge the hate to themselves do not surround themselves, even symbolically, with black imagery, with reminders of what they hate. They try to banish the dread view from their lives, not only in their living rooms but on buses and in toilets and in schools. There is *no* context in which this particular juxtaposition of values might work, no point of vantage from which it could be looked at and believed.

It was apparent that Mr. Ward did mean what he seemed, at the end and below the fantastic surface, to be saying. Once the lights had gone down on the Jemima-surrounded rejoicing whites, they went up again (though we didn't expect this and were confused as to when the play ended). Now we saw the blacks on their way home, he with a switchblade that he was slicing into the empty air, she with a white doll into which she was fiercely sticking pins.

Mutual, total, unalterable hate. Hate is all that can be hoped for. It *cannot* be erased, not by any amount of good will, because the good will itself is only a mask for more hate. That is the concept the play's structure was built to reflect, the premise that gave rise to its particular gestures. It was disturbing that a talented playwright should think the content true enough, absolute enough, to serve as a basis for assent, for quick recognition, for laughter. It was a relief—and the only comfort I was able to take from an uninterruptedly depressing experience—to notice that the notion, when worked out on a stage, stood there as transparently, moment-by-moment and finally in essence, false.

7

LET's be plain about this. Charles Gordone is the most astonishing new American playwright to come along since Edward Albee, and with *No Place to Be Somebody* he lurched at us not like the younger Albee or the one-act Albee but like the already ripe and roaring Albee of *Who's Afraid of Virginia Woolf?*

This time the milieu was black, this time the malice couldn't be made to crumple and die at dawn but had to see its way to as many sprawled corpses as *Hamlet* has, this time the work was called comedy but plunged straight through the paper-hoop of comedy to land upside down and splattered all over with an ugliness that wouldn't wipe off, this time the tongue lashings shaded away regularly into a thumping or a reflective poetry. The construction of the play was complex, rich, garish, improbable, overburdened, defiant, and successful.

Mr. Gordone wished to keep every observable, every conceivable aspect of the black-white love-hate relationship alive in his head and alive in ours, without cant, without bias, without coming to any absolute conclusion except that terrifying contraries exist simultaneously. To do the job, and to keep the violent survey in some kind of control, he presented us with a man—a writer and actor so nearly white that he could not get a job as a black—who carried a whole boiling world of race hatreds and race lusts in *his* head, who conceived of them all as coming face to face, grinning and snarling, as part of a single criss-crossed action in a single Village bar.

He dropped into his imagined bar as he wished, always to over-hear the world at knife's edge. He could, in effect, make the bar vanish when he wished, reducing the whole world to himself, his race-remembered dance steps, his sharp chanted "Yeahs!" that

seemed to function as a rein on the cosmos, his quiet recollection
of what it had been like to get out of the ghetto and away from
those "dirty black people" only to discover that his new friends,
"those clean white people," somehow or other imagined that he
was one of the dirty black people too. (Showering and showering,
he made himself cleaner than anybody, but nobody noticed.)

Functioning as tribal god to the play, and also as one of its
sacrificial participants, he was insider and outsider, all-knowing
and unknowing, cynically curled lip and damaged psyche at once.
Ron O'Neal, an actor who must have the most expressive eyes
since Ronald Colman, played both the poet and the poem superbly.
(The adverb sounds conventional; the performance was not.)

What went on inside the tough, tawdry, bluntly melodramatic
poem, which is to say inside Johnny's Bar? Johnny, played with
unerring skill by Nathan George, was a black man who meant to
become his own Mafia. He had cut out from "goodness," cut out
from whites (though he didn't in the least mind making use of two
white mistresses before the last clatter of gunfire had sounded),
cut out from all the promises in which no urgent man could
possibly believe. He was race in a rage, on the rise, ready for
triumph or for martyrdom, which would amount to a win either
way.

In Johnny's Bar there were white and black whores, competing
with one another and devoted to one another. There were white
and black liberals, jointly guilty in their innocence. There was, to
pave the way for an entirely characteristic scene of Mr. Gordone's, a reefer-crazed white handyman who boasted, between
twitches, of his earlier glories as a musician. He was loved by a
simple, a too-simple, black girl; she bought him the drums he had
yearned for. Once he had the drums, he insisted on playing them,
playing them before the blacks to whom he had boasted. The
blacks surrounded him, waiting. Mouth working spastically,
fingers trembling apprehensively, he began to perform. He gained
confidence, gained speed, lost himself altogether in the rising rattle,
finished manically triumphant—unaware that he had, in the act,
exposed himself cruelly for the nonentity he was, an untalented
child caught showing off before his stern embarrassed betters.

It was Mr. Gordone's habit—an excellent one because it is the
fundamental stuff of drama—to press his confrontations until they

became reversals, until the roles were changed. If on-the-make Johnny was turning himself into his kind of white man, the bad white man who gets everything he wants, so the white drummer was trying—and failing hideously—to make himself musically black.

The humiliation that came of the failed inversion was rammed home—hard—in what was probably the evening's ugliest, prickliest sequence. Johnny's white whore was being discarded by Johnny. Too shrewd not to know what was happening, too drunk to do anything about its happening, the girl began brazenly to black her own face, smearing grease wantonly and bitterly while shocked, angry, and sorrowing blacks tried to stop her.

The moment was vicious in every way, it hurt everyone participating in it. It also summarized absolutely the double thrust of the play, the terrible effort at adaptation on both sides that just now ends in grotesquerie. We have not got through the cruel comedy of adaptation yet; this play was the situation's unforgettable weather report.

Not everything in it was harsh or harshly funny. The author has a great gift for dropping from intense heat to a pleasant chill, from importance to how-do-y'do. An Italian thug who'd gone to school with Johnny and was now going to destroy Johnny—he would get to it in a minute—paused to savor a delicious macaroni salad made, to the thug's astonishment, by a filthy dying black. The girl who had wasted herself on the drummer asked someone to read the clock on the wall for her, then fell into earnest hushed thought. She decided that she would go home and, first thing tomorrow morning, begin to learn how to tell time. (Mr. Gordone's touch here was so light that what might have become obtrusively symbolic was instead personal and affecting.)

And for Mr. O'Neal he had written not only act-prologues that expanded like arias, but at least one passage of deliberate verse that began at doggerel beat and then climbed beyond simple stresses to full orchestration. (Listening to it was to have one's hope renewed that verse theater, clamoring and contemporary, might be possible after all.)

There were flaws, as there are bound to be in any genuinely original play. Mr. Gordone writes a bit sentimentally at times ("Somewhere inside, Johnny's got something, only it comes out crooked"). Occasionally he makes a dramatic gesture that seems schematically planned, unspontaneous: the drummer's turning on his girl after he has failed, for instance. And at the very end of the evening he put Mr. O'Neal through a sudden "camp" bit in widow's weeds, giddily standing in for all the mourning women of the world, that was false to the play's tone; it was too thin and obvious in its humor for the weight and wiliness of the text as a whole.

But what was important was that a writer had turned up who had the nerve of his talent. The overfull play did not sprawl, was never embarrassed by its own appetite. The melodrama belonged to the materials at the same time that it was being theatrically arresting, the bar talk and the imagery relieved one another readily, the inside of a man's head and the outside, outsize, roiling world fused. We had been waiting and waiting all the way down to the end of the season and were at last rewarded. Here was a playwright.

Money and
Uglier Matters

I

PEOPLE are always saying that the theater can never die. Do you
know what? It can't even commit suicide. It's been trying and it
can't. Let me explain.

Just a little while back a nice chap, a fellow with pink cheeks,
spectacles, and very little hair came up to me in a restaurant and
asked if I could tell him how to go about investing in a Broadway
show. He'd like to take a little flier, he said, he had some money
available, he didn't exactly know the ropes. Could I direct him to a
producer who perhaps had some shares of a show for sale?

Now of course, being a reviewer, I couldn't direct him anywhere specifically. Reviewers are pure of heart and above commerce. They also don't know much *about* commerce, or about the
financial hanky-panky that underlies all their esthetic pleasures,
though very few people will believe this. So few people believe it,
in fact, that reviewers are *always* being approached for inside
information on theatrical investment, and, somehow or other, the
people who ask the questions are always pink-cheeked, bespec-
tacled, and going on bald. Maybe that's why they're called angels.

Anyway, over the years I've developed a Standard Evasive

Reply to the question "How can I put money into a play?" I suggest that the potential gambler look over the track records of the various producers, decide for himself which looks most like the man he'd like to lodge his money with, and then write to that producer's office to see if he just happens to be soliciting cash for a project at the moment. (Actually, my man ought to write to the producer with the *second*-best track record, because the managers who really make it big three times out of five are bound to have little bands of more or less permanent investors and it's hard to get on the mailing list, let alone into a probable winner.)

I gave my restaurant acquaintance the Standard Evasive Reply, then, and thought that was the end of it. It wasn't. He sampled the field of producers, got a few turndowns, eventually received from one that wonder of wonders, a prospectus. A prospectus means that shares in a show are available, that you're invited to buy in. And it provides, in logical order, all the facts about the production you ought to know before joining.

He looked it over. He didn't know what to make of it. He sent it to me for clarification. *I* didn't know what to make of it.

You see, he still had—and maybe even I still had—an old, old image in mind, the image of a producer making a get-rich-quick pitch to a possible investor at razzle-dazzle speed, painting beautiful pictures of the profits to come while promising him a spare blonde just to keep him comfy in the meantime. You know the sort of thing I mean.

It doesn't exist any more, not on paper anyway. The prospectus of today, if the one handed me is at all representative, is a brand new breed, a breathtaker. It is issued, I would guess, by the I Cannot Tell a Lie League, probably under orders from someone named Lefkowitz in Albany. It is Boy Scout honest, ferociously honest, even disgustingly honest. It levels. It confesses. It admits everything. It doesn't invite, it warns—and not in that whispered tone of voice that turns up on the sides of cigarette packages either. It screams at you, just in case you're daydreaming of blonds and not paying close attention. Invest money in a Broadway play? Yes, you may, if you wish, these new circulars seem to say, provided you are accompanied by an adult and are certifiably insane.

Chances are you've never seen one of these documents and can't quite grasp, from my generalizations, the full impact of the new style. So let's quote from one. It's for a show that is actually planning to go into rehearsal as I write. Although the producer has only limited experience, the authors of the play have earlier written several Broadway successes and the director has had two hits just recently. Sounds pretty good, doesn't it?

Watch it. Right here on page two of its appeal for funds, immediately after an identification of the producing firm and a statement of what shares cost,. begins a section—a fairly extensive section—called "The Risk to Investors." Now of course any sort of investment, in any industry you care to name, involves some degree of risk. How much here? "In such a venture," the very clear prose of this statement informs us, "the risk of loss is especially high in contrast with the prospects for any profit." Never mind that "especially high." Notice the slight sneer in *"any* profit." They didn't have to have that "any" in there. They could just have said "profit." But if you had *any* notion of picking up *any* profit when you came in here, fellow, go out wiser and go out now.

Next sentence. "These securities should not be purchased unless the investor is prepared for the possibility of total loss." It did sound that way, didn't it? We do seem to have been following the argument.

Next sentence. "While no accurate industry statistics are available, it is claimed that of the plays produced for the New York stage in the 1967–68 season, as high as 80% resulted in loss to investors." Uh-huh. And that's only hearsay. If accurate industry statistics *were* available—where is Lefkowitz hiding them, and why?—would they show 90 percent loss? 100 percent? 120 percent, counting overcall? Do they come and get your gold fillings?

Next paragraph, provided anybody is still in the building. "On the basis of estimated expenses, the play will have to run for a minimum of 13½ weeks (108 performances) at a theater scaled to $45,000 gross receipts per week at full capacity even to return to limited partners their initial contributions." Notice that *"even."* Sneering again. And we're not through with this cautionary tidbit. "More than 77% of the plays produced for the New York stage in the 1967–68 season failed to run this long," the oracle continues. "Of those that did, a handful played to capacity audiences." The brochure is using some restraint here. It doesn't say a "pitiful" handful.

The potential investor who has been keeping up with the arithmetic of all this now realizes that he has approximately a 23 percent chance of running for 108 performances, in case he is personally interested in seeing the show 108 times, but that his percentage-point chances of playing that long to capacity are so infinitesimal that they have not even been figured out by the Penitentes who prepared this statement. And unless it's capacity, it's crash, crash, crash.

All of this, mind you, appears in a statement meant to *persuade* the investor to invest. "I hope you will consider investing," is the way the producer concludes his personal note. It is perhaps the only place he is not entirely open with us. "I hope you will consider investing, you idiot," is the way the sentence should read. It will probably appear that way in the next solicitation that is prepared.

You may think that this one section, "The Risk to Investors," is perhaps required by law and is the only section of the document to display such candor. Nonsense. Broadway beats its breast straight through the nine legal-size typed pages; the promise of disaster is omnipresent. In a section, "Subscriptions," which has to do with the fact that an investor may permit his money to be spent before all of the necessary funds have been gathered, the tone is, I would think, particularly sharp. First the investor is given permission to make such an arrangement. He is then given a good rap on the knuckles and perhaps a bit of a boxing about the ears: "Investors should note that there is no advantage to entering into these agreements. In fact there is a distinct disadvantage since persons who do so risk loss of their entire investment even if the partnership is never formed." You don't fool around with *this* producing unit, trying to give it money for nothing.

In a section called "Return of Contribution, Share of Profits," wouldn't you think you'd get some good news? Or at least a hint of hope? Here's what you get: "Any net profits will be distributed only after the Broadway opening, after all contributions have been repaid and when such distribution will still leave the partnership with a $25,000 reserve (plus any amounts which the Producer wishes to accumulate for the formation of additional companies to present the Play)." In short, this producer absolutely promises to keep those dreadful net profits away from you for just as long as he can think of anything else to do with the money. And he kids you not.

Should you put yourself in his hands? He is now apparently required to display his track record, showing the profits and/or losses involved in any prior productions he has mounted. The information is here. This particular producer has in the past produced two plays. Each lost every dollar spent on it. Welcome to the fold.

Should you *still*, out of loyalty to the theater, out of love of the arts, out of hope of meeting an actress, out of sheer and glorious personal stupidity, go along for the ride, *even* as advertised? After all, there's a lot of excitement about a New York opening night. "The Producers may abandon the production at any time prior to the New York opening for any reason whatsoever."

Well, there you are. That's how the invitation to Paradise, the open-sesame to good fortune, the promise of bliss reads these days. I guess you can say one thing about it. If the theater can survive the form in which it must now sell itself, it's got something.

And I've just looked. There are seven new productions scheduled for next month. The crazy pitch *works*.

2

As I SEE IT, money is something you grab anywhere you can just to get and keep the show on. As other people see it, money is magic, money is invested with moral qualities, money is sacred and shameful in the very same breath, money has a color that can be detected, money is the one true mystery before which we bow our heads in awe.

Or so I gather, having listened to some of those other people.

"Shame, shame," is what the girl was saying—a pretty girl, slender, with long light hair falling over her shoulders—as I waited in line at the box office of a new Off Broadway hit. The girl wasn't talking to me, though I was willing. She was talking to the man selling tickets behind the little barred window and she wasn't angry, she wasn't scolding, she was ever so gently reproving— sorrowful, really.

What had happened was this. Once the show had awakened early in the morning to find itself a hit, prices had jumped. The management had read the notices and taken heed, some seats were now marked up to a breathtaking ten dollars, and the girl who had just been given this information was bleeding for the lost innocence, the rusted integrity, the destroyed *character* of Off Broadway. Off Broadway had betrayed itself by charging what it could get.

I didn't feel quite so scandalized. I don't exactly see why Off Broadway has to have *all* the character. Why can't the customers who are so eager to get in have a little character and cough up? They've got the extra cash. I know they do. I've watched them dig for it. A ten-dollar seat Off Broadway is only four dollars more than what it would have been if the show had been a flop and not worth seeing. And there's no quid pro quo about the matter. That is to say, if the management has a show nobody wants to see, the customers won't come running, dewy-eyed, just *because* it's four dollars cheaper. The management is supposed to be virtuous about hits but the customer isn't supposed to be virtuous about flops. If you see what I mean. Furthermore, *Dames at Sea* and *Boys in the Band* and *Adaptation—Next*, all of which did raise their prices, were every bit as entertaining as their ten-to-fifteen-dollar Broadway equivalents.

But all right, I do realize there are poor starving students who can't afford ten dollars a seat (I could afford exactly 85 cents when I was a poor starving student) and poor starving nontheatergoers who should be encouraged to go to the theater more often by making it easy and marvelous and cheap. I'm in favor of any programs that now exist (some do) or that can be brought into existence to help move the impoverished, the alienated, and the merely young in the direction of the neighborhood playhouse.

But there are various things that ought to be kept in mind. One is that there remain less expensive seats, even in playhouses housing hits, for the benefit of those who choose to be stuffy about, or just can't scrape up, the ten dollars; these good souls simply have to wait a little longer to get the seats of their choice. And it should also be remembered that there are such things as poor starving actors, poor starving playwrights, and poor starving managers— yes, I've even known a couple of starving managers—too.

At ordinary prices, Off Broadway, actors do not make a living wage. They pick up token salaries, tolerated by Equity, in exchange for an opportunity to work and be seen. That is why they hop about so much. Almost immediately after a show opens and is reviewed, its cast will start to change. Instead of settling down to a profitable run, which is normally impossible, the actors are scooting off to join other productions in which they can be seen and reviewed again.

Playwrights and managers don't get a lot of take-home pay either. In houses seating 199 or 299 people, there isn't much room for profit once the light bills have been paid; Off Broadway profits, if any and even with hits, tend to come from duplicate touring companies playing larger houses in the hinterlands. The fact is that there are a number of rather impoverished people up there behind the footlights or roaming about (in rags?) backstage, and any theatergoer who wants to give a writer or manager just enough pocket money to tide him over his next couple of flops, or who even wants to see this play performed by the same actors who opened it, can just tell himself that he is making his present and future pleasure possible by the simple layout of the extra cash. He isn't being bilked, he's investing in a co-op.

Above all it should be remembered that theater—any theater, all theater—*is* expensive. There's no way around it. Too many collaborators, dimensional people who have to be fed daily, are involved in mounting a show and then keeping it running to allow for any sort of inexpensive duplication; there is no way to run off a show on a Xerox. The last gasping actors to play a play in its fourth and final year still have to eat; production keeps on costing money so long as the ushers usher and the marquee lights shine.

This is never going to change. Flops will always cost as much as hits to produce and run, there will always be more flops than hits, the output is always going to run ahead of the intake—unless the intake is increased by jacking up the ante for hits or, in the case of obviously less commercial work, unless the bill is footed by the government or by foundations. The theater will always have to ask for more money from somebody.

Again my own attitude is that I don't care who's fleeced of the money so long as the theater gets it—unless we are perhaps to stop just short of accepting handouts from the CIA. But there are other attitudes, and they bother me. For instance, in talking about the emerging Black Theater in an issue of *Newsweek*, Peter Bailey, a reporter-critic for *Ebony*, insisted that "the most crucial practical issue facing the Black Theater movement" at the moment is not that of finding writers or developing actors and directors. It is getting rid of white money. At the moment most, perhaps all, Negro acting companies at the professional level receive grants. But "it is impossible for true Black Theater to be financed by white-establishment foundations," Mr. Bailey argues, adding that "some way will have to be found to make black people understand that cultural institutions are a necessity in the development of a people and that, this being the case, they must be willing to finance these institutions."

This strikes me as nonsense and a good way to get precious little theater. The black community, with its inherited economic disadvantages, has quite enough on its hands trying to meet the new financial challenges of asserting black power in a hundred vital areas without also struggling to assume a "fringe" economic burden that is already too great for the white community to manage.

Let's not make any mistake about this last point. The white community, with its far more ample resources, is absolutely unable to finance any sort of repertory or resident theater without help from the heavenly founts. Whites may have most of the money in Atlanta, but they have had to close down a ballet-opera-theater complex opened with great fanfare just a short time before. As I write I've been interrupted by what is not at all an unfamiliar telephone call, a cry for help from a resident theater on the verge of going under after four years of activity and dwindling foundation help. What to do, they all ask, where can the money be got? The fact of the matter is that there isn't a single resident and/or repertory company in the country today, white or black or color blind, that wouldn't go under the minute foundation funds, or government funds, or university funds, were withdrawn.

If the affluent establishment whites can't swing it, how are the underprivileged blacks to bring it off? I don't think it *can* be brought off, not in relation to the kind of ensemble companies we're talking about, and I think that insisting on it is simply the fastest known method of tacking up a closing notice. If I were managing a black theater, I'd grab any money going, grab it and run with it. Look at it this way. There are black people and white people. The money is green.

But, then, money seems to me a neutral matter, and the theater doesn't. Although I am a reviewer, I couldn't even get excited about the fact that a recent musical comedy delayed its opening for something like two months doing repair work, stalling off the critics while taking in—from the general public—as much as seventy thousand dollars a week during previews.

A few people I know have been disturbed by this practice—it had happened a couple of years earlier with Sammy Davis' *Golden Boy* too—on the theory that anything being seen by *that* many people must be considered formally open and should therefore be formally reviewed without further delay. I'm opposed to jumping the producer in such cases. It's perfectly clear what he's doing. He's killing himself trying to improve his show. (He may even improve it, bear in mind.) The audience knows that it is seeing a preview, rather than a polished product; if it doesn't complain, I don't see how anyone else can. And I see no point in attempting to review a show, any more than I would a building or a hockey game, until it's *finished*.

But do you know what I think really bothers some people? All that money. All that money going over the counter before the show's had a seal of approval. I don't think anyone ever says to himself, "Oh, those poor people in the audience, they may go and be bored to death, with no one to protect them." I think he more likely says, "That show isn't even ready and they're spending their *money!*" Somehow it's the cash that was hurt, not the customer. I'll bet there wouldn't have been any fuss if that musical had been doing poorly.

Funny thing. It's the virtuous people who worry about money all the time. And it's the practical charlatans who run the business who treat it with the reasonable contempt it deserves. They use it, let who will revere it.

3

HERE is an extremely curious piece of theatrical news. During the first week of the 1968–69 season, Helen Hayes broke a house record in Philadelphia.

Doesn't sound curious to you? It should. Never mind the fact that Helen Hayes has probably broken dozens of house records during her long and astonishingly unbumpy career. The play in which she broke it was *The Show-Off*. The production of *The Show-Off* was the same A.P.A. production that had sweetened the season at the Lyceum in New York just one year earlier. At the Lyceum it played in repertory, with Miss Hayes simply an unstarred member of a generally fine company. The production, and Miss Hayes, received almost universally enthusiastic notices. At the Lyceum, in repertory, it tended to gross in the neighborhood of $27,000 a week.

Fast dissolve. Put Miss Hayes' name above the title, pull the play out of repertory and let it go as a loner, and suddenly, in Philadelphia, it does $51,000 a week. (And $43,000 the week before; the big one was no fluke.)

How is one to explain the perverseness of that? We all of us, on our honor, love repertory. We all of us, really and truly, admire the actor or actress who, having been a star, is willing to forget all that nonsense of glamor and billing and submerge himself or herself in a happy-family ensemble. And how do we express our gratitude, our deep satisfaction that a new theatrical order is in the making? By rushing off to the first playhouse that reestablishes the star as "star"—the same woman, mind you, giving the same performance—in a production that isn't the least bit new but has merely isolated itself from the varied company it once kept. It is possible that you will find something regrettable in the situation. But we'd all of us better face the fact that it's what happens.

Something a little bit similar may have happened at about the same time in Mineola on Long Island. There a generous group of "name" performers (Henry Fonda, Robert Ryan, John McGiver, Jo Van Fleet, Estelle Parsons, John Beal) came together for a month to see what it might be like doing a couple of reliable plays out of the American library without worrying about who was to be top dog tonight. Equals wished to play in one another's company as equals and the devil take the matter of who got the best dressing room.

The first production, incidentally, broke the Mineola house record, though a house record in Mineola is rather more breakable than one in New York, or even Philadelphia. Community theater on Long Island doesn't expect to sell out and the players had deliberately kept themselves to the theater-circuit sidelines, not wishing to challenge the big time until they'd made certain they were having a good time.

The first production was *Our Town*, and they seemed to be having a very good time indeed. As a second production, the company offered *The Front Page*, which returns us to our theme. The play patently stood up well; its local notices were fine; the production added yet another star, Anne Jackson, to the alphabetically-listed roster on the billboards out front. It did not break a house record. It did not profit from the success of the production preceding it. Box-office receipts declined.

In heaven's name, why? There might conceivably have been a slight "star" technicality at work here. Henry Fonda's name was placed above the title of the first play, Robert Ryan's of the second, on a rotating basis. In all probability Mr. Fonda has greater automatic drawing power than Mr. Ryan; the theatergoing public has seen him oftener, known him longer. But Mr. Fonda was in the second play too, playing a relatively minor role in which he was cast severely against type and in which he nevertheless found a way, a sneaky way, of getting every last laugh. The stars were all there again, and the public cared less. (Typically, a restaged, only partially recast, production later opened as a one-shot venture on Broadway and became one of the hits of the season.)

It would seem that the minute a star subordinates himself he instantly diminishes himself—not with his fellow actors, not with critics, not with the angels in heaven, but with people who do (or don't) buy tickets. Suppress an assertive glamor and you also suppress sales. Reduce people to colleagues and you seem, in the public mind, to have reduced them to also-rans.

It's a delicate, even a nasty, problem. Because we *do* care about repertory (in theory, at least), and because we *could* have far better productions if we succeeded in persuading more and more professionals at the height of their powers to put their powers together in an almighty display, we are forced to ask what goes wrong when the motives—and even the results—are so right.

I wish I had nine tidy answers lined up for you. I haven't. But one of these days, if we don't want our joy to die aborning, we'd better get at the questions.

Is it a mistake to drop high-voltage names into a kind of lower-case alphabet soup below the title? Would it be better to put them *all* on top, in staggering caps, to make the occasion sound like the second coming it is? (This, by the way, is often done in London, where the galaxy of names on the marquee sometimes makes you feel that missing the event would be like passing up the climactic ball at the Congress of Vienna.)

Is it a mistake to blur the image of one play by shouldering it too close to another? This may be a vital question for repertory in this country, thus far an unanswered one. We assume that bills must be changed nightly, or weekly, if we are to have honest repertory. I suppose we assume it because that's the way Shakespeare ran his playhouse. But Shakespeare *had* to run his that way; to get audiences across the river, he was forced to offer something new every night. That's not true for us. What saved him may sabotage us.

Are contemporary audiences simply put off, confused, by too frequent and too arbitrary changes of program? Mightn't we still call it repertory if we let a play run long enough to establish itself firmly before following it with another? How long before an actor gets bored with a role and needs a change of pace? I think we should ask some actors, and right away.

Would the quick failure of the Edward Albee–Samuel Beckett repertory at the Billy Rose have been prevented, or at least retarded (and a retard is always a breathing space, sometimes a life saver), if the one new play in the repertory, Albee's *Box-Mao-Box*, had been promoted to a fare-thee-well instead of being relegated to a sometime status, lumped together with a group of standard pieces most people felt sure they'd already seen? Is it the theater's business to sell repertory *as such*, or to sell actors and plays?

Admittedly these are commercial questions. But each of the

ventures we've been talking about is or was a commercial venture—to some degree and out of simple necessity, noble ideals apart. Neither the government nor foundations can possibly finance everything that we wish or hope or intend to do. Seats must be filled if the actors, not to mention the candybar concessionaires, are not to become discouraged. Clarity, convenience, and a high sense of excitement are among the ways of filling them.

Perhaps there are other ways. I don't know the contractual terms involved, but some of the money Helen Hayes earned on the road with a production that never earned as much in repertory went back to help sustain the repertory operation. Is that a clue? Off Broadway productions sometimes make most of their money on duplicate productions, scattered across the land. Can offshoots be handled in such a way as to build bank accounts for the experiment on home base?

I shall plague you with no more questions. But the matter needs looking into—pragmatically, candidly—before any more of our dreams, like the buildings that house them, go dark.

4

IT's NO SECRET that recent Broadway seasons have all been undernourished. As usual, there's been talk of money. Broadway money is tight, 'tis said, and so the available scripts have had to stay there, on the shelf, gathering dust. Well, I've been doing a bit of checking about, informally but with an unengaging persistence, and I find this simply isn't so. Money does not appear to be particularly tight nowadays, except for oversized musicals, those investor-eating mammoths that cost in the neighborhood of $750,000 to get dressed for the evening and that can run a year or even eighteen months without earning the $750,000 back. There's some reluctance here, all right, but I wouldn't call that sort of reluctance symptomatic. It could be just plain common sense. As for ordinary straight plays and comedies, I am told—by people close enough to the production process to spend their lunch hours staring wistfully at empty playhouses—that there is ample financing available. It's the straight plays and comedies that aren't available. The shelf is empty.

The Broadway shelf, that is. Producers have come to recognize the fact that there are two distinct shelves on which to deposit, and from which to snatch, scripts: the big-theater shelf and the cozy-theater shelf. They've learned that it is a mistake to attempt transplants (*You're a Good Man, Charlie Brown* was at one time offered a Broadway house and very wisely turned it down) and now, when they do come across a two-character exercise that belongs in a bandbox they march directly downtown with it, even when all of their previous work has been done uptown. Kermit Bloomgarden has done this after years as a serious uptown man, and he is being followed by others. The Off Broadway shelf is for promising plays that are too slight or too short or too narrow or—to look at the matter in another light—just too new to work well where the expense-account trade and the unions forgather.

What, in these terms, is a Broadway play, a play of the kind that so often seems absent without leave just now? It's hard to talk about what will fill a very big house for a very long time without seeming to talk about mere slickness, spit and polish, sleight-of-hand. It takes a con man to lure so many suckers away from their bars and restaurants for a thousand consecutive evenings, doesn't it? Broadway is so often painted as a heaven for hacks that it grows difficult imagining anyone but a hack wanting to work there. Let's try imagining someone else, something else, for a moment. Imagine a man who has his Off Broadway work behind him, a man able to manage not two characters but ten, a man strong enough to keep ten passions crossed without confusion, a man trained to work at such relative breadth that his written embrace can scoop up twelve hundred people a night and command them to give assent to his continued grip. A craftsman devoted to scale and possessed of authority, let's say. Or, to face a fact that's coming up, a talented and experienced middle-aged man.

That's the man whose plays are missing from the Broadway shelf just now. The plays are missing, he isn't. The Middle-aged Able hasn't simply vanished from the face of the earth, victim of a dread blood disease. I've just tried a little trick. I've run my finger down the list of the twenty-one longest running straight plays (not musicals) in American theatrical history. Do you know that the writers principally responsible for eleven of them are still in the building and not even very old? That's an incredible figure, considering how far back the list goes. But, with a single exception I think, they're merely in the building, they're not giving us plays.

Why not? What has stayed the hands that ought to have been happiest with the rewards the theater brings? I don't think it's fat or living too high off the hog that hits bring home. I don't think it's laziness; most of them are busy doing *something*. Nor do I necessarily think I've got the *real* reason, or all the reasons, cornered. But I've got a strong hunch about one factor that may be operating to paralyze the practicing professional.

Fear. The fear of producing work and being found old-fashioned. Newness is so much in the theatrical air right now, the revolution is so far advanced (in theory, at least), the jumping-jack activity in Off Broadway lofts and garages has sent up so many rockets announcing a radical change of course, that the man who learned how to make an effective play just the day before yesterday is more than disturbed by the thought that he may not be with it. He is sometimes utterly psyched out, inhibited from practicing what he formerly thought of as his craft.

He tells himself he's waiting. He doesn't know, for sure, what the next new firm form will be. When the dust has settled, he may be able to manage it. But a hesitation at the heart keeps him from doing what he used to do, even if he thinks that what he used to do is still open to some growth. The world has passed him by, as indeed in time it must pass by all but the very greatest. But it's passed by him early, when he was just getting ready for lunch.

He is aware that there are some who will be glad to see him fail, if he does try now and does fail. A few seasons ago a considerable array of middle-aged talent, perhaps seven or eight "standard" playwrights, turned up with plays that were all turned down. A friend called me on the telephone in high glee. "It's a watershed!" he cried, meaning that with all of these normally successful people wiped out, the Broadway doors would promptly be opened wide to younger and fresher talent. But it hasn't happened that way. It *was* a watershed, and the doors *are* standing open, but the younger and fresher talent hasn't moved in yet. The younger-fresher group is still Off Broadway, much of the time doing provocative and even astonishing things, but not yet quite ready for the ultimate assault. In the interim, a great gap has opened, another kind of generation gap. A generation that belongs there is missing.

This isn't the fault of the News and the Nows, mind you. They must do what they do, must challenge, must change, must shout, must jump. They must even deride, to call attention to themselves and to what they hold false. If they weren't warming up in the wings, we'd be in inconceivable trouble. The fault is interior and personal and widespread. It is the same fault, I think, that moves most of us to shudder and to shrink as we contemplate the mystical and unfathomable rectitude of youth nowadays. Nearly everyone has bought the bill of goods: the young have seen a sign in the heavens that is invisible to over-thirties and always will be. An over-thirty can do nothing but put his own head on the block. It doesn't occur to him to keep doing his own thing until the new thing is actually produced. He hears the promise, the rhetoric, the accusation, and he steps aside.

Steady, men. There's a place for filler. We've got to kill time somehow, while we wait. Neil Simon knows this (and so, probably, does Arthur Miller). I am persuaded (and I am hopeful) that our theater is going to look different, perhaps spectacularly different, by 1980, maybe by 1975. I also think it would be just jim-dandy if, during the meantime of our great expectations, our playhouses could be kept open and active. We want them ready to hand for the new when the New does in fact become Now.

A man who can write a play, any kind of play, ought to. He owes it to the people who are going to supplant him.

5

EVERYONE spent the first four months of one recent theatrical season reading about nothing but the appalling, perhaps terminal, state the Broadway stage is in. Fewer productions than ever before. Fewer hits and emptier houses. Shy money, nonexistent writers, disaffected audiences, doom, doom, doom.

Everyone spent the fifth month of the same theatrical season reading about nothing but Neil Simon, a gentleman who somehow or other was managing to take home weekly, according to *Variety*, some $45,000, all of it earned in that same disaster area where playwrights don't exist and money can't be had and doom, etcetera, doom.

If you have been listening at all during the past few years, you will have spent a great deal of time hearing that popular comedy of the well-made sort is dead. Comedies that could be described as bourgeois, comedies that could be dismissed as mere ragbags of gags, comedies that appealed to the family and friends and the friends of friends, comedies that weren't black and weren't with it but that came up sunny and silly in a heart-warming way, were old hat. The theater, earnestly making its way forward to far-out, had passed them by. Embarrassing relics, that's what they were, from *Junior Miss* to *Any Wednesday*.

Neil Simon was writing nothing but well-made popular comedies. He was the fellow who was taking home $45,000 a week, or $30,000 if you were going to believe *him* instead of *Variety*. (I don't believe either of them; the money all goes into little underground funnels, one of which is directly connected to Washington, D.C., and is never heard of again.)

Obviously there is something wrong here and it doesn't seem to be Neil Simon: on the one hand, a universally-believed and in fact well-substantiated image of the present commercial theater as impractical, if not already insolvent; and on the other, three commercial ventures *by a single man* running concurrently, all of them smash hits: *Plaza Suite*, *Promises*, *Promises*, *Last of the Red Hot Lovers*. (What if there were four Neil Simons? There wouldn't be a house left in town.) On the one hand, a state of mourning for the money and the glory men like Lindsay & Crouse and Kaufman & Hart used to be able to accumulate writing and/or directing plays about mothers and fathers and dizzy neighbors and darling debutantes. On the other, plays about fathers and mothers and dizzy neighbors and more or less darling debutantes turning Neil Simon, again according to *Variety*, into the most financially successful American playwright ever. (Not just this one year, not just this decade, *ever*.)

You may be used to Neil Simon, you may think him a perfectly normal product of the Broadway system instead of an inexplicable phenomenon flying in the teeth of what has happened to the Broadway system, you may think that I am exaggerating one or another of the despairs and taboos that are thought to operate in order to make my paradox. I may, for instance, be exaggerating the rumored death of pop comedy. Pop comedy is always a saleable item, isn't it? As a matter of fact, it hasn't been just lately, and I'm not making anything up.

Here in one pocket I have a letter from a long since successful playwright whose name you'd know, and the letter, which is cheerful enough in a resigned sort of way, mainly details the kind of comment the playwright has been getting from producers on his last two scripts. He's the kind of playwright, by the way, whose work would normally be snapped up by the first or second producer offered it; certainly by the fourth or fifth. No one's snapping. He is being told that his newest play "would have been a hit a few years ago." It's unthinkable now though, because "critics will no longer go for it" and "the well-made play is dead."

In another pocket I have a letter from an almost equally well-known writer of comedy, a writer who had a smash not more than six years ago. This writer, also well enough off not to be bitter about the matter, is being told that the new play is "charming and well-crafted" (the only thing I doubt about the letter is that a producer ever used the phrase "well-crafted"), but that this is the era of *The Killing of Sister George* and *Oh! Calcutta!*, if not that of the late Joe Orton; at the very least a play has got to have a role that could be played by Dustin Hoffman. See where films are at, the message runs: it's *M*A*S*H* all the way. The stage must keep up. And so, no dice. "Old-fashioned me," sighs the playwright, signing off. (This playwright's last produced comedy, by the way, was no *Junior Miss;* one would have thought it cynical enough for all normal purposes, though it did have that glossy one-set, snappy comeback, morning-sunshine look and feel to it.)

Of course, it's possible that these particular plays are no good. But a considerable body of criticism, including the daily criticism that in part must function as a shopping service, has in recent years not bothered to ask whether or not such plays were good of their kind; it has increasingly dismissed the *kind*. We've all read reviews which said, in effect, "Oh, the damn thing will probably run," or, "Your mother may like it, for as long as she's around," or, "It's awfully funny, if that's what you want to waste your time on." The implication has been riding high that popular comedies might be tolerated by the less than intelligent, but that they were, in an absolute sense, intolerable; no self-respecting theater, on its way to newer, fresher, richer values, could continue to play host to the things of our childhood. Neil Simon himself has been steadily hounded by condescension. Until *Last of the Red Hot Lovers* opened, he had been consistently put down in a good many quarters as an overturned joke file, a stitching machine for linking gag to gag. (I haven't wanted to go back and look, but I think I was guilty of this myself as I knocked out my review of *Star-Spangled Girl*.)

Now that he's made it—and in the current stunned admiration for the scope of his achievement he has become not only rich but respectable—nothing has changed, really. For the form, that is to say. Mr. Simon is now being regarded as an aberration of nature, one of those evolutionary throwbacks that somehow manages to capture our fancy, an isolated instance, an exception, a fluke. *He's* getting away with it, the unwhispered whisper runs, and good for him, he's a nice, hard-working, modest guy; but don't think him representative, don't—above all—think that there could ever be any more of him. You may not have noticed the title that *Newsweek* put upon its glowing, well-written, entirely sympathetic cover story about him. "Last of the Red Hot Playwrights," it caroled. Why last? To be sure, that title is a play upon Mr. Simon's own title; nothing more, maybe. But why *make* the twist unless you're dead certain, in your heart of hearts, that the style in which Mr. Simon works is in fact an exhausted style and that when Simon goes only desert will remain?

A good many explanations are being offered for the double upset—the double *temporary* upset—Simon represents. How has he managed to make the Broadway system work for him when the Broadway system is plainly falling apart and will continue to fall apart in spite of him? According to one theory, by combining with his talents as playwright the instincts of an extraordinarily shrewd business man. "Only Doc Simon can pull it off," comments another writer of comedy, "and that's because he's his own pro-ducer, with Saint Subber willing to take just a percentage for office services." Saint Subber, who began presenting Neil Simon's comedies with the first real smash, *Barefoot in the Park*, has un-doubtedly been a bit more important to the playwright than that;

Simon himself has reported how apprehensively he once waited to hear whether or not the producer, reading a new page of material, would laugh. The fact remains that Simon does most of his own financing (as it is easy to do with six strong hits out of nine tries behind him), mainly manages his own deals, owns his own theater. That mushrooming *Variety* figure of $45,000 per week, which undoubtedly embarrasses the quiet and unassuming Simon, isn't a totting-up of royalties; it got that big out of theater rentals when he put his own hit into his own house, and out of an investor's rather than a playwright's share of the profits.

True as all of this may be, it only explains the dizzying size of Simon's success, not the cause of it. Without owning a theater and without investing in a single one of his own "properties," the playwright would still have three hits running in tandem, would still be a rich enough man for whatever expensive habits he has. Theaters have as often as not been terrible burdens to carry, losing bucketfuls of money when nothing happened to be in them. Lindsay and Crouse, mining a popular comic vein with something like Simon's enthusiasm, owned the Hudson for a time but were, in the end, glad to be rid of it. Successful playwrights often invest in their own plays; they lose, when the play isn't right, right along with the other backers. Simon has a managerial knack, it would seem. The knack wouldn't do him much good if *Plaza Suite*, say, couldn't buck the word about town that this was no time for light comedy.

Well, then, runs another explanation, if not his business acumen, then his simple, if extraordinary, industry. Mr. Simon—you'll notice that occasionally I forget to call him Doc—is known as a man who keeps at it. He doesn't write a hit, go to Bermuda for a rest, then to Europe for inspiration, then to Hollywood for kicks, then to the public library to see if he can find a subject, then to Acapulco just to get away from the public library, and then, some two to three years later, to his typewriter because by this time everyone is asking "whatever became of" him? That's the way most of our playwrights work (?), but not "Doc." He opens a show, probably reads the reviews to see how his investment is going to do, then turns to his machine to tap, tap, tap out the next. He is, in effect, a nine-to-five fellow, daily and for all I know Sundays; in any case, there's always another play ready before the last has begun to slip from capacity. He *expects* himself to produce yearly, he treats his craft as a profession rather than an avocation or a mining expedition which may or may not strike gold, he is a steady and possibly compulsive worker.

The other contemporary playwright officially celebrated for this sort of regulated activity is, of course, Tennessee Williams, and undoubtedly the matter-of-fact, no-nonsense Return to the Machine has *helped* make Williams (*a*) the finest serious play-wright of his generation, and (*b*) the only other playwright I can remember *Variety* making much of because of his incredible earning capacity. Steady work habits are fine; the one thing they do produce is a substantial shelf full of plays rather than the two or three knockouts the average important American playwright manages to squeeze out of his career. But, of course, they don't make Simon's plays playable, any more than they make Williams' the genuine accomplishments they are. I have known people who worked at playwriting four hours a day for twenty years and never got a play produced.

Yes, but see here, still another explanation begins. You talk about Simon operating confidently against the superstition that inconse-quential light comedies are kaput, but Simon doesn't exactly write inconsequential light comedies. He's been mislabeled; what he does has a much more serious, perceptive, *human* base to it than ordi-nary mechanical farce or flyweight comic improvisation. And this is an argument I'm happy to hear being made these days, having delighted in the presence of this lifelike and surprisingly honest substructure in Simon's caprices all the way from *The Odd Couple* up to, though not entirely including, *Last of the Red Hot Lovers*.

There *is* a root, as real as a toothache, beneath the grin of Simon's sunniest work, and it is one of the things that anchors the mere playfulness, ties a kite string to the broadest gags. *The Odd Couple*, in its simplest statement, is already a home truth: two men who don't get along with their wives will probably not get along with each other *in exactly the same way*. It's funny the minute you hear it; a motion picture company paid a million dollars (more or less, and no doubt more) for it in outline alone, before a word of dialogue had been committed to paper. It's a foolproof stage situation that is likely to keep the play around until it's as old as *Charley's Aunt*.

And it's also a sad helpless little commentary on the cussedness of things connubial, indeed on the exasperating nature of *all* relationships. Those two men haven't learned anything from their marital quarrels that will help them share an apartment now, and they aren't going to learn anything from their quarrels now that will help them next time around at home. In fact, they aren't going home. They aren't going anywhere, except into new failures. The fact that they're marvelously funny every moment they're failing doesn't disguise the accurate, and not at all soothing, observation on which their mishaps rest. Hilarity dances on sloppy iceboxes and nights alone in bed.

I have elsewhere expressed my immense admiration for a single line in *Plaza Suite*, a line which may make the first play of that trilogy the most perfectly representative piece of work Mr. Simon has ever done. A husband, married twenty-three years and wretched with his wife during a weekend at the Plaza, is reminded of all he's accomplished in life: got the jobs he wanted, got the wife he wanted, got the kids he wanted, got the home he wanted, got the works. What, then, is he so miserable about? "I want to do it all over again," he explains, grinding his teeth hard.

The line comes as a jolt in the theater; we've been laughing at the foolish quibbles and complaints of these middle-aged misfits, a wife who'd still like the Plaza to be romantic and a husband desperately trying to wriggle his way out, and we've accepted them as reasonably plausible Scarsdale wreckage, tuned up just a little bit to make their jokes bounce off the keyboard harder. But we hadn't realized they were *this* close to our own nerve centers, to the hard perverse core of our own suppressed dreams, and we are startled to notice how easy it was to drop from a laugh into an irremediable loss. The man *can't* do it all over again; the situation is hopeless. And so, with regret, all we can do is return to laughing about it.

What I have particularly liked about this combination of sleekly spaced gagging and seriousness implied but held at just enough distance is Simon's ability to keep his proportions right. At his best he writes a light comedy that has neither too little nor too much seriousness for a light comedy. Enough to guarantee that the material is not being hoked up or faked. Not so much as to call for a weightier play or a surlier attitude. The seriousness, as much as the comedy, is light, deft, not overwhelming, capable of being dealt with in philosophical resignation (followed by a wry grin). What can't be helped is pretty horrible; still, it can't be helped; have another joke. (Doc indeed, reaching into his kit for a line that may make it hurt less.)

If I have a reservation about *Last of the Red Hot Lovers*, which I do, it is connected with a slight self-consciousness that may be creeping into Mr. Simon's head as he realizes, and no doubt gratefully, that the remote sober underside of him is at last being given its due. *Last of the Red Hot Lovers* is also a triad of playlets, in each of which a perspiring businessman, again twenty-three years married and until now faithful, attempts to seduce a woman he's lured to his mother's apartment. The comedy is going to be made of his floundering, his staggering unsuccess in each case.

In the course of the first play, the businessman is given a speech that will adequately, perhaps touchingly, express his state of mind. He's not a particularly lecherous fellow. He really does like his wife. It's just that he has gone for so long doing, uncomplainingly, the normal, the routine, the ordinary things expected of a man in his extremely unspectacular position. And he is, most noticeably, getting older. Any day now it'll all be over for him, sexually sooner than anything, and he won't have had one damn day that was better than another or more colorful than another or more fun than another or more memorable than another. Who wants to subside finally, and without a high kick, into the okay but dreary world that always was?

The speech is a good one. Curiously, though, it's not *also* a funny speech. It is dead straight for as long as it lasts, which is fairly long, and that means that it has been pried loose from the delicate balancing process (now you see seriousness, now you don't) at which Mr. Simon excels, left to stand by itself as a declaration of intent. The hinted ache and the antic compensation are no longer locked together; the fun stops to let frustration declare itself instead of our being given glimpses of the frustration beneath all the happy skittering. For as long as the speech lasts the play is not really a comedy at all, and the isolated seriousness is not of a gravity to make the marked alteration worth it.

Next, having completed and apparently exhausted the "root" speech, the evening moves forward to its subsequent nonseductions without having any further domestic insights to explore. The next two sequences are variations on the first minus the small pain that set the first in motion, with the result that Mr. Simon is now truly forced to invent jokes—mainly jokes about the women, one a pot-smoking chatterbox, the other a semisuicidal Hecuba—in the gratuitous way his detractors have sometimes described. There are still entertaining things in the play, many of them. But, overall, there's been a dislocation. Two strains that normally run together lightly, highlighting one another handsomely, begin to behave like oil and water, retiring to their respective corners.

Be that as it may. Other plays are coming after *Last of the Red Hot Lovers*. The point here is that yes, Mr. Simon is more than a gagman, he does have an eye and an ear for the crazy cruel world about him, and yes, he remains a writer of light comedy, not of anything else. His special victory is to have discovered the exact amount of God's truth a light comedy can properly contain. But, to get back to the thread of our discussion, that blows the explanation that Mr. Simon is successful against the prevailing winds because he isn't really doing what George Kelly once did or what Jerome Chodorov has sometimes done. If he *is* a craftsman putting good one-set domestic entertainments together at a time when theory holds such an act to be unthinkable, if he *is* a fine Broadway playwright functioning at a time when Broadway doesn't support fine Broadway playwrights, how come? What has he done to make a monkey of us all?

Fundamentally, I think, he has learned not to listen. Perhaps he was born knowing how not to listen. There are circumstances in which deafness is an indispensable virtue for survival, and this may be one of them. What has Mr. Simon not stopped to listen to? To the winds, to the soothsayers, to the theorists who see change in the air and announce it before it's settled, to the thinkers, to the mourners, to fashion itself. It has not occurred to Mr. Simon that he had better write a play that is a little bit like Ionesco, that has a lesbian corpse under the couch, that is even as alert to the new candor as the very funny Bruce Jay Friedman is. I doubt that he has for a moment considered doing such a thing. Perhaps he has, perhaps he has. And then decided that, whoever these fellows were, he was someone else.

It is curious how this sort of imperviousness (do you want to call it integrity?) can flourish not only in the face of fashion, but of fact. It is a fact that the theater is in trouble. It is a fact that forms are changing. It is a fact that domestic light comedy seems transparent and antiquated most nights now. It is a fact that virtually everyone else is deeply discouraged about the possibility of doing what Mr. Simon habitually wishes to do (though I suppose one ought to mention, in passing, that the *only* other success of the Broadway season in which Mr. Simon made so much money was Leonard Gershe's *Butterflies Are Free*, which just happened to be a light domestic comedy).

In the face of conditions which would discourage him if he paid them any mind, in the face of fashions which would outlaw him if he worried about what year it was, in the face of earlier (and no doubt forthcoming) attacks on his methods which would curl his soul if he were susceptible to what my children call being "psyched out," in the face of a thousand fingers wagging at him to tell him what he ought to do, Neil Simon considers what he can do and does it.

Ironically, he may be the man—middle-aged, rich, establishment (if there is such a thing)—who has profited most from a younger generation's admonition to do your own thing. That is certainly what he does, stubbornly, blandly, obtusely against the grain. And, lo and behold, the kids are right. It works. Of course, they didn't think it would work that way.

None of us did. We may have to rearrange certain notions. Forms do change. But do they ever really die? If a man comes along who is right for them, even though he comes along ten or ninety or two hundred years late, will they pop up once more for him in response to his right choice? *A Man for All Seasons*, after all, is a chronicle play. *The Great White Hope* can be called, without insulting it, a nineteenth-century melodrama. *The Price* is Ibsen, and it is more than a ghost. For that matter, a case could be made to the effect that Neil Simon was simply buying out Menander's shop, good will and all. (I have a sneaking feeling that he may be better than Menander; the ancient Greek's reputation rode high so long as it was based on a smattering of aphorisms thought to have been culled from his plays, but when one full comedy manuscript finally turned up not long ago it wouldn't have taken a Pulitzer over *The Odd Couple*.) We are always talking about having to learn to live with change. We may also have to learn to live with shining surfaces that go away and come again, like the moon.

In any event, there's news for playwrights. It is the intimidated, inhibited, fashion-fearing playwright who is most likely to fail. Some men will kick the traces and do the New because that is the nervous charge that is in them. All hail. Others may, if they have the courage and the calm, put a sheet of paper in the typewriter and begin typing "Act One. An attic apartment. Leona enters." To thine own hand be true and it will follow as the night the day that *Variety* will be stunned by your grosses along the Broadway God forgot.

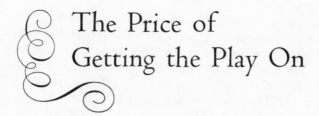

The Price of
Getting the Play On

I

WHEN I devoted a newspaper column to inquiring where all the playwrights were, our theaters being so very uncrowded these days, I was actually asking where all the *hit* playwrights were, i.e., those who'd been markedly successful, weren't yet overage, but had disappeared nonetheless. Naturally, when the piece appeared quite a few letters came flying in, some from those very playwrights I was being nosey about. These good souls explained that (*a*) they were sitting it out in Switzerland until Jerzy Grotowski went away, or (*b*) sweating it out in Hollywood until nudity went away, or (*c*) sleeping it out in Menninger's until *I* went away.

But far and away most of the letters came from playwrights, or at least people who were writing plays, who'd not only never had a hit or a production but had never even been able to get a producer or an agent to so much as *read* a play. This was the biggest yelp of all, and also the most unanswerable. It's one thing to be told that your play is no good, that you are totally without talent, and that it will be better for your wife, your aging mother, and all your children if, this very minute, you go into some other line of work. That's a clean-cut answer, it may come from someone versed in the trade, it may tell you what you have to know if not what you want to know.

But to sit out there in Des Moines or Albuquerque or Stowe or Kenilworth with three or four or six or eight manuscripts heavy in your hands, your heart even heavier with all the labor and the longing, and not to have any way of knowing whether the stuff is any good or not is insupportable. Stone walls do not a prison make, but they're awfully hard on the head. The Berlin wall comes to seem fluff alongside the Broadway wall, and the frustration can build to a fury. (Some of the letters I got were angry enough to suggest talent.) Moreover, the one thing desperately needed at the New York center just now is new writers with new scripts, and, since *some* of the work presently languishing in San Jose and Grand Haven is apt to show promise and perhaps even be performable, the obvious, anguished need on both sides is to bring the right parties together. How does one arrange this if producers and agents won't read unsolicited scripts?

Let's get rid of one thing right off. Producers *won't* read unsolicited scripts. They won't do it for a single fearful reason: they are terrified of plagiarism suits. All a producer has to do to run into a plagiarism suit is to produce a play six years from now that just happens to bear a slight resemblance to pages 14–17 of a little turkey that came in a large envelope and was opened and acknowledged by his office boy yesterday. (I once did a television adaptation of Mary Chase's delightful play about a witch, *Mrs. McThing*, only to spend the rest of the Sunday evening on which it was shown trying to get rid of a woman who phoned from Vermont to say that she *was* that witch and was suing for the theft of her life story.) Envelopes containing manuscripts go back unopened. Plays do bear resemblances to one another and resemblances can cost thousands. Forget about this ploy and don't blame the producers.

Plays must come to producers' desks through official, responsible, safe channels—meaning agents. But agents won't read *unsolicited* manuscripts either. That is to say, you can't pack your latest treasure into a binder and pop it into the mail unbidden, expecting it to be read upon arrival in New York. The reason for this is that there aren't enough agents in the world with enough time in the world to read all the scripts in the world. It's a mathematical impossibility. Thousands of new scripts are copyrighted

annually at the Library of Congress and there's no agency on earth
big enough to get through them all properly and still stay in
business.

Playreading takes time, costs money, and is most often profitless.
Ten years ago one of the most distinguished agents in the business
estimated that it cost his office approximately ten thousand dollars
to get the out-of-town curtain up on *each* new play accepted and
optioned. That's to say, maintaining an office and serving the
playwright creates that much overhead just to open a play, and if
the play doesn't work the office gets nothing back. Agents, like all
other guardian angels, can and do go broke; they'd all go broke if
they tried to cope with everything that threatened to come in.

How much *can* they read of all that's offered them? Their
estimates vary, as their tastes and their staffs and their appetites
vary. (You can get lists of reputable agents any time you like
simply by writing the Dramatists Guild, 243 West 44 Street, New
York, N.Y. 10036, or the Society of Authors' Representatives,
101 Park Avenue, New York, N.Y. 10017, if you don't want to
just copy one out of *The Writer's Yearbook*.) After a little poking
around, not exhaustive but I hope reasonably representative, I'd
estimate that agents are able to read fifteen to eighteen percent of
the material offered them. How, then, do they select the fifteen or
eighteen percent they'll actually read?

By mail, by hearsay, and by hard evidence. Take them in turn.
The first indispensable step for a writer who wants to get rid of a
play he's hatched is not to send off the play but to send off a letter,
asking politely if the agent would like to see the work in hand.
(Politeness helps; some writers have been known to storm into
agents' offices and demand to be represented as though it were a
birthright, just as they have stormed into producers' offices and
shouted *"J'accuse"* when their very first one-acter wasn't
promptly booked into the Booth. Never mind modesty. Sanity
helps.) The letter should be brief enough, but it should suggest the
sort of play that's been written and it should say a little something
about the writer's background.

Admittedly, as a screening device, this is chancy. It means that a
little click will have to sound somewhere in the back of the agent's
head as he reads the letter, that some whiff of charm or intelligence
or common sense will have to drift from the page like perfume. It

might take almost as much talent to compose such a letter—
straightforward, unpretentious, and yet tantalizing—as to write a
play. But some get through that way.

More get through by what I've called hearsay and you could
call "having contacts" or "knowing somebody" or just "luck."
Audrey Wood first heard of Tennessee Williams from Molly
Kazan, wife of the director, and Molly Kazan came across him
because he'd submitted a couple of one-acters to a contest being
sponsored by the Group Theater. (As a result, Mr. Williams got
an agent, and a great one, though it was six years later that he got
his first hit.)

It works by phone and by friends and by any remote control
you can cook up. Which means that that first letter can also contain any recommendations that are going—from university professors, from local theater directors, from newspaper critics in the
community you chafe in, from unwary playwrights accosted in
hotel bars. *Anyone* who has seen a playwright's work and is willing
to speak up for it can and should be pressed into service. It's
legitimate and it carries weight.

But now to the hard evidence, which does involve hard work.
The playwright himself, if he really wants to come to attention a
hundred or a thousand miles away from where he's sitting and
waiting, can't sit and wait. He's got to create the circumstances in
which those recommendations become possible. In short, he's got
to get produced—not in New York, not yet, but in Tallahassee or
Twin Forks. The opportunities for this are approximately twenty
times greater today than they were when I was a young teacher
some twenty-five years ago—and it was possible then. (I am myself a failed creative writer, but I was being produced all over the
place by the time I was twenty, in Elks' Lodges, in American
Legion halls, in church basements, in university theaters, and by
the time I was twenty-seven I had a fine flop on Broadway; my
wife, starting in university theaters, managed her first Broadway
flop by twenty-three.) Today there are theaters wherever you
look, including some you can't see behind the dirty storefronts,
and where none exist they can easily be made. The one thing every
small town on earth is full of is actors; you don't even have to
whistle to get them to come in nights and do your play.

Nagging the director of a local community or university theater to do your play, and getting it done, isn't the end of the road, only the beginning. The first play may, but probably will not, get you the kind of recommendations, the word of mouth and word on paper, you need to push further. You'll have to risk it and go on. (By the time I did have an agent, another great one, I asked him, in a moment of mild despair, how many flops I'd have to get through before I could expect a hit. He said twelve.) But all the time you're failing, you're learning. (You may even learn that wisdom says get out.) And, if you've got anything, you'll be getting better, getting closer. In due time you'll have the evidence to back you up.

Certainly there's nothing simple about this, nothing quick or comfy or ego-sustaining (although the production process is always interesting, no matter where it takes place). But why should *becoming* a playwright be simple or easy? Some years ago (in 1953, to be exact) Sean O'Casey wrote in *The New York Times* of how he'd tried to get Shaw to do a preface for an early book of his, this no doubt on the "recommendation" theory. Shaw refused, wisely according to O'Casey, telling him that he'd "have to go through the mill like the rest of us." As O'Casey says, "Shaw went through the mill, and came out bounding; Yeats went through it, and came out with a wide-brimmed hat, a great black coat, and a flowing tie; I came out of it tattered and torn, like a man tossed by the cow with the crumpled horn, but still sparring, ready for defense and a forward blow. But it isn't a nice experience, and it leaves one wondering."

He goes on:

I always warn beginners who write to me to get to work in field, factory, or workshop, and stay there as long as they can. Beginners should be told the facts of life. In drama schools, they should be told that merely to step on a stage isn't the advent of a great actor or actress; that a brush in the hand and a beard on the chin doesn't compose a great painter; that everything has to be learned through years of work; that work, work to make an artist is as arduous as the work that makes an editor or a stonemason; the one difference being that if either editor or stonemason weren't excellent at their work they'd have to go; while the incompetent artist can go on forever and ever, deceiving himself, though he deceives very few others.

Amen, amen. And then there's the reverse side of the coin. When the work does get done, when it happens, it's noticed—noticed very quickly even if it takes place at the Long Wharf or the Alley or the Arena or in a school gymnasium in Connecticut. People are apt to come running at the first real whisper. And at that point, the agent you need, deserve, and get will not be a fairy godmother, which he or she was never meant to be, but—as you will discover—a valuable friend.

2

EVERY once in a while in Enid Bagnold's enchanting *Autobiography* there is a cry from the heart against the theater's massive and unending demand for collaboration. "The theater is a gross art," wails the author of those far from gross plays *The Chalk Garden* and *The Chinese Prime Minister*. The theater is "built in sweeps and over-emphasis," and "compromise is its second name." A writer writes; what the writer has written is then handed over to producers, directors, designers, actors, each of whom inevitably, helplessly, humanly alters the stir of the words on the page. "What I do," Miss Bagnold says in her straightforward way, "cannot easily be remade in the bodies, movements, voices of human beings. Ah, if I had known the delicate and bitter labour far far ahead. . . ."

And if Shakespeare had known the delicate and bitter labor far far ahead? I have got Bagnold and Shakespeare all mixed up in my head at the moment because, between devouring the book and going back to see Moses Gunn's *Othello* for a second time, I have been reminded of an absolutely overpowering conviction I had while watching *Othello* for the first time, in Connecticut, three months earlier. I know, I swear I know, just how Shakespeare got Iago's motivation all muddled.

He started out plainly enough. In the opening few lines it's perfectly clear. Iago hates the Moor because the Moor has passed him over and given Cassio his command. That's simple and it's really adequate. Nothing will be entirely adequate to explain the evil in Iago until the evil in the universe is itself fully explained. Short of that, this will do. Accept it as a formal motive and get on with the interesting play.

But Shakespeare didn't let it rest there. And do you know why? Somebody got to him. It may have been the actor playing Iago, who didn't feel firmly "grounded" in his villainy. It may have been one of his partners in production. It may have been someone in his first audiences, grumbling on the way out that he didn't see exactly why that Iago fellow had to go and make all that fuss.

Whoever it was, *someone* said to Shakespeare, in effect, "Can't you give him a little more to go on, make him *really* hate the Moor, something personal, something everyone out front will understand, something like—I'm just talking—having Iago think maybe the Moor's been fooling around after his wife?"

And Shakespeare bought it. He didn't buy it with any interest or enthusiasm. For instance, although he'd been meticulously careful to base Othello's suspicions of Desdemona and Cassio on actual meetings and exchanges between the two, he never did go to the trouble to drop in a scene between Othello and Emilia, one in which Iago might at least scent a remotely possible betrayal.

Instead, he tucked the additional motive into two lines of dialogue during a soliloquy—that is to say, into the spot where it'd go easiest, with least bother. Iago, almost as an afterthought (and don't tell me it wasn't an afterthought), mentions that he also suspects the Moor of having slipped between his sheets, rather as though he were more worried about the laundry than the lady. And then again, some time later, two more lines in another soliloquy. The work—obviously work Shakespeare didn't want to do— was now done. It was done to satisfy a collaborator. It confused the motivation rather than strengthened it, the two motives actually tended to cancel each other out, everything became half-hearted, apologetic, and patently insufficient thereafter, but Shakespeare had obliged a colleague, and in the theater all colleagues must be prepared to oblige. They make trades.

Now it's no use telling me this may not be so, or that, so or no, it can't be proved. I smell it. And I am now as intractable on the point as Miss Bagnold is on most of hers. *That's* intractable. She disposes of someone who has told a story differently from her version of it thus: "If he says in his book he wasn't there I don't believe it. He is dead: I am eighty. There's no arguing with either of us."

Just how vulnerable an author is to a producer or an agent or a player is made clear in a horrendous incident in Miss Bagnold's chips-down, chin-up memoir. She had written a play, not long after *The Chalk Garden,* in which the hero was a scientist, a mathematician. And he had, mathematically, discovered God. "He had worked Him out. He wanted proof. So he wanted to die. His brother, treating him as an ordinary suicide, tried to prevent him." Intriguing idea.

But what was essential to the final scene of the play, Miss Bagnold goes on to say, "was that the suicide should be by poison. I had my eye on Socrates. Death by the raising of a cup can be a fascinating secret between the playwright and the audience. Not 'Will he die?' but 'When?' The audience, allowed the privilege of knowledge, is agog: the peopled stage in ignorance. Also (Socrates) one can talk while dying. And in parables that the audience alone can understand. This was my carefully-worked-out drama for the play's end."

She wanted John Gielgud to play the part. Mr. Gielgud, then out of the country, responded through his agent that he would play the part provided, in the last scene, he be permitted to shoot himself. Mr. Gielgud is among the most intelligent of actors; there is some thought that it may have been his agent who bore down hard on the change. But, come production, Miss Bagnold did rewrite the scene so that the hero put a bullet through his brain. If ever a colleague's demand blew a scene, and perhaps a whole play, to smithereens, this was surely the time. *All* values destroyed in the switch. And if Bagnold could not withstand Gielgud, do you suppose Shakespeare often withstood Burbage? No, it's always been that way. Give and take.

Why should anyone have to give to an actor? Because the actor has his own instabilities, fears, right and wrong instincts to contend with. Because his reputation is fragile, because his life is precarious. Look at Moses Gunn. Those few of us who go off-Broadway with great regularity have known, for some years past, that Mr. Gunn is one of the finest actors in the country. But the general public hasn't known it, hasn't seen the man. He hasn't Landed (as James Earl Jones hadn't Landed until *The Great White Hope*, as Sada Thompson, brilliant as she is, still hasn't Landed).

The opportunity came, or seemed to come. Mr. Gunn was cast as Othello in Connecticut; his first reviews were in the main extremely favorable; the production decided to move for a two-week trial run into the Anta in New York. This, now, should have been It for Mr. Gunn. The world should have found him, identified him permanently.

On opening night in New York it didn't happen. Why? I can't tell you that, I can only guess. During the three months he had played in Connecticut he might have overdecorated the role somewhat; there were many more, very restless, gestures with those incredibly tapering fingers now. But that could only have been a small part of the matter. His first act remained beautiful, stately, stylized, resonant. The second was fine, passionate but still firmly framed. The third was seriously off, overpitched, beginning in a reedy vocal agony that could only go higher, bypassing the open diapason tones that had earlier made his final two set-speeches such somber miraculous music.

Opening night nerves? The accumulated strain of a young lifetime of reaching? The need to make it all come true Tonight? Something was too much; and now Mr. Gunn, somewhat better known to be sure, has to do it all over again. There is heartbreak on the actor's side too, you see. Anxieties grow up, defenses harden, hides toughen, protective demands increase—just as they do with playwrights. And so finally the two, writer and actor, become locked in mortal, sometimes magnificently fruitful, combat.

Miss Bagnold is an honest recorder of combat, plain about the pain, candid about her own good and bad habits, aware of her idiosyncrasies, and proud of the use she has made of them. She writes a gaily capricious prose, first-naming everyone in the world so that they must be identified in footnotes, breaking off sentences, paragraphs, and time itself to tell you what's going on in her head *right now*, leaping the leaps that metaphors make, funny and bold and armed to the teeth. Her charm is exceeded only by her strength of mind and will.

And so, summing up her experience of theater, she says: "If I had known the agony, the lost and spilt meanings—well, I would have done it all the same. Almost now, at my age, I would write for no public. I would sit like a woman lost in the pleasure of her game of patience until she falls dead face down upon the cards."

3

PAY close attention now.

One warm July night during the summer of 1969, Josef Bush, adapter of a play based on the Marquis de Sade's *Philosophy in the Bedroom*, marched into the off-Broadway Bouwerie Lane Theater not too long before curtain time and, armed with a bucket of white paint, proceeded to disfigure all the scenery he could reach—the scenery for his very own show. The producers had changed his show without his consent, dispensing with certain actors, parting with the director, dropping various photographic projections, introducing a thirty-second nude scene. The author could not, would not, tolerate these changes in his text, and, to show who was boss, he exploded.

A month or two earlier the two principal authors of a Broadway entertainment known as *Hair*, who were also engaged in playing two of the principal roles on stage, were ordered out of the cast and out of the theater by the producers. Why? Because they had changed the text. They'd spent some time appearing in a West Coast company of the show, they'd thought of a few new things to do and say that struck them as bright, and they'd slipped them in. No dice. The producer was going to stand on the text he'd bought. You might conceive of him as Galahad, champion of the authentic, preserver of the true.

In both cases you'll notice it was the playwright who lost. One playwright was unable to keep the management from making changes, the others were unable to introduce changes the management didn't want. Playwrights may be creative, but they don't exactly seem to be in charge.

This goes directly against the grain of the ethos and the mythos of the contemporary theater. Whenever someone, exasperated beyond endurance, asks "Whose play is it?" we give a ready

answer. All of us do. We say that the play belongs to the playwright and that the playwright is the one, onlie, and true begetter
of the work, that he remains lord and master of his property
forever thereafter, that the work cannot be altered without his
heartfelt approval, that his words belong to him at least until death
and expiring copyrights do them part. That's the legend we sub-
scribe to and, for the most part, the law we make.

Reviewers, even critics, assume that what they are seeing and
hearing is the work of the man whose name is listed on the
program and they bestow approval or issue condemnation on that
basis. They are not necessarily idiots, they have probably heard
that there was tinkering done in Boston, they may have read in
Variety, or barring that in Jack O'Brian, that Neil Simon was seen
slipping quietly through hotel corridors in a town where some
other man's play was trying out. *Someone* may have added a
comma or subtracted a coarse phrase before the show came in. But,
the assumption runs, it was done with the knowledge, the permission, and no doubt even the gratitude of the playwright. He's left
his name on the work, hasn't he? The ultimate authority of the
playwright, at least to accept or reject, is preserved in our habits of
thought and in the words we type out. Commentators who are
farther removed from the practicing theater and who may not
even read *Variety* no doubt assume, without thinking about it, that
the Tennessee Williams text they are reading is the text Tennessee
Williams first wrote, as in fact the Edward Albee text they are
reading *is* sometimes the text Edward Albee first wrote. Close or
distant, near or far, we stand with the playwright. His is the ultimate power. Whatever hanky-panky may have gone on during the
hideous production process, we believe that he has ultimately
exercised that power.

Contracts generally make sure that he can and will do so. Most
authors and producers, upon coming lovingly together, sign what
is known as the Minimum Basic Agreement. The author now has,
in writing, the right to approve of the players, the right to approve
of the director, the right to insist that his play be played as he
wrote it unless he himself approves such changes as may be proposed. Of course, none of these approvals may be "unreasonably
withheld," it says in the fine print, and "unreasonably" is a wide-
open word that only a battery of psychiatrists could define, but

you'd still think a playwright could move confidently forward, bolstered by the support of the community and the heartening language of his contract.

Naturally, he can't. Naturally, it doesn't work that way. The theater is a human institution as well as a commercial one. The commercial aspects and pressures—the need for name stars, the need for salable subject matter, the need to woo theater parties, gimmickry of every kind—are overly familiar to all of us and I won't burden you with recapitulation here. But the human aspects may be less apparent from a distance. The playwright is human, the producer is reportedly so. The first thing to be recognized about a human producer is that he has a human mind. The most notorious thing about any human mind is that it is subject to change. The producer *may* change his mind about doing the play and it may never get on at all.

This is the First Terror that haunts the playwright, that cripples him and begins to take his play away from him before he has so much as signed a contract. It is a psychological matter entirely. The producer hasn't really threatened him or been mean to him, hasn't risen from behind his desk like a bogey about to devour him. The producer has, thus far, been nice to him. What else would he be? He is even about to give him some money, some option money. But inside the playwright's head an insidious and diminishing little theme has begun its march: "I must be agreeable. If I am not agreeable, he may drop the play. If he drops the play, no one else will ever touch it. It will be mine again."

You see, so long as the play is the playwright's and his alone, there is exactly one thing he can do with it. He can take it home and put it in a desk and leave it there. If there is one thing more than another that he *doesn't* want, it is to remain sole proprietor of his play.

And so he gives away a little something of himself, spiritually, simply by entering the production process. He is now marked for surrender and is going to give away more. (Lillian Hellman finds the simple act of entering the production process so fundamentally distasteful, such an invasion of creative privacy, that she can rarely bring herself to write about it; one senses that she does not wish to remember it.)

The theater is human and temporal. There is a clock on the wall.

Presently it begins to tick. The kind of thing it begins to say, after a few preliminary weeks or months, is this: "*If* I do not accept a star or director I don't want, and *if* I don't agree to make the changes *they* want before signing their contracts, they may not sign their contracts, in which case we will not be able to go into rehearsal on time, in which case we will lose the theater we have booked, in which case the play will have to be put off until next year, in which case we may not find any better star or even any star, in which case the play won't be done." The First Terror has a long reach. The playwright agrees with the director that a few structural changes may be advisable. The playwright agrees with the actor that a new third-act scene or speech or exit is necessary. The playwright agrees because the price of going on is giving in, and not going on is unthinkable.

Rehearsals may be better or worse, depending on luck. The director who was available at the time may prove to be just right for the actors who were available at the time. The actors, comfortable and becoming creative, may charm the playwright enormously. Or exactly the opposite may happen, with changes being made either way (a perfectly good actor may not be able to read a perfectly good line well, rhythms being idiosyncratic and in frequent need of adjustment). Whichever way things are going, matters do not as a rule reach the panic stage during rehearsal. For one thing, it isn't absolutely clear how they *are* going yet. The play hasn't been performed before an audience. The mix may be right or wrong, the playwright may be hopeful or apprehensive, no one can be certain of what will happen on the out-of-town, or preview, first night. Furthermore, during this period the playwright is aware that he retains a certain prestige. Being a playwright, he is still the only man in the building capable of *writing* the changes being requested.

This last link to glory will be promptly attended to the minute the show opens wherever it opens. Occasionally a show opens in a condition that can be called right, but very rarely. Most shows, even those that are eventually going to succeed, open imperfectly. That is to say, the playwright has now been *proved* imperfect. Until now, officially if not in fact, he has functioned as sole creator; it now seems that he didn't function terribly well as sole creator. He is suspect. To himself. Again, this is first a state of mind. The actors do not attack him in the theater lobby, the producer does not sneer as they pass in the aisle—not unless things are *seriously* wrong. But the playwright looks at himself with a shade of distrust: the effect he'd intended in Act Two doesn't work, the line he'd thought hilarious gets nothing at all, the character he loved most moves no audience to tears. He is now enrolling in the Unsure of Himself League, which means that he is ripe for what comes next.

What comes next is help. Help comes in all forms. It comes from the director, who suddenly sees the play in a new light because the producer is going to fire *him* if he doesn't quickly see the play in a new light. It comes from the producer and the actors—on the telephone, in hotel rooms, during rehearsals—and friends who have come for the opening and enemies who have come for the possible early closing. It comes from reviews, it comes from ticket brokers, it comes from press agents, it comes from perfectly ordinary people who have seen the show and have loud things to say about it in the lobby. The playwright is the beneficiary of an endless solicitude, all of it well intentioned in the sense that the people giving advice sincerely want to save the show (although it doesn't necessarily follow that they are trying to save the *same* show), all of it given on the simple unquestioned assumption that the playwright wants help and is going to accept it. And he is going to accept some of it, not because there is so much noise around him but for a much more urgent reason: that show needs fixing.

If a playwright is clever, devious, and quick-witted enough to persuade everyone at hand that he is taking their advice while actually and instantly substituting new material of his very own that will play perfectly *the first time it is tried*, he may hold some ground in the situation. If he is not each and all of these things, and blessed by the the gods besides, he is ready to be enveloped by the Second Terror, which is only an extension of the First Terror but much more absolute in its effect. A while ago, in reviewing a new show, I mentioned certain oddities of development that were utterly inexplicable given the premises of the evening, the casting, etcetera. I soon received a thirteen-page, reasonably calm, wholly persuasive letter from the author saying that he found these oddities very odd too. In fact, none of them had been his work. A director, taking over from the original director out of town, had insisted upon them.

Why had he permitted them? Simple. The original director was gone. A new director of some standing was required. But the new director, when approached by the producer, said that he could not possibly guarantee to redo the show effectively in a hurry unless he were given full command, final word on everything. The playwright gave him full command to get him. He had to do it because if he did not do it the producer would not bring the show into New York. The show would close on the road, which is even worse than not getting it done in the first place, because after a show closes on the road the chances of its ever being picked up for production again are nil, or extremely minimal. And so it goes, as Kurt Vonnegut would say.

The playwright, contractually, can still say no, can always say no. But by saying no he will put everyone, including himself, out of work. You might think that this chipping-away process, reducing real ownership to the posture of begging for favors, would end or be reversed once a show is a success in New York. Surely the playwright's power is returned to him once he produces a smash. Well, Mary Chase's *Harvey* opened as a smash, one of the biggest straight-play smashes of all time. Within a very short time its first star, Frank Fay, was adding a little something of his own to the proceedings. At the final curtain he was doing a monologue, a monologue that became rather longer and more important as time went on. The play never needed it, of course. Apparently Mr. Fay, an entertaining but insatiable man, needed it. Its effect, in the playhouse, was to suggest that it was Fay who had been responsible for the play's success, not the play proper: monologues are generally added only when shows are desperate. I have no privileged information on how hard Miss Chase worked, or had her agent work, to get that monologue out of there. If she did try, she tried quietly: there was never any hint of trouble. Whether she tried or not, the monologue stayed, the actor's authority came first. Could Miss Chase have overruled Mr. Fay, insisted he be brought to heel? Yes. And she would have rocked the boat on a hit. Not many people care or dare to do that. The authors of *Hair* dropped the new material their producer didn't want and went quietly back into the playhouse.

What an intolerable place the theater must be, you say, and how unseemly a place for literate, intelligent, sensitive people to be working in. That isn't the point I wish to make; we know the whole roster of horrors, and if we don't we can read William Gibson's *The Seesaw Log* or William Goldman's *The Season* to get more than a glimpse of them. The point I would like to make here is that as the playwright surrenders his play piece by piece he is always surrendering it voluntarily.

He doesn't have to. He can always do what Elaine May did with her first commercially produced play. The play, with Mike Nichols in the starring role, opened out of town and was in transparently poor shape. Obviously it would have to be rewritten in part, and quickly. Miss May declined, refused to alter a word. The show closed. It has never been seen in New York. That's the option.

Then it's just not worth it being a playwright, is it? Wrong again. It's worth it provided you are a *play*wright. A play is not simply something written, it is something written to be performed, which means that it is subject to alteration under the experience of performance. It cannot be otherwise. Until a play is exposed to an audience, adjusted and readjusted to achieve its right and maximum effect on that audience, it cannot be called a playable play. That is not horrible, though the labor involved may well be. It is the nature of the beast. I would say that seventy-five percent of everything we've been talking about is inevitable and that perhaps fifty percent of it is healthy.

A play trying to find its shape in rehearsal and performance is doing nothing more than going through, in public, the editing that a novel goes through in private. The process is much more complicated because performance involves so many more factors: actors to speak the lines, directors to arrange the movement, a thousand auditors present and reacting openly at the very same time; but the process is not in itself more disgraceful. A novel undergoes changes too, not always amicably. Editors and publishers ask for cuts and revisions and novelists do not reject all of them. Novelists sometimes publish portions of the work in trial-flight magazines and rearrange a bit on the basis of reader response. Along the way there may be serious disagreements. Philip Roth changed editors at Random House during the writing of *Portnoy's Complaint*, which, in the theater, is the equivalent of changing directors out of town. Reworking is standard in the arts, even if it is more spectacular in the theater.

Probably it has always been just this spectacular and just this exasperating, or nearly so. Certainly Shakespeare, sure of himself as he should have been, went through it: he needs only one line, "let those that play your clowns speak no more than is set down for them," to let us know that he would not have been unfamiliar with the problem a Broadway author had several seasons ago. This author's play varied its clocked running time as much as fifteen minutes per night, depending upon what the leading actress chose to say on a given evening. (There was never any public protest, the show was successful.) Molière has left us a *Tartuffe* that is not the *Tartuffe* he first wrote. However superior the original form may or may not have been, whatever agonies Molière went through battling for and then amending his text, *Tartuffe* is a great play. Pressures changed it. They did not destroy it. Aristophanes could be quite snappish about the reworking he had to do, hated to do, but invariably did. We know that the only text we have of one of his comedies is a late text because it contains a complaint about the maltreatment given the first text. Playwrights have always seethed and have always fixed.

Even so, wouldn't it be a good idea to try to find or invent a form of practical theater in which the playwright could do his necessary work without so much personal pain and so much sacrifice of his first-born? Of course it would. You invent one. People *are* inventing, or trying to invent, such forms all the time. A playwright can, for instance, become his own director, as Sidney Kingsley and Arthur Miller and dozens of others have at one time or another done. That eliminates one problem, though it creates a new one: when the show is before audiences and in need of adjustment, will the playwright be able to get the new material written if he's in the theater all the time rehearsing the actors? Playwrights have become their own producers. On the whole, this hasn't worked out terribly well. The Playwrights' Company did flourish for a time, though after a while it relied heavily upon the written work of outsiders. Producing takes time and energy too, time away from writing. Some playwrights have owned their own theaters. Usually they were glad, after a while, to get the problem of maintaining real estate off their backs. Each of these gestures may have helped; each took its own toll.

Today's playwrights, despairing of solving the problem inside the clock-ticking urgencies of the commercial theater, have tended to move away from the New York center. Off to the resident reps, off to the universities, off to the Berkshires come summer, is the cry. There's merit in it, so long as we don't hide the fact that the same kind of work goes on. I have on my desk a prompt copy of Robert Lowell's version of the *Prometheus Bound* as it was first performed at the Yale University Theater. Scarcely a page passes without cuts or alterations. Who made the cuts? Did Lowell, in the calm exercise of his authority, make all of them? I hope he did. But I daresay that director Jonathan Miller suggested some of them, that the professional actors in the company may have urged others, that the sheer pressure of an audience to be pleased or at least held in the playhouse dictated others.

Howard Sackler benefited enormously from having his *The Great White Hope* first done by Arena Stage in Washington, a year before its New York appearance. The Washington production, which was approximately as good from the beginning as the ultimate production in New York, gave the playwright a chance to see what had to be done to the text before taking it elsewhere. One thing that had to be done was cut an hour out of it. That's a long time, and the play changed shape and implication in the process. The principal virtue of having a resident theater tryout, and then a year to do the tinkering, is, of course, that that clock has stopped making its threatening sound. The playwright still has to rewrite, but he can afford to think while he is doing it.

And yet taking away the clock is no guarantee that agony will go away with it. If ever there was a modern playhouse that ignored the clock, that could afford to work on a project without pressure from the outside until the project was ready, it was Stanislavsky's Moscow Art Theater. Stanislavsky frequently took months to prepare a production; he was free to take years. And Chekhov, the beneficiary of this process, constantly complained that Stanislavsky had ruined his plays. A case can be made to say that indeed he had, or that he had at least misinterpreted them. Not even Chekhov, given all that lovely leisure, could get what he wanted or thought he wanted.

Some of the agony is simply institutional-temperamental and will always be there. What playwright will ever see on the stage what he saw in his head? No playwright will, ever. He may upon occasion see something better, but he will never see his vision made tangible without alteration. The shape of an actress' eyebrows alone will alter it. Collaboration cannot be escaped; it is one of the theater's imperatives. And collaboration with the audience, during early performances, is imperative, too. I said a few paragraphs back that I thought a considerable part of it was healthy. Perhaps I can get at this backwards. After a string of early short-play successes, Edward Albee crashed through with a successful large-scale work, *Who's Afraid of Virginia Woolf?* Since that time, however, he has been in trouble; four or five plays have come and gone with only one being modestly rewarding or rewarded. I think a part of the trouble here comes from the wall Mr. Albee was able to build about himself during the production process. Thanks to his first successes, he was in a position to assemble the kind of staff he wanted. He went into partnership with two producers who would be unswervingly loyal to him. He used the same director again and again, no doubt for the same reason. All of these people, producers and director alike, were first-rate craftsmen. They remain among the best in the business. But they may have succeeded too well in their task. Their task was to erect a buffer state about the author, a closed corporation that would protect the play's text. The situation was meant to serve what the playwright had written. One gathers that cuts and changes were made very rarely during the rehearsal and preview process. The shows, even the most disastrous of them, were always ready well in advance; no preview was ever canceled and Mr. Albee's productions were among the first to permit critics to drop in early, everything having been "set" for so long. Substantially, Mr. Albee had arranged for himself an ideal world in which *no* pressures other than friendly and precommitted ones would be applied to mar a manuscript. And this is, of course, the dream all playwrights have dreamed.

If it did not seem to serve Mr. Albee well, if his work has diminished rather than grown under the happy dispensation, I can think of only one reason: he has been made too secure and the security has invited self-indulgence. By shielding the playwright too thoroughly from the existential give-and-take of the public arena, by isolating him from audience response to the point where he could pretend indifference to audience response, the dream creation has put him out of touch—or permitted him to put himself out of touch—with certain hard realities of the playhouse, with the need to go to the audience and do battle. I think Mr. Albee does need to do battle again and that his work will very likely profit from it.

Do battle. The play is the playwright's, as we all agree. Everything that can be done for the playwright to make the battle at least bearable, unabsurd, not automatically damaging, should be done. But the play that comes to be *is* born of a battle. The battle goes on inside the playwright as he measures what he can have against what he must have. It goes on within, and with, his many colleagues as a group mind comes into being to make public what has hitherto been private. It goes on within, and with, the audience as the experience is tested to see whether a thousand minds will hold it true. And when all of this rough-and-tumble is finished, the playwright whose play has survived it can sit back and gasp, "Yes, it's mine," remembering to thank in secret the actor who has salvaged a key scene or the director who has invented one, while the playwright whose play has not survived it can only rage (truthfully), "No, it's not mine," and take a paint brush, or an ax, to the scenery.

We don't have to praise this condition of life, this possibly unacceptable profession. We do have to recognize it for the unavoidable contest it is, and cry accordingly.

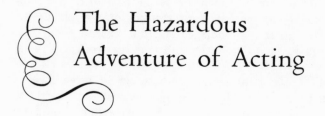

The Hazardous Adventure of Acting

I

IT SOMETIMES seems that all you have to do to turn a great clown into a great actor is teach him to do less.

There are endless theatrical stories, involving everyone from George M. Cohan to Menasha Skulnik, in which the key to the sudden success of an old vaudevillian in a straight role is nothing more than the paring away of surplus effect. In *Ah, Wilderness!* George Cohan was permitted to play front, as he so often had, but forbidden to wink at the audience. In *The Rivals* Bobby Clark was allowed to play all sorts of games with a bottle of ink and a quill pen, but forbidden to gargle. Just a little less camp made Frank Fay fit for *Harvey;* in films an Ed Wynn parted from his giggle or a Victor Moore deprived of his wide-eyed whine instantly produced a first-rate character actor. Take something away, take almost anything away, and what's left is astonishingly legitimate.

True of Bert Lahr, too. In the candid, harrowing, ultimately very moving biography that John Lahr has written of his father, *Notes on a Cowardly Lion,* the transformation from burlesque zany to stunning interpreter of *Waiting for Godot* began on a movie lot in 1938. Bert Lahr had been cast, much to the surprise of anyone who'd seen him work, as Claudette Colbert's loyal manager in a film called *Zaza*, and when the film was finished the talk of the trade was all about the "sincerity and skill," the "unsuspected ability" at creating emotion the comedian had displayed. Where had it come from? On the set, the director, George Cukor, had taken Lahr aside and said, "Simple, Bert, simple. Cut it down to half. Give me half of that." Lahr gave him half of that and the half he gave him was God's truth.

Now what this suggests—it is very easy to sentimentalize the principle—is that clowns, in their outsize and even outrageous behavior, are something like explosions of truth, bizarre fireworks-displays of truth, that they begin by possessing more truth than do other performers and need only lop off a bit here and there to show you an integrity at the core that Laurence Olivier might envy. A great clown can do it with his hands tied; all you have to do is tie his hands and see.

It would be nice if that were uniformly so, nice if things could be as easy as that, because then all fine comedians could be quickly diminished into fine actors and we should be theatrically rich beyond our fondest dreams. Of course it isn't entirely so, of course clowns fail as actors occasionally, of course the philosopher's stone hasn't been found. But because the alchemy has succeeded so often, surprising the daylights out of us each time it does, we're honor bound to ask: is there *some* kind of comedian who is very naturally an actor, *some* kind of comedy that at first blush seems fantasy but strips down readily to naked fact?

I think there may be. I can't prove it, and don't even wish to: not all of the men I'm thinking of have put themselves to the test (it's usually an accident that any of them ever are; Lahr himself was dragged kicking and screaming beyond his ambition), and comedy itself likes to make a fool of the man who pursues its categories too doggedly. But there is a kind of comedian who works so closely to his own nerve ends that his comic shudder is scarcely a mask: if it didn't get a laugh it would be a nervous breakdown. This kind of comedian makes all his comedy out of his discontent. He pretends to the anguish he feels. He shows you his symptoms, and you laugh. "All right, *you* laugh, but that's funny!" Lahr once screamed at a group of professionals who were enjoying watching him work. Clearly, for him, "funny" was an abstraction. It was what he did with the truth to make it visible, a matter of hanging an ache up to dry. He wasn't inventing, he was exorcising, though not consciously for self-therapy. He was respecting, and insisting that you respect, the facts as they existed.

Many comedians keep the facts just inside them as they fake fantasizing. In this country Mark Twain was their father, funny until the bile finally came up. (And good on the platform too.) Several years ago Groucho Marx finally prowled out onto the stage of the New York theater where the Tony awards were being televised. It was clear to anyone listening attentively that Groucho had had a bad day backstage, that he was now fussed if not fuming at the long and exhausting wait, that he hadn't had so much as a chair in the wings to sit on. If you'd met him at the stagedoor you'd surely have felt his temper. What was he doing now? Making hilarity out of the ineptitude of the programming, the long day's delay, the very lack of a chair. We are so used to Groucho's name now that we quite forget there is a "grouch" in it. But there is one, and it is only partly concealed by the arch the clown's eyebrows make as they lift—literally lift, as though it were dead weight—an actual exasperation with the world into a professional dyspepsia that is comic in its range, its rage, its compulsiveness, its quickness. The growl glides, and enchants. There are performers whose humor depends upon articulating and only slightly ridiculing the way they do feel this very minute.

Bert Lahr made his entire stage image out of what he felt and could never stop feeling. He was a man beset by fear. The actor Larry Blyden, who should write a book himself, is perceptive about Lahr as he is quoted in *Notes on a Cowardly Lion*. Having worked, and worked hard, with the comedian in *Foxy*, he remarked that "Bert needs three things. One: he needs to be loved. Two: a thing he needs a little more than that is to be served. Three: he needs to be acclaimed. He doesn't need to love; but he needs to receive it. Laughter is like that. Bert comes from a hungry time. When they laughed you were going to eat; when they didn't, you starved. If they're not laughing, he panics. There's nothing vicious or greedy or selfish; they are conditions of his life. He had terrible things happen in his life; and yet, he has succeeded and become Bert Lahr by making people laugh."

Hearing the laugh was more than having proof of the love. It *was* the love. He didn't think he was going to get any other. He hadn't got it from his father, who'd brushed him away from a moving streetcar when he ran after him begging for money. He distrusted his mother, a good woman but a prudish, complaining, sometimes "unexpectedly violent" woman. With his first wife and partner, the other half of the burlesque and vaudeville team of Lahr and Mercedes, he knew love. He saw it freeze into dementia praecox before his eyes. A terror that haunted him was that his perfectionism (his fear of failure) about their stage work had contributed to her disintegration. One kind of love had helped destroy the other. In time, from his second wife and—mysteriously—from his children, he received a completely giving love. But he no longer asked for it or seemed to believe it likely: he was not affectionate at home, he was only anxious about the likely failure of his next work on stage, preoccupied, intent upon "protecting the laugh." It was too late to count on anything else and, to make matters worse, the work had never, never, never been good enough. "Sure. I've done O.K., but never as good as possible," he said late in life. The love out there hadn't been all it might have been either.

This is knowing love in fear instead of knowing it in confidence. The warmth of love is passed over because the death of love is foreseen. "A comic is like radar," Abe Burrows explains as he reminisces about working with Lahr, "he sends out a laugh—his personality—if nothing comes back, it's death. Literal death. Comedians always used the phrase, 'Boy, I died last night.' That's no accident. They are literally comparing it to death. On the other side, they use terms like 'I killed them,' 'I fractured them,' 'I had them laying in the aisles,' 'I murdered them.' This is really like a bullfight, but it's more than a contest, it's a life and death battle."

For a man like Lahr, walking onto a stage knowing that he was going to his death or to a mere temporary reprieve, performing became an ultimate existential statement. It was all there was to him. His close friend Jack Haley says of him that "His whole life was show business. His *whole* life. . . . There's a difference when you've got mileage on you, and you've been all down the road. You know you're not going to go any place. There's not going to be a bigger Bert Lahr than Bert Lahr was. . . . You're not going to get bigger—just older. . . . [But] in the early days, those were the times when he was fired with ambition. Fired with ambition—and fear."

And so, having no place else to test or to use or to measure what he was, he brought the ambition and the fear onto the stage with him. The Lahr who leapt from the wings without warning, in his perennially repeated vaudeville act, to interrupt Mercedes' dance and to savage the floor with the tattoo of his cop's nightstick, was a bull out of pasture, a bull crosseyed with intensity and very close to letting you see the steam from his nostrils, a throbbing image of assault. He insisted on his presence, insisted on circling the stage to be certain he commanded all of it, insisted on absolute attention out front to each and every mangled word he used, insisted on the rectitude of the mangling. Inside the insistence was instant terror, which is why, after every roar, he flinched. He wasn't even afraid of the person he was roaring at. He was afraid of his very own voice. The throb outward was a quiver within. The bull bellowed and turned into a cowering beastie. The Cowardly Lion in *The Wizard of Oz* was more than a piece of happy casting. Although *The Wizard of Oz* was never a very good film, it was not surprising that he should have been the immediate hit of it or that such children as now remember him will remember him just that way. He was just that way, it was a happy piece of what made him unhappy. A coward determined to be a lion was the sum of it.

John Lahr is admirably open-minded about his father. He can look at him and call him Lahr and persuade you that that is how he thought of him. (No doubt the comedian's detachment from his children bred a genuine objectivity in them; luckily it seems not to have bred resentment.)

For the book he prodded his father about all that had been difficult in his life—the prolonged mental instability of his first wife, his subsequent insecure experiences with women, certain of his unhappier relationships on stage—but he has plainly got more ample and more exact information from the Haleys and several dozen other colleagues than he was able to pry loose from the man who played a phonograph loudly through meals in order to discourage unnecessary conversation. Bert Lahr didn't necessarily wish to conceal these things. He simply preferred not to remember them, to pass the agony over into his work.

The material has been gathered, though, and presented dispassionately. "I'll throw it out of my mind," Lahr had a habit of saying as he was confronted with the fact that his mentally ill wife was pregnant while the woman he was seeing was in all probability disreputable. His son says: "On stage, as he sang about the success of Rusty Crouse, he was able to forget his failures as Bert Lahr. His coarseness and his betrayal of his family he understood, but felt compelled to continue. There is no justification for his attitude; he had an ethical naïveté that is paralleled in his stage roles. The baby and the nurse stayed in his apartment; but he usually spent the night with Rachel. 'Sometimes I'd come home and go into the child's room. I'd look at him, but I couldn't pick him up. I felt dirty.' " He was emotionally obtuse about people he ought to have been close to, his practical jokes were almost always cruel rather than funny, he could be ruthless with fellow performers when those laughs were at stake. The portrait is complete and calm.

In some respects John Lahr's book is quite clumsily written, though problems of diction and syntax and structure are eventually brushed aside by the scale and intimacy of our acquaintance with a troubled, understood, at last endearing man. Having said that his father "was the most inarticulate man ever to consider himself adroit with words," John Lahr proceeds to give him a little competition in the area. He writes that Beatrice Lillie "was not below using a Seltzer bottle or wearing a pair of roller skates underneath an evening gown," when obviously he means that she was not above such idle practices. I cannot imagine what he holds the word "limpid" to mean: "The comedy Lahr and Moore provided gave *Hold Everything* the necessary originality for a long run that the book, limpid and often sentimental for all its ingenious turns, lacked." He is fond of the word "profusion" but never seems to sense the need for a profusion *of* anything: "They shared, like Lahr and other Broadway journeymen, a boisterous faith in America's profusion."

He dumps fragments of medical case histories upon us, without suggesting where they have come from, as freely as though he were doing a discontinuous television commercial. He omits vital steps he has prepared us for: for many years Bert Lahr concealed from his children the kind of work he did; suddenly we discover the children frisking about backstage; the moment of revelation, of discovery, is nowhere to be found. He contradicts himself carelessly: having told us that both the Shuberts and Ziegfeld had proposed New York shows for Lahr and then dropped their plans (the Shuberts had even had him under contract), he announces, one paragraph later, that "Nobody had suggested Broadway to Lahr before." Stylistically, the fat book is sloppy.

But it is a fat book and it eventually embraces us. Whatever serious irritations we may feel, we feel keenly for only about a third of the way; after that, the sheer weight of the evidence catches up with us, makes us feel bound to a dimensional human being and the dilemma in which he has placed himself. The account is not all dilemma, I should add. There are agreeable, even lighthearted, glimpses of Beatrice Lillie at work, of Fred Allen being friendly, of Abe Burrows being generous, of vaudevillians summering at Lake Hopatcong, of a fund-raising wartime caravan of stars gathering nightly in Laurel and Hardy's dressing room. But the dominant tone is otherwise: Beatrice Lillie crying, Oliver Hardy trying not to. By the time you are through with the book you may have a feeling that you might just cry yourself.

For we are brought very close to a man who was himself close to the dark heart of comedy; we are brought close to his perspiration, close to his rage, close to what was funny about him. (Kinescopes of his cop act still exist; the act remains hilarious.) And we do sense, in time, what there was in him that made him able to play Molière and Aristophanes (he was never given time to do either of them properly, but he clearly could have been magnificent in both) and to arrive at the honest desolation, the grimace become spasm, of *Waiting for Godot*. He had been telling the truth about himself on stage all along, embellished only with fierce darts and feeble cringes and reverberating ong-ong-ongs that stylized his insecurity to the point where we could enjoy it. When he modulated these things, we could still enjoy what we saw because what we saw was so. But we were looking at terror.

2

It would somehow or other have been insulting not to tell the truth about Tallulah Bankhead on the occasion of her death—no one would have wanted that horse laugh hooting at him from the heavens because of some indecent piety he'd put down—and so great gobs of truth, or at least of candor, were dispensed in her unfawning obituaries. (Obituaries are getting rougher lately; we must all watch out.)

She was nowhere near a great actress, though once in a while a surprisingly good one. Her career never came to the shapeliness promised for it by her early and varied success in London. Most of her energy seemed poured into her flamboyant private life; after a while she was having to borrow back on the flamboyance to get her through a performance. Backstage, she was known to be rough: authors and producers were reported hospitalized by her tantrums, while she herself proudly announced that she'd never read or heard a line of *The Little Foxes* outside of the scenes in which she appeared. *The Little Foxes* was her greatest success and she claimed not to know the plot.

Very often *she* told the truth about herself, in a quick hoarse gabble with a "darling" stuck like wet punctuation wherever she punctuated and with an extraordinarily pleading look in her eye. (What was she pleading for? Simply to be believed? To be recognized as honest? To be trusted? Why?) And now all the truths had to be set down, given back, added up—even if they added up to an image of on-the-whole failure, of fabulous waste. Give a girl as good as she gave, and don't fool around.

Glamor gone over the hill to the doghouse, then—that was about the size of it. And yet, finishing out the record this way doesn't account for the record at all. Tallulah was a special kind of theater person. Failure, for instance, never diminished her. She could go year after year turning up in disasters—plays that slapped her down savagely and wrapped themselves up in a matter of weeks—and remain Tallulah.

After you'd heard what a mess she'd made of *Antony and*

Cleopatra, weren't you just as interested in going to see her the next time around? Did you ever stop being interested? After all, there is such a thing as a flash-in-the-pan performer, the star who excites us tremendously and then, after a couple of failures, loses all fascination for us. Performers of that kind are being washed out every year. But Tallulah wouldn't wash out, or didn't. Each new graduating class coming out of high school had to find out who this witch was, hear the voice, grin back at the skeptical, wicked, and yet in some way wistful, smile. (I don't want to overdo this wistful or pleading business; but it was there, it was moist enough to wash windows with, and it is almost never mentioned.) Career seemed irrelevant. Even strict professionalism seemed irrelevant. Tallulah was always something To Be Continued.

Now what kind of a performer is that? I think Miss Bankhead belonged to an odd tribe—a peripheral tribe and yet a valuable tribe—that never did interest us in acting as such. I don't think we expected to see her give a good performance. I think we expected to meet her some day. Really meet her. In person. I think she was too real to us to be good in most parts. She lacked camouflage. There was no chameleon in her. That is why people used her first name all the time—not because it was an unusual name, but because they'd always meant to speak to her privately.

She reminded us—and this was her value—that theater is a personal matter: face-to-face, tone-to-tone, toe-to-toe. She made the theater personal, carrying it out into her life and back onto the stage again. She made us feel personally about it, about her. We didn't say to ourselves, "Would I wish to meet her?" or "Will I like her when I do?" We said, "She'll come—around a corner, around someplace, and when she does, she'll be exactly the way she is!"

She was a presence who insisted upon being present. The theater begins in this kind of astonishment.

3

IN A WAY, it was lucky that Conrad Bromberg's bill of three one-acters called *Transfers* didn't have a long run off-Broadway. If Ron Leibman had been permitted to play it eight times a week for very many weeks, he'd have killed himself.

Mr. Leibman is a very fine young actor possessed of extraordinary equipment. His voice is so clean, resonant, and naturally incisive that he doesn't have to raise it to rivet an audience. His eyes are alive and more than that; they're forest eyes, and can see in the night. His body is lean and supple, his arms and hands are free and expressive, he is always present in the whole of his person. (So many actors are part-time persons, eyes without bodies, voices without feet.)

However, Mr. Leibman has a problem, an odd one. He has so much equipment that he's got to learn when not to use some of it. He's got to hold something back for us to feel. You see, if the actor himself feels absolutely everything—quivering, retching, crying, clawing at himself in total commitment to his pain—he leaves the rest of us in the playhouse with very little to do.

In *Transfers* he did it all, consuming all of the emotion that was going, draining every last ounce of agony that could be forced from his fingertips, not simply displaying imagination but using it up. With nothing to imagine for ourselves, nothing to suspect or infer or intuit or guess at, we simply sat there, fascinated but essentially neutral nonparticipants. The actor who succeeds in hurting us, or concerning us, or perhaps making us cry is usually the actor who is making a pretense of trying not to. He hides something, whereupon we provide it for him.

Mr. Leibman was not overboard, not false, not ham. What he did was right; his mistake was in being right without reserve. When, as a psychiatrist called into a classroom as a guest lecturer at a time when his own life and mind were being hopelessly shredded, he first made a nervous, clammy professorial joke (he shucked off his shoes, remarking that "they hurt from sitting all day"), his coy candor, his fey good-guyness, was perfect. Leaving sentences unfinished to suck frantically at a cigarette, gesturing so forcefully with his eyeglasses that you felt certain they were going to be smashed, hiking up his trousers as though they were bedclothes and then transferring his helplessly busy hands to bloodshot eyes, running nose, flying strands of hair, he was accurately describing in space the unhinged state of his psyche.

Even when, having done everything, he was compelled to do everything again because there were no new worlds to conquer or new props to mash, he repeated the patterns with belief and constantly increasing intensity. On opening night, in fact, his preoccupation became so total that when, having inadvertently tossed a still-lighted match away, a small but quickly developing fire broke out on his desk, he never noticed it at all, though, as I've mentioned earlier, several dozen members of the audience were literally raising hands to point it out to him.

Concentration is a virtue in an actor; forgetting oneself while carrying a performance forward into the house is a virtue too; complete immersion, absorption pressed to the point of oblivion, may not be. This actor was honest, but he had extended himself so far into playing that playing had nearly turned into being; along the way he had become unaware of factors with which a performer must always deal and over which he has got to exercise conscious control. Good work, Mr. Leibman, and less of it.

4

WHEN Zoe Caldwell was good in *Colette* she was very, very good and when she was less good she was florid. The line between the two was thin because Miss Caldwell is, by nature, a magnetic overdose of an actress, equipped with double everybody else's machinery. Her voice, to begin with. In *Colette* she did not have to project her voice into the auditorium, on principle, with practice. She simply opened her mouth and a high wind passed through her, instantly reaching the far brick walls of the Ellen Stewart Theater, whistling through its crevices and returning as echo.

As a result, director Gerald Freedman was able to place her anywhere at all on stage as he went about charting the course of

Colette's life from schoolgirl ("with braids long enough to let buckets down a well') to neglected wife to imprisoned writer to vaudeville performer to novelist to aged lover to national monument. He could put her behind a scrollwork piano, so that you could see no more than the glass of red wine she held above her head, and still you could hear her. He could put her behind screens, frantically changing costumes, and you could hear her. He could even put her directly behind her first husband, a giant oak of a fellow, and though you now felt you were likely never to get a glimpse of her again, you could hear her. She didn't pronounce words, she propelled them, and did so precisely. Find the American theater ten more Zoe Caldwells and the end of amplification is in sight.

She is also a devilish technician, a kind of seething snakepit of skills. The very finest thing she did in *Colette* was to tick off in ever-quickening syllables an entire vaudeville performance while her fingers were whisking this way and that, to piano accompaniment, applying makeup. The evening was composed of excerpts from Colette's autobiographical writings, which accounted for the fact that the description was in the third person, and what Miss Caldwell was doing was racing the clock to finish her own dressing while all of the other acts were doing whatever it was they did.

Thus she rattled on about Russian acrobats and greyhound dog acts, exactly timing their leaps and their smiling bows to the amount of mascara she had or hadn't got into place yet, and as she competed with composer Harvey Schmidt (doing his own accompaniment at that piano) to see which could tinkle fastest and brightest, she was brilliant. She could have called it quits at the end of the episode and collected full pay for an evening's work.

It might even have been a good idea if she had. For, not too long after, she leapt into a pantomime sequence which was *her* part of the vaudeville show and while she made it extremely funny indeed, she (and/or Mr. Freedman) lost sight of where she (and/or he) was. Suddenly a realistic scrapbook full of odd memories and small truths (Colette so loved the dawn that her mother "granted it to her as a reward") turned into broad parody that resembled one of those television programs called Fun with Flickers, and the silent-movie pastiche skittered out of frame, bounds, and focus. It was not in control any longer, and though Miss Caldwell could hoist a dainty foot backward with pained aplomb when she was clasped at the waist by a villain with a whip, we realized that we were no longer attending to legitimate reminiscence but to campery that was not playing fair. Serious "mime" turns in vaudeville may often have been bad; but they weren't bad like this, they were bad in all sincerity. What we saw now was mere kidding, and kid stuff.

Of course, if Miss Caldwell *had* cut the evening off while she was still fully its mistress, we should have been denied the final sight of her: stocky walk, head ducked down on one shoulder as though it now needed something to lean on, eyes flashing with a still-youthful madness, hair in gray ringlets blown to dandelion fuzz.

The second act did stretch out, though, taking the form of an interview in which the doyen could make teasing remarks (the one thing you must hang onto is your "self-doubt") and could reminisce about her mother's preference for flowerbeds over love (Mildred Dunnock, in a quiet, charming performance) but in which the assorted loves—male or female—who came and went were insufficiently characterized to allow the evening to stand up as "play."

I do find myself tiring of the recited memoir, patched together of dramatically incomplete scenes, as a substitute for an acted-out whole, and I rather yearn for the days when Paul Shyre was doing such adaptations (O'Casey mainly) as lectern readings, candidly and without claim to play status. This one, put together by Elinor Jones, was about as satisfactory and unsatisfactory as most, given an extra charge, when it was not an overcharge, by Miss Caldwell, cousin of the sting ray.

5

THE musical comedy *Coco* purported to be about a dress designer named Chanel—Coco to intimates—but it was nothing of the sort. It was, as an evening, plainly and simply about a phenomenon called Katharine Hepburn. Not that the events dramatized, or undramatized as things turned out, had anything to do with Miss

Hepburn's past history. Her own life could not conceivably have been so lifeless. But each time the actress came down the up staircase—she came down it scowling, came down it serene, came down it like a cavalry attack, came down it drunk—she was coming down it to *be* Hepburn, to be present before all of us, to stand with her feet apart and her hands in her pockets and her chin tilted high as the balcony's eye because that was the image we had of her and she wanted to assure us that it was absolutely real. It was.

The character of the evening was personal, and the person was not Chanel. We had all been in love with Miss Hepburn since she'd first hurled that sandstorm of a voice at a disintegrating John Barrymore in *A Bill of Divorcement,* since she'd suggested in *Christopher Strong* that the Wright Brothers had taken up their work so that she could one day play an aviatrix, since she'd ruefully but resolutely sent Douglas Fairbanks, Jr., away in *Morning Glory,* since she'd made such a mess of dinner at Alice Adams' house. Our love might have stumbled a bit from film to film; astonishingly, she hadn't been a good Babbie in *The Little Minister.* But we'd been able to know it as love, the real thing, because it could be so quickly restored; it had never been hard to say "All is forgiven, come home." And she was always, at all ages, coming home, usually in better shape than ever.

Yet she was never as good on the stage. (Or almost never. We've got to except *Philadelphia Story,* carefully tailored to her traits by Philip Barry, in which she was both lovely *and* good.) The reason for her stage difficulties was quite simple. Beneath the voice and the stance, the soar of the jawline and the teeth that seemed to have been cut out with a scissors and pasted on coloring paper, beyond all the mannerisms existed an actress, a fine one: that had been clear all the way from *Alice Adams* to *The African Queen.* But the equipment and the mannerisms were themselves so exaggerated by nature that to exaggerate them once again in the process of projecting them from a stage was to destroy them, to make them rigid and monotonous. Miss Hepburn must be one of the very few living performers who must be caught at half mast, listened to at low tide. Everything about her, from her energy to her angularity, from her brusqueness to her delicate beauty, is too much.

Still, when you've got a love affair going there ought to be *some* way of making an actual date with the girl—once, anyway. Having seen her at the screen's discreet distance forever, which was more or less like carrying on a romance by telephone only, you at last wanted contact, if only to pay your personal respects, if only to get to your feet at the end of the evening to let her hear your *private* applause. And so librettist-lyricist Alan Jay Lerner had arranged a meeting in which such a salute was possible by openly acknowledging his star's idiosyncratic extravagances, by letting herself display herself at greater size than any reasonable play would decently contain, by clearing the stage so that she could take over *all* of it, by permitting her and even commanding her to roar, fret, howl, stomp, cry, keen, and high kick in celebration of our long lives together.

He probably didn't mean to do this in the beginning. He probably intended to write a musical about Gabrielle Chanel. There were all kinds of Coco-isms stuck into the script like glazed candy cherries thumbed onto a cake: take a line like "In most cases equality is a step down" or a note to Picasso that runs "Dear Pablo, forgive me for not answering your letter sooner but I had nothing to do and couldn't get to it." The limping plot line (Chanel trying a comeback after fifteen years away) did have something to do with clothes, rather dispiritedly imitated by Cecil Beaton; and the star's final tears were called for because Coco was losing a girl she wished to "mother" to a man.

But it was now all those rehearsals and all those previews later, and something else had come into being. Composer Andre Previn had opened up, or closed down, his songs so that Miss Hepburn's indulgent cackle could manage them; there were marches to keep an obvious beat, there were spaces for handclapping, there were voices from the wings to serve as supernatural controls. A dance had been arranged so that Miss Hepburn, in a black dress that looked like a licorice brownie, could do her finest quadrille since *Little Women* at twice the speed. Director Michael Benthall had been careful to see that Miss Hepburn was close to us, flipping a scrapbook gaily at the footlights while dancers in "basic blacks" whipped through a precision routine that seemed to suggest that Zelda Fitzgerald had been trained at the court of Hammurabi; when she rose, she rose to stalk the curtain line from left to right and back again so that she could look at us and confide in us and, though whipless, behave in general like a musical tamer.

The show had become a showcase, a form of endearment, a gesture of assent, an open palm of respect. Obviously Miss Hepburn would never be old enough or tired enough to undergo one of those official evenings of tribute at which everyone gathers to summarize and reminisce. And so it had been arranged right here, with her doing all the work. If *Coco* was anything, it was Miss Hepburn's gala Benefit Performance, for our benefit.

6

Hello, Dolly! gradually turned itself into a permanent national institution, one that invited anybody who was anybody to drop in and play it some time. It threatened to become, for all star performers who could wear red on red, a kind of test match, a rite of initiation, an ordeal by fire and an election by accolade: either you did it right or you didn't get into heaven, or Sardi's, or sixth grade.

I mention sixth grade because Ethel Merman finally entered *Dolly* and also, I do believe, fifth grade, where she was to be seen plugging for sixth. Consider her walk. She didn't walk like a crumpled adult, badgered by burdens, harried by time, made cautious by too many collisions. She walked like a kid who had just won all the marbles (they were in her pocket and nobody was going to get them back) and she was on her way home, king of the cracks in the sidewalk. Her arms swung back and forth jauntily, her head was up and her eyes straight forward, and you'd have known she was singing even if you couldn't hear her. Put a paper hat on her head and a wooden sword in her hand and you'd have had the ultimate image of Triumph at Age Ten, male or female, vegetable or mineral, sink or swim.

If I mention knowing that she was singing even if you couldn't hear her, it's because half the time at the St. James I couldn't hear her. This had nothing to do with the quality of her voice, which was exactly as trumpet-clean, exactly as pennywhistle-piercing, exactly as Wurlitzer-wonderful as it always had been. Right from the first notes, the first words ("I have always been a woman," I think they were), you knew that it was all still there, dustproof, rustproof, off and aloft and ringing. The only thing was that she was just one woman, alone on stage, and one woman alone simply could not make more noise than a thousand people in the auditorium standing up and screaming at her. At the St. James they stood up and screamed during the first number, they stood up and screamed louder during the second, and by the time she got to the "Hello, Dolly" number they didn't bother to sit down between notes. I'd have liked to make a deal with them. Equal time for Miss Merman.

My God, what a woman she is! Her comic sense is every bit as authoritative, as high-handed really, as her singing voice. At the very opening, as she was offering one of her calling cards to a horse, she made the gesture with such confidence that you expected the horse to take the card. Later on, when she was stuffing up Horace Vandergelder ("Have some more beets, Horace") preparatory to turning down the offer of marriage he hadn't made, she didn't bother looking at Horace and she didn't bother playing to the house. She concentrated on the beets, as though they were the gang of rowdies that had to be controlled, and she tackled them and dished them out and returned to stare them down with such abstract concentration, such tenacity of purpose, such total and ruthless devotion that you'd have sworn she was Florence Nightingale reorganizing the Crimea. (Why has Florence Nightingale always been played by languid heroines when she must have been a whole lot more like Merman?)

Merman is odd. She has won love by never asking for it. She does what *she* does, on her time and in her tempo, and it's up to you to decide when you want to come around. Everybody had come around by this time, and there she still was, cocky, chin tilted, half-dollar eyes sprouting sunburst black lashes, power flowing from her that would still light the town when Con Edison failed.

7

Home was an evening of endings. John Gielgud, the white hair at his temples fluffed out into miniature wings, entered an empty world sedately, erect in his own absence. He was, perhaps, on the grounds of a summer place, but a summer place from which summer had fled, leaving no more than a sandy sky behind. There was a balustrade, there was a flagpole, there were a few cream-colored chairs; othewise there was no telling where earth and horizon met.

He was followed shortly by Ralph Richardson, testing the ground before him with a cane to make certain it was there, putting each foot down as though it might not quite match the other, managing to suggest in the vacant oval of his eyes and mouth that eyes and mouth had lost all definition. If God once painted him, he had run.

These two were at the end of their lives, perhaps a little past that, still breathing. They exchanged counters from an ancient piggybank of words.

GIELGUD: "When I was in the army—"
RICHARDSON: "Oh, really?"

The thought was over, stopped. Not because Mr. Richardson had terminated Mr. Gielgud's sentence with the finality of his phrase, one more bead in his litany of embalmed responses, but because Mr. Gielgud would not, could not have completed the sentence if he had been given time and air in which to do it. The completed sentence no longer existed. Wherever it had been going, it was gone. "You wonder how there ever was time for it all" was all he could say, wondering not where the time had gone but what all was. Crinkling his moist eyes in the far light, he saw things—amusing things that made him break into a perverse smile, disturbing things that began aborted tears—but things that could no longer be articulated. This was conversation on a subject that had died.

Mr. Richardson had resources. Put to it, he could do card tricks. He did not impose his card tricks on Mr. Gielgud, he offered them as an aged puppy might offer to play a half-remembered game. It was a social gesture, well intentioned, without thought or joy behind it. But there was a moment of feeling in Mr. Gielgud's look of regret, of depressed sympathy for his entertainer, when a card that should have been a three of spades turned up as a two of hearts. Mistakes could not be retrieved, the game could not be improved, the hand was at last slower than the eye.

Moments of inadvertent humor slipped out of their locked-off interchanges. Mr. Gielgud was painfully alarmed by signs of senility in Mr. Richardson when Mr. Richardson spoke of a friend who'd met George VI at Waterloo. A bit of questioning cleared the matter up. Waterloo Station. Mr. Richardson, who had once marketed jam, truly believed that jam packaged in cardboard tended to reduce anxiety in the housewife; glass, and the prospect of its shattering before the jam was gone, could only make her nervous.

Now and again they joined two ladies on the grounds, Mona Washbourne, whose face seemed to have been done up in as many curlers as her hair, and Dandy Nichols, who seemed to have been blocked out on the stage by the creator of the comic strip "B.C." Miss Washbourne was friendly, Miss Nichols was not. Nevertheless they all went to lunch, and came back. When they returned, a chair had gone, spirited away by a young athlete who had had a frontal lobotomy. We knew now, as no doubt they did, that their silent salt-and-pepper void was a mental home. What to do about the chair? Nothing. If lives and sentences end, chairs end too.

How did the evening end? There had been another exchange.

"Amazing thing, of course, is the—"

"Oh, yes."

As the two men stood apart, immobile, the lights faded.

Stalemate from first to last. If we could not take our eyes from the image before us, or ever turn our ears away from David Storey's play, it was because we were in the presence of two of the great actors of the age and were being steadily instructed in what had made them great. They *could* create *ex nihilo;* they were doing it now, sustaining the terminal cancer of their dead-end exchanges ("In the blood," "Bound to be") with an interior command that said "Wait now, I've almost thought of something." There was a stir of Gielgud, a promise of Richardson, inside the glaring white blank before us that bound us to life and personality and movement even as these things were being formally interred.

The two men were overwhelmingly good, uninsistently perfect. Mr. Richardson, trying to laugh but finding no sufficient impulse; Mr. Gielgud, remembering that he might have been a dancer if he hadn't been the only boy in the class; Mr. Richardson, slowly working out in his mind the mathematics of a proposition, "In the nature of things—one fails"; Mr. Gielgud, replying before he had heard the question because answers no longer mattered. These were the achievements of actors whose craft lies endlessly open before them, actors who have *not* arbitrarily ended the search. To them must be added an extraordinary moment of Miss Washbourne's, one in which she tossed her head to God with a sharp " 'Oo does He think He is?"

The play, as a play, was another matter. It was a carefully tooled example of its kind. I do not like the kind. For one thing, all of its moments were exactly equal to one another; the author's checkrein, putting a period to everything the moment it had begun, kept them so. The calculated stasis seemed to me both wearying and artificial. And to keep all moments equal, most lines had to be equally spaced. We were listening to spondee forever; inevitably, our senses were dulled. The play was like Beckett without the anguished poetry, like Pinter without the tension. It was, really, *domesticated* Beckett, Beckett tamed to a tabby cat.

As it happened, the matter was easily checked. At the Public Theater an Irish performer, Jack MacGowran, was then engaged in reading blended excerpts from Beckett's novels, poems, and plays (novels mainly) and one had only to listen to the first resonant cries of anger that came from the same near-naked stage to know that what bothers Beckett is not endings but the fact that *things do not end.* They go on, damn it all, is the burden of Beckett's fury, here given body and bite by yet another superb player.

True, Beckett's figures—certainly the Molloy of the novels— would prefer the fragmented stillness that had overtaken the residents of *Home.* They wouldn't mind sitting eternally in a vast space with nothing but a pendulum clock for company. The glint of the pendulum, passing without alternation, would be preoccupation enough.

But Beckett's men are denied such repose, the peace that comes when understanding has passed. They are agitated, infuriated, by the fact that things, themselves included, continue to move, to grow and change, to *busy* themselves when there is no point to the busyness. Mr. MacGowran was maddened to sense the movement of slugs in the earth beneath his feet, driven to baying at the moon, ludicrously and long, at the sound of chestnuts falling, of children walking. "Let me say before I go any further," he snapped at the beginning of the evening, "that I forgive nobody!"

This restlessly, wrathfully surviving man was angry because there are no terminations, only continuations. His anger and its object plainly affected the language tumbling about. Instead of coiling back upon itself, persistently folding itself up like card tables put away for the night, it lurched forward, out into the open where it could flay and sear. It clattered onward into imagery ("Crows have done this, ducks are perhaps the worst"), required a longer rhythmic line ("And unhappiness like mine, there's no annihilating that!"), boiled with an unexpected comic energy ("And every fourth year the February debacle!"). A man can detest February because February changes. His fury can be funny. It is also a moving principle. Sentences advance as life does.

Mr. MacGowran, with the head and hunch of a hawk, with parchment creases beneath his eyes to fold up tight in inflamed resentment, persuaded us without effort to endure, and to enjoy, his bill of metaphysical complaints by stressing the active rage in Beckett and by threading together in his particular arrangement of materials passages that would sustain that rage. It was—and is—the rage of men who do not despair of having lost life but of having been given it. They know that they are condemned to go on, and the knowledge drives them wild. It also drives them into words, words with more strength in them than existed in the mannered cancellations of *Home*.

Interestingly, Mr. MacGowran's success also suggested something else: that Beckett seems more vigorous when he is read *solus* than when he is acted out.

8

ONE of the rewards of constant theatergoing is flushing out the hidden actor.

What's a hidden actor? Well, he (or she) is someone who's very, very good and who is at the same time, for one wicked reason or another, virtually invisible. The theater is a tricky, rather malicious, place, and it can manage a dozen or so most inventive ways of seeing to it that a performer, though plainly there, isn't seen.

Let me give you an all too obvious sort of example. When I first saw *Your Own Thing*, no member of my family accompanied me. Deserted for the evening, I got all the dessert. The show turned out to be the freshest, friskiest musical then running in New York. This meant, of course, that various members of my family had to buy their own tickets and pack themselves off to the entertainment at a later date, while I arranged to drop by and drive them, happy creatures, home.

I drifted into the theater somewhere past the halfway point, stood at the back, and was at first thoroughly confused, then enchanted. I was confused because Sebastian seemed to be chasing the wrong girl. When I'd seen the show, Sebastian had been enamored of a tall ample blond. Now, as the strobe lights batted their manic eyelids and the whole company hotfooted it through shattered space, he was plainly trying to get his hands on a diminutive brunette. (This showed good taste on his part, if an unexpected infidelity.)

I figured it out in no time (or in four minutes, which is no time for me these days). A cast replacement. The original actress had clearly flown the coop (to Hollywood, I later discovered) and a small, left-handed, slightly lunatic sparrow had come out of the psychedelic woodwork to take over the role. The newcomer's name was Marcia Rodd, she made the most ordinary line extraordinarily funny by seeming to wave it away with a lofted left hand, the show was even better for her splendid imperviousness to its rush, and who—apart from a few professionals—had ever heard of her? When the show was being welcomed by reviewers, she hadn't been there to be reviewed.

Show business is full of people who are perennial replacements and I am constantly filled with wonder that, given their frustrations, they don't burn down their dressing rooms. Their frustrations are not routine frustrations; they don't just stem from having failed to get a job. They work. They please thousands of people. And they never—or rarely ever—see their names in type in New York. (Agents and producers tend to be affable with people whose names have been in type in New York.) Occasionally a performer who is known to be a "good replacement" breaks through into the opening night circuit as Joel Grey did in *Cabaret*, or as Kenneth Nelson, who'd been roaming the road forever less a day or two, did in *The Boys in the Band*. Mostly they are present but not accounted for. Marcia Rodd should have been accounted for, late perhaps, but loudly. (She has since appeared on Broadway in *Last of the Red Hot Lovers*, from whence she was snatched for films.)

Performers can *be* there on opening night and still be hidden. They can be hidden by so simple an enemy as numbers. In *The Prime of Miss Jean Brodie*, for instance, there were four principal schoolgirls to trail like a colony of drugged ducks in the wake of Zoe Caldwell's sibilant skirts. They were one and all splendid and, because there were four of them, they one and all blurred. Not as they were passing, only in our minds afterward. It was very hard, after all, to keep rustling through a program trying to figure out which schoolgirl was "Jenny" and which was "Monica" and which was the chubby one, particularly when you didn't want to take your eyes off Miss Caldwell anyway. And so you settled for saying "Weren't the girls good?" as you took stock of your enthusiasms later, obliterating even as you praised. I had a sneaking suspicion that Catherine Burns wasn't just one of "the girls," but a serious and composed young actress who wouldn't let a line pass without making certain she'd had it in for a private talk and perhaps tea, and I found myself hoping that next time around she'd have a second name on the program and no one in her age group near her. She was Monica. I mean the chubby one. (And you may since have seen her in the film *Last Summer*.)

Players can even get notices, get their first fair share of attention, and still be swallowed up by their shows. The very nature of the entertainment—sometimes the sheer excellence of the enter-tainment—tends to drown them out in memory. Paul Hecht was astonishingly good as the cheerfully bitter, resigned and ruthless Player King in *Rosencrantz and Guildenstern Are Dead.* I think everyone said so. But *Rosencrantz and Guildenstern* was about Rosencrantz and Guildenstern, wasn't it? And when we'd been caught up in the cold golden sweep of the show, expanding and expanding until the whole world burst into a sick flame signifying death, did we really go back and count out-of-joint noses?

In *The Boys in the Band* Laurence Luckinbill played a homo-sexual whose façade was so commonplace that he would never have been taken for a homosexual. He might possibly, in his adopted colorlessness, have been giving the evening's best perfor-mance. Was it likely, considering that the company as a whole was doing the most striking ensemble work in years, that anyone was going to pluck him out and get his name right?

You may think I'm forcing a point here, dropping a few croco-dile tears on behalf of adequately recognized performers. But in point of fact—let us pause for a blush—my own newspaper that season ran a picture of Mr. Hecht that wasn't a picture of Mr. Hecht, and not long after *Time* magazine ran a picture of Mr. Luckinbill that wasn't a picture of Mr. Luckinbill. In such circum-stances, actors find it hard to feel that their work has been noticed. And what do they do to fill their scrapbooks toward the future?

Speaking of scrapbooks, and the pasted-up records of hopes and failures and fears and dreams, do you know those little biographi-cal notes which appear in the backs of the playbills, identifying the actors? They run something like this: So-and-so has been busy in the Twin Cities playing Macbeth and the First Gravedigger, breathlessly occupied with de Ghelderode in a summer stock company that seems to have survived anyway, intermittently rushed from Canada to the Coast for special appearances in tele-vision series you have certainly heard about but just as certainly not seen. The same galloping performer has also usually been featured in a film, though almost always in a film "due to be released in the fall." It is a career that you have missed, but it has plainly been an active—even a bustling—one, rising of course to its peak in the production you are about to sit through.

I want to record my favorite such note. It appeared in the

program of what turned out to be a successful Off Broadway play and it confined itself to a single sentence. It said that the leading actor had "spent the last two years in constant amazement and ever-mounting wonder."

I admire that program note because I believe it. I think that's what the actor *had* been doing for the previous two years instead of working. It was clear enough that he must have worked some-time, somewhere, or he would not have been as good as he was. But *I* hadn't seen him in all of my wanderings, which are moder-ately extensive, and I can't suppose that he had been leaping from starring role to starring role in phantom films and secret smashes that had succeeded in eluding me. I think he'd been sitting with his mouth open, gaping at the astonishing spectacle of the contempo-rary world and, what is more to the point, at the equally astonish-ing spectacle of the contemporary theater.

What probably astonished him, as it continues to astonish me, is the quality of work that keeps popping up out of apparently no preparation at all. Our theater simply isn't a training ground. It doesn't offer regular work of a systematic kind to keep promising performers directly engaged in the pursuit of their promise. Those stock companies we read about are there all right, and now a number of resident repertory groups have been added to the list. But the stock companies mainly do retreads of standard or even ancient Broadway work, offering the actor very little opportunity to vary what he does, and the resident reps can absorb only a limited crop of newcomers each year—not to mention the fact that these reps cannot yet guarantee the newcomers many di-rectors capable of training them. The whole thing is still a flotsam and jetsam operation, with talented youngsters surfacing for a brief while here, vanishing there, popping up in a sea roll again a few years later perhaps, drowning perhaps when no one is looking. Certainly there is no plain safe path to maturity available, even when work of a kind is available.

But our actors mature nonetheless. In secret, I guess, while they are sitting and gaping. To take the three most obvious examples of one recent season, where did Marian Mercer, Al Pacino, and Ken Howard acquire the breathtaking authority that made audiences light up at the sight of them? Something certainly happened in the theater when Miss Mercer opened her mouth—her altogether unexpected, slyly unstable mouth—in *Promises, Promises.* The show had been going wonderfully as it was; no surprises were needed. Then Miss Mercer leaned against a barstool, somebody's cast-off baby doll who'd just received a brain transplant (from Mars, possibly), and said a number of exceedingly forthright things as though she were wishing everyone a happy birthday. Where had she ever had the time or the chance to acquire that raffish sunny tone? You don't get a witch's brew like that without experimenting.

We'd seen Al Pacino do some of his experimenting off-Broadway, moving not as human beings do but as an anxiety-ridden octopus might—itching forward and back on undercoils. We knew, before *Does the Tiger Wear a Necktie?*, that he could seethe in silence, suppressing switchblade hands. But where did he find the ten or twelve shadings, the harried half notes, that were needed to make a living jitter a companion for a full evening?

Probably everyone knows by this time that Ken Howard, the Thomas Jefferson of *1776*, was playing a bit part in the secure *Promises, Promises* when he decided to take a chance on the more experimental musical. But does anyone remember him from *Promises, Promises?* I don't. In which case, on what unpremeditated midnight did he summon up in himself all the quiet élan, the easy grace, the manly seriousness that now defined the young Jefferson and that would, sure as Hollywood, wind up making Mr. Howard the country's next, or next to next, matinee idol? (The process is now under way and is, I suspect, irreversible. I don't sneer at the notion of up-and-coming matinee idols, by the way; Charles Boyer and Ronald Colman were matinee idols and excellent actors besides.)

But these are three who may have made it by this time. Straight across Broadway, and reaching readily down into the Bleecker Street caves, a caravan of supporting players keeps coming on urgently, proudly equipped beyond anything that can quite account for them. Occasionally an entire company startles with its uniform capacity for characterizing absolutely. *No Place to Be Somebody* had a company like that. It seemed to have been culled from a highly selective Who's Who Among Actors, inviting each member of the company to polish a role he had patently been born to do. It hadn't been put together that way, of course. Heaven knows where the players had come from, heaven knows what their rightness was made of. It was simply there, impossible in theory, effortless and shining in practice. Add one more thing. The company was mainly black. But black actors, surely, are the very actors who have had the fewest opportunities for training, the very least preparatory work. Some performers, it would seem, grow when the sun isn't up, grow in idleness and subliminally, grow when they are doing nothing more than living in ever-mounting wonder.

The actor whose biographical note I quoted earlier was Ron O'Neal of *No Place to Be Somebody*. Ironically but no doubt appropriately, he may have been the best of them all.

How do these people finally come to attention? Is there anything about them that *helps* impress them on our minds, supposing we've had a chance or two to see them? I know of one thing, but to explain it, in a somewhat roundabout way, I'll have to pick a bone with William Goldman. Mr. Goldman is, in case you hadn't heard, the author of *The Season*, a book I liked except for one little patch of slander. In speaking of established performers, Mr. Goldman claims that there are such things as critics' darlings, creatures who are "always overpraised, overpoweringly, regardless of the caliber of their work." He lists a few of them: Sandy Dennis, Carol Channing, Mary Martin, Beatrice Lillie. And then he adds:

They are also all freaks. All of them. All the time. Mr. Webster says a freak is "oddly different from what is usual or normal." That is certainly true of the people under discussion, but I would like to push the definition a good deal further: these are people that never breathed on this or any other planet. It is not possible that anybody ever met anyone like Carol Channing on the street. With those crazy popping eyes and that bizarre speech pattern, the lady would be hatched up on sight. And rightly so. Critics' darlings all share this in common: extravagance of gesture. They gesticulate; they overdo. They are, in all ways, enormous. And they are all women.

Actually, we can throw that last little remark out of court immediately. All women indeed. Bert Lahr was a critics' darling if ever there was one, by anybody's definition. Ditto Ray Bolger, and why not Bobby Clark? But, of course, even if we succeed in sneaking a few men onto the list, we're still dealing with what the ungallant Mr. Goldman would call freaks. I wish to say a word on behalf of freaks. They aren't freaks. They simply have stage faces.

Now it is perfectly true that a stage face is not like your ordinary, meet-someone-on-the-street face. In fact, if you took those everyday believable-on-the-street faces Mr. Goldman professes to admire so much and put them up on a stage, I think you'd be in a bit of trouble. I think the stage would go blank. I think perhaps nothing might happen at all, except that you yourself would be back on the street again in no time, looking for Carol Channing. (I have met Carol Channing on the street and I didn't want to hatch her up; I wanted to hug her for improving the sidewalk.)

You see, it *takes* Carol Channing's eyes to blaze bright enough to be seen in row Q in the balcony, and it *takes* the incredible curve of Mary Martin's cheek to make her seem the same person from all points of the house, and if Beatrice Lillie's nose weren't so severely lofty we'd scarcely know she was the headmistress in charge of our education tonight. In fact, if a young performer wants to get anywhere in the theater he'd better have something odd, something oversize, something not quite this-planetary about him or he's not going to come on strong enough to mesmerize that befuddled crowd out front. Lacking a nose or a rasp or a trick of the heel (it needn't be preposterous, whatever is oversize about Mary Martin makes her come out seeming normally pretty), the beginner had best go into the movies where a closeup may do the trick or get in touch with Mr. Goldman about other employment.

I think of this frequently because every so often, on this evening or that, a performer—perhaps an unknown, perhaps a half-known—strolls or bounds out on stage and, before there's been a peep out of him, occupies your eye as though it were conquered territory. The scenery drops away around a shape that is stronger or stranger or more assertive than it is, and you know on the instant that you are looking at a stage face. When I finally went to catch up with *Jacques Brel Is Alive and Well and Living in Paris*, for instance, I was really going to catch up with Elly Stone and Mort Shuman, who were, it so happens, entirely delightful. I wasn't looking, however, for an apparition named John C. Attle who apparently hadn't been in the original company and who was, in my ever-so-showwise circle, unheard of.

Mr. Attle does a song very slyly, very dryly, as it turns out. But that isn't the essence of the matter. The essence of the matter is that he absolutely doesn't look like anyone else you ever came across, which means that you instantly sit up to get a better view. You want to record what is unique. Mr. Attle is unique in that, somehow or other (and no doubt it is the carousel echoes of the Parisian evening that brought the image to mind), he resembles both parties to the French Revolution pressed together. I mean, he looks as though he were standing nobly upright in a tumbril suavely waiting to be beheaded, and he also looks like a trim young greengrocer smilingly but sternly waiting to help the execution along. It's as though history had run over him and left him two-dimensional but totally there: his nose is aggressive now, his mouth a thing of doubt, his eyes lidded with lead. He is odd, smooth, compact, *definite*. God stylized him and let him take it from there. What he will manage to do with his curious gift I don't know (a great deal, I hope), but God, at least, was on the right track.

Hattie Winston, in *The Me Nobody Knows*, had a face that blinked on like a light bulb. If she simply passed by in a chorus line, your head swiveled to see what had happened back there. Boni Enten, leaping from a seat in the auditorium to join the onstage fretwork of *Salvation*, moved straight as a bullet to the target of center stage, instantly drilling a hole in the proceedings. She wasn't by any means the star of the occasion, but it was hard for her *not* to be because she was more than merely present, she was perceivable. A young man named Terry Kiser turned up twice in a single season, once as an only slightly mad scientist, once as a routine juvenile in *Paris Is Out*. Both times you were aware of him because of the strange buzz in his eyes; his eyes weren't as big as Carol Channing's, needless to say, but there was a degree of amiable ferocity in them that fixed on something—on the idea at hand, on another actor, on you.

A stage face doesn't need a Broadway or even an off-Broadway showcase to frame it. You'll just naturally react to it anywhere: at Yale, for instance, where, in a rather trivial adaptation of Ovid's *Metamorphoses*, a gravely formed clown named Louis Plante first appeared as Vulcan, sweeping the floor with the hair of his favorite goddess, then as Pygmalion, blowing the marble dust away from between the toes of his just-chiseled Galatea; in each case an innocent open countenance lapsed into expressions of adoration and chagrin that might have been photographed and marketed as Cruikshank caricatures; when the American Conservatory Theater brought its San Francisco company east, you spotted Paul Shenar beneath the heavy eyeglasses and fussy mustache of a Baron von Tusenbach as readily as you did when he appeared, undecorated and conventionally handsome, in *Tiny Alice*.

Nor is it all a matter of cheekbones or unruly noses. (Al Hirschfeld, in his majestic and indispensable collection of theater drawings, *The World of Hirschfeld*, remembers that he once did a perfectly recognizable drawing of Jimmy Durante with no nose at all.) Sometimes a personality proclaims itself—in billboard-size letters—in its animation, or in what our friend Mr. Goldman might call "extravagance of gesture." Certainly a brittle young acrobat named Tony Tanner, who seemed a Harlequin four centuries out of place as he skittered in and out of the quickly slammed doors of a failure called *Little Boxes*, so proclaimed himself. And, in one of the truly fine "lost" performances of recent years, John Castle's in *Georgy*, the fusion of intellectual attitude and physical aptitude was staggering.

Mr. Castle's performance was lost because *Georgy* was a near-miss musical, and near-misses get missed by everybody these days. But, as leapfrogging master of the put-on and the put-down, Mr. Castle cocked a snook at contemporary mores and obligations of every sort with his entire body, starting an impudent song by dancing on his knees, leaping over tables as though he were trampling lightly on all domesticity, whipping his dressed-up stick and bowler into place only to glide without warning out a window. You could call this a stage presence rather than a stage face, if you wished. It's all the same thing—more than the rest of us have got or could manage.

The oversize can simply be a matter of intelligence. When J. A. Preston came on as a messenger in a revival of Aeschylus' *The Persians*, there was nothing to forewarn us that anything exceptional was about to happen. The entrance was unspectacular; a messenger is a messenger and generally a bore to boot. Suddenly, and without exerting special energy on our part, we were listening more intently than we'd planned to. A panoramic battle was expanding before our eyes, though the man was standing still, speaking metrically. An interior pressure surfaced; though little obvious acting was called for, we knew we were attending to an actor.

Much the same thing happened toward the end of a minor Off Broadway venture called *A Scent of Flowers*. Only a gravedigger, a bit player, was talking, idling philosophically while waiting for the principal mourners to appear. An actor named Jeremiah Sullivan startled us into renewing our concentration; whatever the play was about, these particular words seemed curiously underlined, given quiet stress by the quality of a mind. I could list you others. Let this do.

The truth of the matter is that none of these people are supposed to be people who ever breathed on this or any other planet. They're supposed to breathe on the stage, a world with laws and hat sizes and sunset eyebrows of its own, and to make us gasp when they do. May they never cease coming.

The Heritage

I

We do a great deal of talking about the nature of the stage when it is fully itself and only itself, uncorrupted by alien decor, unfussed by borrowings from film or any other medium, undiminished by temporarily profitable surrenders. We are going to do a great deal more talking as we continue to experiment with mixed media and as we try, in honest desperation, to rediscover the root of theater in everything from calculated barbarism to infinitely refined, carefully contentless, form. Before the conversation goes any further, though, and without prejudice to whatever conclusions it may reach, we must take into consideration the production of *Tartuffe* mounted by Jean Gascon in Stratford, Ontario, in 1968.

Mr. Gascon's staging of Molière's play was not just a superb *Tartuffe*, though it was that. A man would have to have been mad to expect a better production in his lifetime, or even to have hoped for so good a one. It was, furthermore, not simply an extraordinarily funny *Tartuffe*, slapping us awake and into laughter where we'd always dozed before. It was a *seriously* funny *Tartuffe*, deriving its comedy from fierce concentration on what may reasonably be expected of dimensional human beings. And it was something

more again than a particularly effective production of a particularly interesting play. It was the stage at peace with itself, quietly
proud of itself, sensually aware of itself, uncluttered, uncompro-
mised, serenely at home with its simplest methods and most pro-
found materials. It was the stage satisfied to be the stage and
making the glorious most of it.

There was nothing here to "help" the text. The acting area was
an open space, with a dark entrance above from which the sober
and wily Tartuffe could emerge—routinely flogging himself with
a knout—to seduce the religiously susceptible. There was a stair-
way down, there was a vast rug to play upon, there were a few
pieces of furniture to intimate a beige-and-gold world, even
though the all-important table under which a husband eventually
had to hide if he was to hear Tartuffe make certain proposals to his
wife was tidied away unobtrusively at the lower reaches of the
platform. The stage was free to breathe, on its breath came words,
the words would do the work.

Not even the traditional, and entirely legitimate, comic shudder-
ings and grimaces were much indulged. Orgon, that husband and
householder who is infatuated with his guest's false piety, spent no
time slavering or being crotchety or slicing the air with his stick.
Once, he meant to whack a sassy servant and hit a pillar instead,
just as Tartuffe attended to bits of business that *had* to be there.
Tartuffe does, after all, have to do something about covering his
hostess's cleavage. That he chose to make her modest by deftly
tucking a handkerchief directly between her breasts was no more
than sensible—given his instincts. No vaudeville was sought, no
extravagance was ever stressed. These fools *thought*. They did not
require artificial respiration.

Having thought, they spoke, and what they spoke described
them utterly. Perhaps a word about Elmire, the wife Tartuffe so
lusts after, will help make this clear. Martha Henry played her as a
woman who could not be surprised. She was herself reserved,
immaculately self-contained, gently delicate. But she was informed. She had a body. She knew precisely its various possible
uses, understood without pretense or dismay Tartuffe's crafty
designs upon it. She was a good woman but never an innocent one.
He might be evasive, circuitous; she was too supple and intelligent
to engage in affectation. She would have smiled knowingly at his

overtures and never humiliated him, if he had been any other man, any less devious man. As it was, she stood her ground, cool, worldly, and in her worldliness as generous as a woman dare be.

Miss Henry, who was most remarkable, gave us this woman whole; because she did, because she created a many-sided creature who had to be circled to be approached, she gave us a great deal of Tartuffe too. He was indirect and treacherous in the patterns he was forced to make if he was to surround her. We saw, in the counterdance of intelligences, the contending shapes of the play. And because Miss Henry was all of these things, she could, unpredictably but inevitably, make suddenly explosive comedy out of a perfectly ordinary straight line, a mere exit-and-entrance line. She had told her husband of Tartuffe's lust and her husband had defied her to prove it. "Send him to me" was the line, and it was merely meant to get a servant off and Tartuffe on. "*Send* him to me!" blazed Miss Henry, appalled that any aspersion could be cast on her ability to provoke lust, confident as a lion tamer unafraid of the cage, seeming to roll up her nonexistent sleeves and look prettily forward to a contest from which she was bound to emerge triumphant as Minerva.

But it is not to the point here to single out any one performer or line. What happened during the course of the entertainment was that we became committed, word by important word, to the verbal interior of the play, coiling through the rhymed couplets as though we had got very tight hold of a thread in a labyrinth, pursuing the twists and turns of mind as though they were our only salvation.

The director had been patient. Were the long expository passages in which Orgon described his first sight of Tartuffe sniveling on his knees near him in church, or the philosophical passages in which a brother-in-law discoursed on the difference between true and false piety, mere set pieces to be got through, distractions from the fun? Not at all. They were the bone of the play, its origin and its upshot, and every syllable was treated as crucial. By bonding us to background, to implication, to overview, the performers taught us not to ask for incidental laughs, not to hurry, not to anticipate dessert. We were there for all courses, lodgers in Orgon's house, residents of Molière's imagination as he so painstakingly composed the play.

Deeply embedded, we were then startled to hear ourselves roaring in new places, at inflections of the psyche rather than quick tricks of voice. Pat Galloway, as a maidservant with a compulsion to talk back, now needed only to join two surly lovers' hands together and notice in passing that the two hands made "a perfect fit" to bring down the house: we had long since grown accustomed to the kind of connections her mocking head made. William Hutt, as Tartuffe, could instruct Elmire to "preserve her body and soul" and, with the very faintest pause after "body," draw a thunderclap out front. We walked the whole play with these people, in intimate understanding.

The company was virtually flawless: Mr. Hutt, a hypocrite put together out of a bust of Beethoven and the remains of Mr. Hyde, sat erect and trembling as a grasshopper while he waited out a woman's virtue; Douglas Rain, as the gullible Orgon, fastened his attention so fiercely on his mentor that he seemed a reflecting pool, dancing insanely to another's rhythm; Barbara Bryne played the eternally obtuse grandmother of the family like an eagle in severe mourning; Mia Anderson's quivering daughter, a wrinkle-nosed rabbit with almost enough courage to nip at one corner of a cabbage leaf provided no one told her not to, was delightful; and Leo Ciceri's reading of the common-sense speeches that measured out and then framed the play could not have been more persuasive.

Richard Wilbur's excellent translation had been used and finally done justice. The players neither engaged in sing-song nor tried to suppress the end-stop rhymes, so unfamiliar to our ears; they absorbed them instead, keeping them just within consciousness and leading us to look for them, subliminally, as bright little tenpenny nails in an advancing structure. No doubt the feel of the evening can best be indicated by its two act endings. For the first, Tartuffe, at last alone onstage, simply seated himself comfortably, locked his fingers over his yearning belly, and smiled the smile of a very-soon-to-be-satisfied man. Laughter and applause came up like a geyser unleashed. For the second, Orgon, very much alone now onstage, stood at the edge of the apron blinking off into the void that his departed friend, proved a fraud, had made of his life. His face twisted a little; he would almost have liked to call him back. The lights faded to a standing ovation. Out of nothing but space, text, and people, all firmly and exhaustively honored, we had arrived at a complete experience of the stage—complete, unique, unrepeatable. One wished to add nothing, go nowhere else.

2

THE QUESTION in Los Angeles in 1970 was not how the visiting British National Theatre seemed to be functioning (splendidly, we knew that) but how Maggie Smith and Robert Stephens would shape up as the unannounced Lunts (they are husband and wife) of the company. Both were opening in a brand new production, the gentle, graceful, mezzotint revival of Farquhar's *The Beaux' Stratagem*, and then, a few nights later, taking over prominent roles in an already aged and much recast mounting of Chekhov's *The Three Sisters*. There was no mistaking them. They did nothing to jar the very nice balance of the acting company as a whole, they were not whetting backstage knives to become superstars. But they were severely present, palpably up there on stage.

Miss Smith's presence is always a severe one. She looks like a pair of scissors, to begin with, a closed pair that cuts even when closed. She must be, I think, the narrowest creature ever to come through a stage door—perhaps they have a special slit in the side of the building for her, much as they have special doors for cats—and she doesn't really own the usual kind of stage face (forehead of a mama doll, Indian-brave cheekbones, exaggeration everywhere or at least somewhere). Look for a particular feature and I don't think you'll find it.

But you'll see her. You'll see her as something over five feet in height with a three-acre range and a velocity just beyond the speed limit. The range comes in part from her hands, which occasionally seem larger and more mobile than she does. She is, for instance, constantly painting murals on an invisible wall in front of her, dramatizing whatever she's talking about with a slap, slap, slap of paint right in our faces, whooshing those craftsman's paws about as though she had dipped them in buckets of color and had to get rid of the stuff (and maybe the hands) instantly. She must be awfully good at waving goodbye to people in trains or at getting taxicabs.

The velocity comes in part from her speech, which seems to

have been recorded at 3¾ and played at 7½ without the least loss
of intelligibility, in part from the fact that her body, even at rest,
seems scarcely to have quieted down. There was a passage in *Three
Sisters,* for instance, during which she was seated near the footlights while the action proper—and it was very busy—went on
without her upstage. But it was she who seemed to be in motion.
The line of her body, in a long tight black gown with only a bit of
white lace on it, was such a serpentine line as it fitted itself to the
curves of an open-backed chair that we seemed to be looking at
one of those theater-marquee signs in which the block letters remain stationary while inside them little additional lights run up and
down dizzyingly. Perhaps Miss Smith is what is meant by alternat-
ing current.

All of this without loss of poise, mind you. In fact, when her
Mrs. Sullen, in *The Beaux' Stratagem,* all bronze-tinted cream and
sly eyes, lifted a teacup to her lips it was hard to tell which was the
porcelain. And she was exquisite as she set off for church of a
Sunday, tying bonnet strings beneath her chin and accepting a
hymnal from her servant in an absentminded rhythm that suggested she'd been born on an escalator and was going straight to
heaven on it.

Mr. Stephens, jolly as he was, was still a bit out of focus in
Stratagem, out of focus, that is to say, with the others who were
being so warm and so plausible and so understanding about Farquhar's play. Director William Gaskill had realized that *The
Beaux' Stratagem* is not a Restoration comedy but a transitional
piece in which the heartless snap and crackle of the old style was
giving way to the more humane and reasonable manners of what
eventually became "sentimental" comedy. (Not necessarily a good
trade; but it did happen, and this play is caught in the evolutionary
crunch.)

It had been staged, then, as placidly, as precisely, as patiently as
its scenery was first assembled: beginning with an empty stage, we
watched a landscape dribble dreamily into view in bits and pieces,
summoning up a lost engraved world in which all views were river
views, terminating in handy inn yards. There was nothing more
perfect in the production than the reading given a line by the inn-
landlord's daughter, Helen Fraser. We'd become comfortable in
the drowsy village to which a couple of London rakes had come

looking for wives (or, more properly, fortunes). I think we'd even come to trust the landlord, whose name was Boniface. But there was some question about the identity of a stranger. "He don't belong to our gang," murmured the landlord's daughter, calmly, almost piously, certainly without ruffling an invisible feather. Instantly we knew that we were inhabiting a den of thieves, and instantly we knew that thievery was going to be taken as the nicest of commonplaces, as an occupation befitting the honorably rising middle-class. It was the placidity that was delicious.

Mr. Stephens was not yet willing to play his particular rake in that key. He felt the need to go back to Restoration decor—a triple flourish with his hand as he sank, jaw set, into a bow—and to read the lines as though he were popping grapes into, or out of, his mouth. What might have done beautifully for Congreve, where the speech *is* both richer and more unreal, was a bit much here, particularly since the comedy was already working so nicely at the carefully lowered temperature.

Mr. Stephens, however, was masterly as Vershinin in the Chekhov play, the most dimensional and yet translucent Vershinin I have ever seen. He came on a bundle of breath that had to be expelled, a man ecstatically happy to have words at his disposal because he had so little else. One understood at once that his ardent, sometimes stammering, puppy-dog agreeableness was the one necessary mask that kept him alive; if he had not been able to believe in his own optimism, his enthusiasm bubbling high in a vacuum, he would have had to face the dismaying facts of his life and go down. He was not in all ways obtuse; he knew that his wife would try suicide again; he could say "What a mediocre person she is" and mean it. But life had somehow to be good and meaningful; he *willed* it to be; and his will made the babble that was so pitiful and so endearing.

Mr. Stephens sustained this complexity—we never saw what was wrong with his life in the dramatic action on stage; we had to discover it in the course of his camouflaging it—without interruption. And with Miss Smith as the Masha to whom he turned in his tired need for love, a particularly revealing and very right scene could be put together. It occurred as Masha, married to a third-rate but self-satisfied schoolteacher, and Vershinin began to acknowledge the passion they felt for each other.

The passion was real enough. But it was founded on their mutual need for more extraordinary lives, it fed on an illusion that nothing about *their* love could ever be "mediocre." And that was the heartbreak Mr. Stephens and Miss Smith were able to put into the reaching out. Even as they tried to escape the dullness their respective marriages had forced upon them, even as they kissed with an ardor that seemed to make this new relationship truly singular, we realized that, in all truth, they were not less mediocre, a loving life between them would never have been less mediocre, than what they were flying from.

The two performers subtly signaled to us throughout that they were fighting hard for an eternal promise that was surely going to turn out to be a false promise. The futility was as real as the grappling, and the grappling was very real; indeed, when these two lovers were at last torn apart, Miss Smith arrived at sounds below the level of speech that would have interested, and perhaps surprised, Jerzy Grotowski.

Miss Smith's Masha was no ordinary Masha, languid and sorry for herself. Miss Smith was *furious*, unable to tolerate for one more moment the absurdity of a life that was worse than sluggish, that was goalless when it did move. She was at her startling best when she literally ripped herself from a sofa, savagely carrying away her pillow as though she might shred it as she would a face, rather than listen any longer to a thoroughly stupid household wrangle. The burden of languor and foreboding shifted to the youngest sister, Irina; this Masha, under sufficient pressure, would have become a Hedda, just as, given the right wrong opportunity, she might in time have become Regina Giddens.

The performance was not all cat. Miss Smith's very first fury stemmed from her exasperated disappointment that her younger sister shouldn't have had a nicer birthday. And when her brother, with whom she was dancing idly about the living room, was pulled from her arms abruptly, she went on dancing alone, not ruefully but with a high heart, caught up for a moment in the energy that might have made her life a thing of grace.

3

WE ARE accustomed to thinking of British actors as better equipped by tradition and better prepared by training than our actors are to do Shakespeare and the range of classical roles generally. That is why we are so eager to see them, particularly in repertory companies, whenever they can manage to come. I now have a notion that we'd better get them all over here quickly, for one last yearning look. While they last. For, on the evidence of Nicol Williamson's *Hamlet*, the British theater is entering a new state of permissiveness that will, in the end, make their local boys no better Hamlets, and perhaps in some ways worse, than those we can readily scrape up here.

Mr. Williamson is known to be a fine actor of a kind. We grew to know the kind, and to applaud loudly, when he was here in *Inadmissible Evidence*, facing each new day in his lawyer's office glassy-eyed, paralyzed with fear that the world would find him out for the fraud he was, rigid, pale, panicked, whining. As John Osborne's image of the contemporary career man, collapsed with guilt for want of principle but unable to imagine a principle that would steady him, he was brilliant. He was failure feeling sorry for itself on the other end of a telephone.

He then came to *Hamlet* as though it were the same part and could be performed with the same equipment. He *has* performed it with the same equipment and has been acclaimed for doing so in England. Shouldn't *Hamlet* be given a contemporary cast, rescued from all that was once aristocratic, consciously styled, formally poetic about it? Shouldn't the new England, the England of an emerging lower-class determined to make room at the top for itself, be given a voice in the proceedings? Is *Hamlet* relevant at all unless it is directly relevant to clerks and delivery boys and bus conductors, to flower children and drop-outs? Why should not each of these perform their own Hamlets? Or ask that it be performed for them by a talented stand-in, Mr. Williamson? In this country, working on the same principle, we should feel honor bound to give the role to Steve McQueen or Jim Brown.

Mr. Williamson has intelligence, of course. He can take a line apart, almost as though it were a watch or a motorcycle, to see what all of its little parts are made of, how they came to be assembled, what purpose they were meant to serve. He can show this to us in the theater. The soliloquies were virtually diagrammed on an invisible blackboard, and the diagramming did make their meanings clear. Dry and choked a bit with chalk dust, but clear. When he came to telling of the letter he had written arranging the deaths of Rosencrantz and Guildenstern on altogether legal grounds, he could expand each "as" (the equivalent of a pompously intoned "whereas") with a fine mocking glee. He knew how to do a put-on. He could, suddenly, mean deeply what he was saying. Pausing and looking at Horatio before assuring him that he was held closer than close—"aye, in my heart of hearts"—he took time not to be glib but to be certain that Horatio believed him. An attentive mind was always present, measuring words.

But what of the tension and force of the words, what of the colors in which they distinguish themselves one from another, what of variety as they all come marching forth, so meant and so measured? Except for one or two fine group scenes—director Tony Richardson had made the play-within-a-play passage a nervous and bristling thing—Mr. Williamson's performance was without physical tension of any sort. It was as though he had confined himself to an analysis of words and had exhausted himself in the process.

Mainly he stood loosely, even limply, at one side of the stage, readying his next thought, while no play went on without him. No *Hamlet can* go on unless Hamlet is willing to drive it. Hamlet is not, as written, a drop-out. He is the man most savagely bent on getting in, finding out, upsetting, overturning—one at a time perhaps, but all in due time.

During the prayer scene, Mr. Williamson, rapier in hand, displayed no impulse—ever—in Claudius' direction. There was no urge in him to kill. But that did make the interior argument—kill now, or kill later?—entirely academic.

Mr. Williamson's arms hung idly from shoulders already idle. His was a pale flattened face, with kinky uncut hair billowing out so far behind him that it became his head, robbing his features of dimension; it was also a face that seemed to have severed association with the listless members that might have been expected to carry it anywhere. Criticism had been made that the balance of the company was surprisingly slack for a much-heralded British import. It was slack, but not surprisingly. How should Elsinore energize itself when it had no impetuous, demanding cock-crow to wake it up?

Watching any one of Mr. Williamson's exits, you could see where the essential desultoriness lay. Whenever Mr. Williamson left, usually slipping away unobtrusively at a lower portal without putting a period to his scene, the temperature on stage remained exactly the same as it had been while he'd been there. His coming or going made no emotional difference, only to some degree an intellectual one.

The intellectual degree was less than it might have been because of the particular noise Mr. Williamson made. I don't mean that he was noisy. Far from it. He was generally subdued and generally monotonous. I do mean that a sound came from him, consistently, that could not be described in musical terms (it must be remembered, no matter what, that the lines he was reading were written as a kind of music) but that had to be thought of as a penny-whistle or a tea kettle is thought of.

Generous reviewers had described this as a Midlands accent, implicitly suggesting that it had been deliberately adopted to freshen the sound of the text. I don't believe it had been deliberately adopted at all, if only because its adoption made no point: Hamlet was not the illegitimate son of a tailor's daughter got by a king passing through the ill-spoken outlands. But as best I can remember—and it's hard to remember *Inadmissible Evidence* exactly, because the actor fused magnificently with the role and the merger did not invite separate analysis—this was the same quality of voice that Mr. Williamson had used last time around, which is to say that it was simply his voice (when raised to the demands of a large auditorium).

The voice was a quick whine, the sort of sound a man might make if he spoke rapidly while carefully pinching the bridge of his nose. Because we had admired the actor before, because we wished to admire him now for those sensibilities he did certainly possess, we tried desperately to blot out the intolerable nasality, tried to shunt it into the far background by forcing thought forward. But it wouldn't blot, wouldn't stay shunted. We no sooner became immersed in a scene than it was there again, and as late as the "If it be not now" passage it was freshly leaping up to assault our ears. The passage came out as "If in bea naht naow." Thought had a hard time getting past it.

The performance, as a whole, seemed one given by a museum guide who obviously knew what he was talking about but was severely crippled by a blocked sinus. Much as we wished to see *Hamlet* anew, much as we wished to make *Hamlet* relevant, much as we wished to rid ourselves of dusty and/or overly delicate tradition, it just wouldn't do. In honoring whatever is contemporary about ourselves we have also got to honor what is there, what is written down, what is demanded. It has got to be possible to see *Hamlet* through twentieth-century eyes—remember what Robert Hirsch was able to do, so superlatively, when he intimated the defiant drop-out in the Comédie-Française production of Molière's *Scapin*—without abandoning all technical requirements and surrendering to a sentimentalized democratic procedure in which every urchin in *Oliver* gets to play a *Hamlet* of his own, in which every *good* actor is given the go-ahead sign, ready for this particular chore or not.

I hope that the British theater isn't resolved on this course as a matter of new policy. It is only our old policy, whereby Walter Huston or Tallulah Bankhead or whoever it might have been brought their special and valuable equipments to projects asking for other equipment, and our old policy has never worked out very well. What we used to tell our own actors whenever they stumbled was that they needed a spot of the training and a dash of the tradition that British actors came by naturally, but we are not truly going to be able to help them any by sending them to see the likes of Mr. Williamson's "mod" manner. They can do that sort of thing already, with their tongues tied.

4

WHAT shall we talk about, the big things Irene Worth did in *Hedda Gabler*, or the little ones? The big ones were staggering in their arrogance, and in the authority with which that arrogance was supported. When, at the Canadian Festival in Stratford, On-

tario, in 1970, we returned from an airy intermission on a twilit
lawn to attend the second act, the house lights went down and in
the complete darkness a pistol was fired, apparently directly in our
faces.

While we were quickly adjusting to the shock, the lights rose on
a smoke-wreathed Hedda, standing on an open balcony, back
arched like Diana the Huntress, head held high as Juno's, smiling
malice in her eyes, the pistol still thrust forward. She *had* fired it
directly at us, and the pretense that we were—in this so-adaptable
auditorium—in the garden to which the lady often retired for
pistol practice was, we realized, the merest formality, no more
than pretense. She would have killed us all if she could. There was
nothing personal in the matter. This Hedda simply did not know
how else to deal with a universe that had supplied her with an
energy for which there was no known use.

The device was very showy. As Grand Guignol, if you like, as
letting us see Hedda bloodied after she had finally put that pistol to
her temple. But it was strong and right. It accepted the theater as a
place in which exasperation might legitimately be allowed to explode, it strode past melodrama into the sheer noise impotent fury
must inevitably make. "From now on I'm not going to make any
more noise," Hedda said in Christopher Hampton's translation,
much, much later in the play—as she was drawing a few curtains
and placing a few screens between the rest of the world and her
suicide. In the play proper she *should* have made noise.

As it happened, Miss Worth did not need gunfire to get the
noise made. She could make it with her body as, left alone for one
wild moment of privacy, she thrust her arms high above her head,
fists half clenched, straining toward an ultimate gesture of release.
What was most remarkable about this extravagance was that it was
an unfinished extravagance, deliberately so. Her muscles strained
while the aching posture was held, then they stopped straining.
Without help from a line, Miss Worth had let us see that for her
there never could be an ultimate gesture, that whatever passion
raged inside her had to stand forever unexpressed.

Burning Lovborg's manuscript, she double-dared her author.
Ibsen had given her an appalling, virtually unbelievable, thing to
do, no matter what the circumstances. She did not make pauses up
to it, hoping to intimidate the audience into a quiet acceptance of

the act. She settled to the task, but made it one not confined to
spite. She literally made love to the manuscript, crumpling its
pages in the act of kissing them, destroying them before she had
burnt them by the ardor of her embrace. Love and spite, passion
and emptiness, were all the same thing to her; each had led to the
other, each blocked the other now, there was nothing to do with the
dead heart in her hands but to put it directly into the fire. The
scene as played was entirely risk, devil-take-you bravura; most
actresses would have been much too intelligent to chance it. Miss
Worth was magnificent.

But it was the little things that did not allow you to recover
your breath between flareups. Miss Worth was not stingy, not a
performer saving up effects for a rainy second act or a tired-out
third. She didn't bide her time between "moments" the better to
bludgeon you with them. The fires of her intelligence were burning all the time, as dangerously when the furnace doors were
closed as when they were thrown wide open. With her back
turned, with her presence nearly obliterated in the busyness of
someone else's urgent scene, she was there to sear with a single
unexpected word. She did have her back to us when her husband,
agape over Lovborg's manuscript and drowned in admiration for
it, remarked casually that he could never have conceived such a
book. Her unbidden "No," read without force and without intend-
ing to interrupt the conversation, but filled with the precise
measure of the hopelessness that overwhelmed her, seemed a lightning stroke in a storm we had only dimly sensed was brewing. We
jumped, and we laughed, and we were frightened.

The wonders she could do with two words, two entirely conventional words, were displayed like diamonds on a shelf when,
hearing that Tesman's tiresome old Aunt Juliana couldn't come
over to visit tonight, she quickly, forcefully, with instinctive
irony, rapped out, "Can't she?" The house thundered with laughter on the instant. For into the sudden, almost unthinking, response
she had packed loathing, delight, mocking innocence, false sympathy, monumental impatience. Overtone upon overtone reverber-
ated from the swift question so that her exasperation with Aunt
Juliana became the least of it; her self-hatred and her contempt for
a husband who could hear what she was saying but not understand

what she was meaning took over, usurped the intention of the phrase. In a sense, the entire play had been packed into an inflection. It was a lot for two words.

The actress was brilliant at every turn, and she was never not turning. She could straighten her spine in swift silent alarm, telling us in the hushed movement that she had known all along there was to be no professorship for her husband, no crowded future for herself; from the beginning she had intuited that life would walk away from her without warning. She could glide past Judge Brack, smiling but nonetheless going, as though to say that she understood and enjoyed him but was permanently not his. She could give a terrible shrug, when asked why she had always had impulses to torment other people to no purpose, and simply say "I don't know" in a candor that was shattering. Miss Worth is just possibly the best actress in the world.

Could she save *Hedda* from the ultimate skepticism, the unwanted laughter as opposed to genuine character humor that has always dogged it? No, she couldn't do that. When Hedda announced, rather too late in the play, that she had always wanted to control a destiny, the information was dramatically unsettling. That hadn't seemed to be Hedda's character at any time earlier. When Hedda gave Lovborg a pistol and asked him to kill himself beautifully, one's snicker had to be forcefully suppressed. When Hedda was dismayed to learn that Lovborg had been shot in the lower abdomen rather than the temple, the romantic nonsense of the role passed over into romantic nonsense in the play proper; one could not say who was being foolish, Hedda or Ibsen. I've been seeing Heddas all my life, from Nazimova on, and these particular jolts to the audience's sensibilities have never been properly smoothed away or absorbed into a living organism known as *Hedda Gabler*. I conclude that they cannot be, that the play does not satisfactorily contain all of the gestures that are made in it. Some belong to another woman, in another household, in another country.

But Miss Worth was the best of them, came closest—so close that you were willing to brush away what was unbelievable in your fascination with the urges that stirred, and flickered, and burned high wherever she walked. She even woke up properly, lying still long after you knew she was listening, turning and opening her eyes when she decided to *be* awake. I had never seen an actress do that before. It was astonishingly true.

5

I HAVE rarely had so strong a sense of the physical presence of words as I did while watching Moses Gunn overmaster *Othello* at Stratford, Connecticut. Words are intellectual constructs, they come dry from the mind and we try to keep them dry, like powder. Tools to be bandied about swiftly, used for our bland busy projects, little efficiency experts to be sent trotting down hallways on trimly shod feet. Words are coin, hard to the teeth, not custard or ever cream. We expect them to hold firm, make sense, and go back into our heads where they came from.

Mr. Gunn, patently and justly and joyously in love with Shake-speare, treated them otherwise—as sounds formed by lips, with the lips lingering over the birth rite, as pulsations from a larynx that was soft and giving to begin with, as reverberations from cords that might have a twanging toughness of their own but that made their first impact on flesh. Words came from a *body*, came from it and through it, and when they reached us they carried with them something of the warmth and moisture and internal music of that body. So far from being products of a sterile machineshop in the brain, they came with the regularity and astonishing color of pumped blood. They belonged to the whole man, and the man was wholly enmeshed in them.

Thus Mr. Gunn, thus the singing *Othello* that began a summer season. There was no dismissal of sense, no fumbling of the point of words. It was clear from the early moment when Mr. Gunn—a giant Moor in a whorled orange robe that a tiger would have felt at home wearing—turned to his overeager guards and wryly, but sharply, ordered them to "Keep up your bright swords, for the dew will rust them," that the actor could go on playing the part at this intelligent, sardonic, strong-willed level and all would be well enough.

He didn't let well enough alone, praises be. There is more to a

line than the mental luggage it is meant to carry, and as soon as
this Moor was confronted with Desdemona's father and the elders
of Venice, he seemed literally to stop, clear a vast air space around
himself, and then wrestle with his own musculature and his own
sensual harmonies to bring to the surface words formed in his
fingers, in his enormous open palms, in an intestinal tingle and a
pressing in and out of lungs.

The words were tasted before they were permitted beyond his
teeth. They were savored not only for sense but for syllable, with
each piece of a word given its separate, surprising value. When,
having explained to the assembly that he had not so much courted
Desdemona as simply told her of his travels and strange trials, he
came to "She thanked me, And bade me, if I had a friend that
loved her, I should but teach him how to tell my story," the words
"teach" and "tell" and "sto-ry" seemed to lift themselves on stilts
to tower over the council chamber and to make in the air a kind of
seawave of sound. The words are so plain that there was no need
to study them. It was the melody we were borne on, buoyantly,
breathlessly.

We knew, in this moment, that we were listening to an aria. We
also realized, at the moment, that *Othello* is in very large part
composed of arias. That is an easy thing to forget when we busy
ourselves with character motivations and all the paraphernalia of
textbook criticism. And we intuited—correctly—that Mr. Gunn
had made a particular point of elevating caressed sound at this
early juncture because he meant to use it and to build on it again
and again in the play.

He did it in the growing restlessness and disbelief and dismayed
fury of his intellectual seduction by Iago. So interlocked were
speech and thought, the physical process and the cerebral prodding, that Iago's "I see that you are eaten up with passion" no
longer qualified as metaphor. The eating up was actual, Othello's
body had been chewed to ribbons by his mind; the spasms of hands
clenched and shaken together as though shaking could discharge
the disease, the wracked agony of a doubled-up frame contorted in
exact proportion to the convolutions of a treacherous brain became not the tatters of passion but the whole of passion seen
simultaneously. Not the signs, but literally the throes. Everything
was expelled by a fit; in this production it was no excess to bring

Othello's convulsion to an end by forcing a stick into his mouth. Body and a voice had to be gagged together.

And the sensual melodic scale was ready for the end of the play, the "Put out the light" passage, with Mr. Gunn staring into a flickering candle flame held directly before his eye, and the ultimate "Soft you: a word or two before you go." It was easy to imagine someone unfamiliar with the bold cadencing and the unabashed resonance Mr. Gunn was using in the production regarding the conscious styling as "old-fashioned," though I doubt that anyone who imagined such a thing was old enough to have actually observed the fashion. I had heard something like it twice in my life, and then at the very ends of the careers involved. I once heard Margaret Anglin do it, and I later heard Nazimova do it. In a sense, I have been starved ever since. I can only say that the "Put out the light" and the "Soft you" passages, as Mr. Gunn was then reading them, were the two most beautiful moments to be savored anywhere on the American stage.

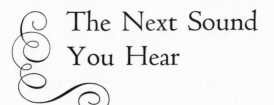

The Next Sound
You Hear

IT IS quite remarkable how successfully we manage to keep in our heads, simultaneously, two entirely different things: the theater as we imagine it to be, and the theater as it is. You see, we really know the facts all the time. We know that most theater is humdrum, if not a good bit worse than that; we can be fairly certain, on setting off for a playhouse, that the experience will be less than worldshaking tonight. Yet we always go with that worldshaking sense alive and alert, ready to be tapped, begging to be tapped. We honestly believe it's going to happen in the face of certain knowledge that it won't. I don't know whether this is good of us or treacherous of the theater, but it's true.

Before going to the first off-Broadway opening of a recent season I had dinner with a friend, who, without really knowing anything about the bill of one-act plays I was on my way to see, tended to commiserate with me. He wondered if I wasn't tired of the whole bit, did I honestly want to leave the dinner table for what would probably add up to a dreary two or more hours, could I honestly have faith in the approaching moment in the light of long years of experience? Possibly?

Without thinking, I replied, "But I want to go. I'm curious." (I see no virtue in this, only a quality rumored to kill cats.) And that was the fact. If I'd cared to dredge up out of memory the probabilities facing me, if I'd cared to rerun in my head all the hopeless bills of hopeless one-acters I'd sat through in the months before summer, if I'd *wanted* to scare myself to death, I could have. Easily. And one's knowledge is not deeply buried, not covered over. It's right there in the open to be examined at any time, fingered like tarnished silverware. One doesn't forget, not at all.

One simply wonders what the new night—the new disaster, if that's what it's to be—may be like. Even disasters are different. They're imagined by different men, come coiling like toothpaste out of different containers, reflect different moods in the changing months, states of grace, wracks of soul. This year's bad play is *not* like last year's bad play. It loses a whole new ballgame.

New sounds—aborted, perhaps, but aborted in the struggle of *trying*—seep across the footlights (that is a term we must some day stop using, no one having seen a footlight in some fifteen or twenty years) and they fall on, if only to offend, ears that listen differently because June and July and August are over. Not even the seats feel the same. The playhouse, visited before, is subtly altered. (What *did* they ever do with the men's room?)

The conversation on the sidewalk does not have last year's expectations, it has this year's, if only because of what everyone has done, endured, or read during the summer (I may have read *Bech: a Book* and *Play It As It Lays* and *Maltaverne* and *Our Mutual Friend*, making me a different man; one fall George Oppenheimer had finally finished *Martin Chuzzlewit*.) The world (do you remember a play called *The World and His Wife?*) is yearly altered.

And so the first new bill of that season was dreary and I was glad at last to get out of there. But it was dreary in *its* way, and it left one asking: Why this way? I could tell you a little bit about it. I could tell you that a woman rented a hotel room, stretched out in bed with her knees high and apart (her knees were all we could see of her at this instant), and gave birth to three lighted glass globes, the first the size of a street lamp, the others progressively smaller. She took each to the window, cut the cord with a pliers, and dropped them to the street below, where they made no noise.

There is no great point in my going on with this because the plays quickly vanished and are unlikely ever to return, you have no need of the information. Still, that isn't the way the previous season had opened. The previous season had opened with incest, in Russia.

The kind of curiosity I am talking about is not entirely predicated on the possibility, ever teasing, that one night, one miraculous night, the play will be suddenly good, fresh, and welcome as a footprint on Crusoe's island. That does happen. Without particular hope, you walk into *No Place to Be Somebody* and then and there the season is made. Or into *America Hurrah* or *The Effect of Gamma Rays on Man-in-the-Moon Marigolds* or one or another gift from the thrifty gods. You are thrilled, or delighted, or in some sense rewarded for your patience.

And that was part of what you were being patient about. But not all of it. You were really being patient about the theater as such, about an activity with a thread to it, about a kind of behaving that stretches all the way back to Aristophanes' sometime failures and Menander's lost manuscripts and Seneca's nonplays and the university drama that thought itself so much superior to Shakespeare. And Sheridan's theater burning down and *The Dragon of Wantley* with its sequel *Margery, or a Plague Worse than the Dragon* and on up through the whole thirty volumes of American "lost" plays, potboilers nearly all, that Barrett Clark so tenderly and so expensively found and bound.

The theater isn't its successes, though of course they help give it a certain position in polite circles. The theater is its continuum, a living muddle of good and bad that takes its vitality from the equally muddled world about it. It's a hand held out to meandering man as he makes his way through swamps and over cloverleafs, now mired, now soaring, always in motion. It's the motion that's recorded, both by design and by accident, and the speedometer never, never reads the same.

I find the motion, including the swamp sloshing, interesting. (Did you know that when Shakespeare was having his hits at the Globe, you might have seen, cheek by jowl with *Julius Caesar*, or at least next door, such plays as *The Devil's Charter, How a Man May Choose a Good Wife from a Bad, The Miseries of Enforced Marriage,* and *The Weakest Goeth to the Wall,* along with what would then have been the equivalent of an Off Broadway produc-

tion, *Sir Giles Goosecap?* Have you ever seen any of these plays?
Would you like to? I would. I know I'd squirm through most of
them, but I'd never be able to resist the temptation to look.)

The true successes survive, and we base our notions of a period
and a people and a playhouse upon them. But the plays that did not
survive, including some that were loved for a little season and then
vanished with the season's tan, also had something to do with the
way the earth was turning, the way folk saw themselves or were
willing briefly to picture themselves, the way particular nights fell
and particular days dawned. They may not have been good. But
they belonged to the complexion of the time; the time threw
them up.

One may very well be curious about the worst that is to come.
Look, and you will see that the worst is part of you. You will also
see the best trying to make its way through the worst. You will,
with luck, once in a while see the best, triumphant, shaped,
finished. But unfinished business can be as interesting as finished.
Unfinished is malleable, still warm even if sticky, subject to error
and risking everything nightly, foolish and grotesque upon occasion but desperately trying to get on with it, on with the business
of reading the clock by which we all make our appointments, for
dinner, for drama, for dalliance, for death.

Index